Drugs

Using the best scientific evidence, *Drugs: America's Holy War* explores the impact and cost of America's "War on Drugs"—both in public spending and in human terms. Is it possible that US drug policies are helping to proliferate, not prevent, a multitude of social ills including: homicide, property crime, the spread of AIDS, the contamination of drugs, the erosion of civil liberties, the punishment of thousands of non-violent people, the corruption of public officials, and the spending of billions of tax dollars in an attempt to prevent certain drugs from entering the country?

In this controversial new book, award-winning economist Arthur Benavie analyzes the research findings and argues that an end to the "War on Drugs," much as we ended alcohol prohibition, would yield enormous international benefits, destroy dangerous and illegal drug cartels, and allow the American government to refocus its attention on public well-being.

Arthur Benavie is Professor Emeritus of Economics at University of North Carolina, Chapel Hill, and has won multiple awards for his work in economic theory and teaching excellence. He has published several books, including *Deficit Hysteria: A Common Sense Look at America's Rush to Balance the Budget* (1998), and *Social Security Under the Gun* (2003).

Drugs
America's Holy War

Arthur Benavie

Routledge
Taylor & Francis Group

NEW YORK AND LONDON

First published 2009
by Routledge
270 Madison Avenue, New York, NY 10016

Simultaneously published in the UK
by Routledge
2 Park Square, Milton Park,
Abingdon, Oxon OX14 4RN

*Routledge is an imprint of the Taylor & Francis Group,
an informa business*

© 2009 Taylor & Francis

Typeset in Sabon by
Book Now Ltd, London
Printed and bound in the United States of America on acid-free paper
by Walsworth Publishing Company, Marceline, MO

Library of Congress Cataloging in Publication Data
Benavie, Arthur.
Drugs: America's Holy War/by Arthur Benavie.
      p. cm.
"Simultaneously published in the UK by Routledge."
Includes bibliographical references and index.
1. Drug control—United States. 2. Drug legalization—United States.
3. Social problems—United States. I. Title.
HV5825.B435 2009
362.29′1560973—dc22   2008024012

ISBN10: 0–7890–3840–4 (hbk)
ISBN10: 0–7890–3841–2 (pbk)
ISBN10: 0–203–88659–3 (ebk)

ISBN13: 978–0–7890–3840–1 (hbk)
ISBN13: 978–0–7890–3841–8 (pbk)
ISBN13: 978–0–203–88659–5 (ebk)

To my wife, Marcy,
With all my love.

Contents

Preface

In 2014 America's longest war—the war on drugs—will be 100 years old.[1] Has the war been worth it? What would constitute victory? More specifically: Has it protected our children, diminished drug addiction, quelled drug-related violence, promoted public health? These are the kinds of questions tackled in this book.

Until around 1996 I had been only dimly aware of the war on drugs. My first exposure to social harms attributed to the war—its very real collateral damage—came from an article that year in one of our main economics journals.[2] My research had always been in the area of macroeconomics. I knew little about U.S. drug control policy. But I was so disturbed by this article that I was driven to scour the scientific studies on the impact of the war. Eventually, I felt that I had to write a book both for the general public and for college students because I discovered that the gap between what the experts know and what the public knows is enormous. It's no wonder we are so ill informed; there is an eerie silence about the war on drugs in the United States. Our political leaders are afraid to touch it.

My original intention was a typical one for a college professor, namely, to help readers understand the costs and benefits of the drug war and to apprise them of possible reform options. But it didn't turn out that way! The more I studied the issue, the more appalled I became. There were *no* benefits I could find, only costs! The damages generated by the war, many of them unintended, are horrendous. The evidence is overwhelming that the drug war is a major cause of violence, property crime, drug overdose, the spread of AIDS, the contamination of drugs, the erosion of civil liberties, the corruption of public officials, and the punishment of thousands of nonviolent citizens—especially blacks and Hispanics—for ingesting the "wrong" substance. We waste billions of tax dollars in what our government admits is

---

1 I take as my starting date the first recorded instance of the United States enacting a ban on the domestic distribution of drugs the Harrison Narcotic Act of 1914, which dealt specifically with opium and coca leaves.
2 Jeffrey A. Miron and Jeffrey Zwiebel, "The economic case against drug prohibition."

the impossible task, rhetorically described as "interdiction," of preventing certain drugs from entering the country. In addition, we pour billions down a rat hole in the absurd attempt to eradicate cannabis plants, coca plants, and opium poppies, plants that can grow almost anywhere. *Drug researchers know all about these damages, but the public does not.*

What about the government's rationale? For several years I've conducted a seminar on the drug war for first-year students at the University of North Carolina at Chapel Hill. In one segment of the course I assign my students to study the government's defense of the war, embodied in DEA and ONDC white papers and the like. My students are invariably shocked, angry, and insulted at a policy based on nothing more than harsh moralizing and lies.

After studying the scientific research, I've become convinced that the United States should end the war on drugs and focus instead on reducing the harm caused by drugs. This view is consistent with the mainstream views of scholars who have spent their careers studying drug policy. *The implication of the evidence presented in this book is that our society would benefit if the various levels of government controlled, regulated, and taxed all psychoactive drugs, allowing consumers some type of access. This policy reform would destroy the market for mob-controlled drug cartels, who currently rake in enormous tax-free profits in black markets, and who routinely engage in turf warfare.* Note that since alcohol prohibition was ended in 1933, violent, illegal alcohol cartels have disappeared.

I find myself having become an advocate for regulated drug legalization, because there were no benefits I could see to balance against the costs of the drug war. Being an advocate is new for me. In my two previous books written for the general public I could play my usual role as professor. In *Deficit Hysteria*, I explained why all deficits were not bad, and instructed the reader as to how to distinguish good deficits from bad ones. That was just standard economics. No advocacy there. I was delighted that students who read the book were curious to find out whether I was a Republican or a Democrat. In *Social Security under the Gun*, I spelled out the costs and benefits of the proposal of President George W. Bush and many Republicans to privatize Social Security, as well as the plan of former President Bill Clinton and many Democrats to free the Social Security trust fund to invest in stocks and corporate bonds. I gave both sides as fair a shake as I could even though my heart was strongly against both plans. My efforts to be an honest broker were acknowledged by an economist whom I have admired since I was a graduate student, Robert Solow, a Nobel laureate, who in a blurb for my book referred to my "unprejudiced account of the various proposals for 'saving' the [Social Security] system."

So, you've been forewarned, Reader! I have nothing good to say about the drug war. It's all bad. Read on at your peril.

Acknowledgments

I'm indebted to Richard Froyen, Richard Koffler, and an anonymous referee for critiquing earlier versions of the manuscript. My thanks to the following people who generously shared their expertise with a complete stranger via phone and email: Anjuli Verma, Bruce Mirken, Peter Reuter, Mitch Earleywine, Bruce Carruth, Michael Males, Faith Boucher, and Tom Maher.

Without question, though, my greatest debt of gratitude is to my wife, Marcy Lansman, who spent many weeks working on the manuscript with me. To the extent that the writing is lucid and well organized, she deserves much of the credit.

Part I
Background

Introduction

On June 18, 1986, a young black athlete, Len Bias, died of heart failure. He was an outstanding basketball player for the University of Maryland and had just been a first-round draft pick for the Boston Celtics. Celebrating the good news, he tried cocaine for the first time, and his death was publicly attributed to the drug. Bias was not just an ordinary superstar. He was perceived as "a clean-cut kid from a religious family."[1] If it could happen to him, it could happen to anyone, or so it seemed.

At that time the country was in the midst of a panic. The media had discovered crack cocaine and proclaimed that it was instantly addictive and deadly. The *New York Times*, in a front-page story, announced that crack was spreading from the inner city to "the wealthiest suburbs of Westchester County."[2] A *Newsweek* editorial broadcast that "an epidemic is abroad in America, as pervasive and dangerous in its way as the plagues of medieval times."[3] The highly publicized death of Len Bias added to the hysteria. In the following month, the TV networks presented seventy-four news segments about the dangers of cocaine.[4] Congress reacted quickly to the perceived crisis by toughening the punishments for drug law violators. Now, even small-fry pushers, arrested for the first time, would be sentenced to ten years in federal prison without parole. It was an election year and no politician wanted to appear soft on drugs.

The media stories scared me too. I remember being appalled by stories of mothers abandoning their babies because of crack. It looked to me like the politicians were doing the right thing to incarcerate the traffickers of this new virulent drug. The information we had was that these criminals were peddling poison.

For the next several years I was barely aware of the war on drugs. I had no contact with illicit drugs since I use none, and I don't even drink anything containing alcohol. What opened my eyes to the realities of the drug war was a 1996 article by two economists spelling out its social costs.[5] They argued that the government's drug control policy was a major cause of homicides, property crime, the spread of HIV, drug poisonings and overdoses, the erosion of civil liberties, and the arbitrary confiscation of assets. The article was a shock, and it led me to begin researching the drug war.

The subject is immense; its boundaries reach far beyond economics, the area in which I was trained, covering almost every discipline you can imagine, from law to criminology to political science to pharmacology.

The more I studied the more I discovered that the war on drugs is a holy war, a crusade aimed at eliminating certain "evil" drugs and punishing their sinful users. Costs and benefits be damned. This finding is the major theme of this book. The war is supposed to shrink the consumption of selected drugs, but study after study—many by our government—has concluded that it's a failure, and that treatment, not arrest and prison, is the way to combat drug abuse. Researchers overwhelmingly agree that the war causes incalculable damage to our society. Here are a few examples, which—along with many others—will be fully documented in subsequent chapters:

- The war has been estimated to have caused about 10,000 homicides a year, most the result of turf warfare between rival drug gangs. Suppliers in this immensely profitable underground market obviously cannot appeal to the legal system to resolve disputes.[6]
- Over 100,000 people are in federal, state, and local prisons for simply possessing (not selling) illicit drugs.[7] It costs an average of $20,000 to maintain a person behind bars for a year.[8]
- More than a third of the AIDS patients in the United States contracted the disease by using dirty needles to inject drugs.[9] The federal government refuses to support the supplying of clean needles to illicit drug users, claiming—contrary to its own studies—that drug injection would be encouraged.[10]
- African Americans feel the impact of the drug war disproportionately. Of the 265,000 state prison inmates serving time for drug offenses in 2002, about 47 percent were black, while blacks constituted about 15 percent of illicit drug users.[11] (The majority of traffickers are white.)[12]
- Heroin is superior to morphine for alleviating some types of pain and marijuana is an effective anti-nausea drug for those on chemotherapy. Yet, in spite of the recognized therapeutic value of these drugs, physicians in the United States are prohibited from prescribing them.[13]

Crusades demonize the enemy and the drug war is no exception. Going back to the 1986 media stories about crack, the experts have pointed out that they were filled with misinformation. According to sociologists Craig Reinarman and Harry Levine, "most of the people who have tried crack or smoked cocaine have *not* continued to use it. ... Daily crack smoking, like daily heroin injecting, occurs mainly among the poorest, most marginalized people in American society—and only among a small minority of them."[14] In 1989, the *New York Times* finally reversed its view, saying that crack was "confined mainly to poor urban neighborhoods," and in 1990 *Newsweek* admitted that "a lot of people use it without getting addicted."[15]

As for the death of Len Bias, it was unlikely to have been caused by cocaine alone, but rather cocaine mixed with alcohol, a potentially lethal combination.[16] (Interestingly, the danger of combining alcohol and cocaine is not mentioned on alcohol packaging.) As Judge James Gray pointed out, "What is not widely known, however, is that Bias was having his third convulsion before his friends sought medical attention. They were too afraid that Bias or they themselves would be arrested that they did not take him to a hospital. If not for our drug prohibitionist laws ... more people like him would probably still be alive today."[17]

You may think my views are extreme. You rarely hear them expressed in the media, since politicians and journalists can't risk appearing to be soft on drugs. In fact, *I'm in the mainstream of those who have studied the drug war*. In researching this book I scoured the current literature on this topic. Of all the books, articles, and websites I found that claimed to be based on scientific research, the only material that favored the war came from the Office of National Drug Control Policy (ONDCP), whose director (the drug czar) is responsible for crafting the nation's drug control policy. Drug researchers from such diverse fields as law, sociology, history, and pharmacology overwhelmingly condemn the war. In addition, all twenty-three of the blue-ribbon commissions that have studied the topic over the past century have opposed a war on drugs.[18] Law enforcement officials who have been on the front lines almost always come to view the war as futile as well as harmful. In a 1995 survey of 365 police chiefs, police officers, prosecutors, and judges, 90 percent in each of these groups reported that the United States was "losing the war on drugs."[19] In the 2006 annual national survey of 22,587 chiefs of police and sheriffs, conducted by the National Association of Chiefs of Police, 82.0 percent of the respondents answered "no" when asked if the drug war had "been successful in reducing the use of illegal drugs."[20]

Here is a sampling of the opinions of some of the experts and public figures:

- "We are presently spending $50 billion a year on the war on drugs. I'm talking about police, courts, and jails. For all the money that we're putting into the war on drugs, it is an absolute failure ... Should you go to jail for simply doing drugs? I say no ... People ask me, 'What do you tell kids?'... You tell them that by legalizing drugs, we can control them, regulate them, and tax them."
  Gary E. Johnson, the Republican former governor of New Mexico[21]
- "We are speaking of a plague. ... The cost of the drug war is many times more painful, in all its manifestations, than would be the licensing of drugs combined with intensive education of non-users and intensive education designed to warn those who experiment with drugs. We have seen a substantial reduction in the use of tobacco over the last thirty years, and this is not because tobacco became illegal."

William F. Buckley Jr., conservative columnist, and founder of *National Review*[22]

- Our supply reduction strategy is "a colossal failure" and our demand reduction policy is one that "can never produce a victory."

  Steven B. Duke, professor of law at Yale University, and lawyer Albert C. Gross[23]

- "America's highly punitive version of prohibition is intrusive, divisive, and expensive and leaves the United States with a drug problem that is worse than that of any other wealthy nation."

  Robert J. MacCoun and Peter Reuter, behavioral scientists at the RAND Drug Policy Research Center[24]

- "Our country's attempts through the criminal justice system to combat drug use and abuse, and all of the crime and misery that accompany them, were not working ... Our so-called War on Drugs was our biggest failure."

  Judge James P. Gray of the Superior Court in Orange County, California[25]

- "About $500 worth of heroin or cocaine in a source country will bring in as much as $100,000 on the streets of an American city. All the cops, armies, prisons, and executions in the world cannot impede a market with that kind of tax-free profit margin. It is the illegality that permits the obscene markup, enriching drug traffickers, distributors, dealers, crooked cops, lawyers, judges, politicians, bankers, businessmen. Naturally, these people are against reform of the drug laws."

  Joseph D. McNamara, former police chief of Kansas City, Missouri, and San Jose, California. He has a doctorate in public administration from Harvard and is currently a fellow at the Hoover Institution[26]

- "The day in the fall of 1988 that I was mandated to sentence Luis Quinones, an eighteen-year-old with no prior record, to ten years of real time because he was a bouncer in an apartment where drugs were being sold, I faced our national drug policy and ... concluded that our present policy of criminal prohibition was a monumental error."

  Robert M. Sweet, a district judge in New York City and former deputy mayor[27]

- "Blanket prohibition is a major source of crime: it inflates the price of drugs, inviting new criminals to enter the trade; reduces the number of police officers available to investigate violent crime; fosters adulterated, even poisonous, drugs; and contributes significantly to the transmission of HIV. These are not problems that are merely tangential to the war on drugs. These are problems caused, or made substantially worse, by the war on drugs. That is why I have long advocated that the war on drugs be fought as a public health war."

  Kurt Schmoke, former mayor of Baltimore, Maryland, and U.S. attorney for the district of Maryland[28]

- "Deterrence strategies have not been successful in reducing drug use. Enforcement strategies have consumed resources, aggravated health risks associated with drugs, and increased the levels of violence surrounding drug markets. Drug policy has also increased profits for drug dealers and attracted other young people into selling ... Severe sentencing laws applied broadly and indiscriminately have undermined, rather than reinforced, the moral authority of the law."
  American Society of Criminology[29]

- The war is "lost" and "making drug use a crime is useless and even dangerous."
  Raymond Kendall, head of the international police force, Interpol[30]

1 Overview

Since the war on drugs is so severely criticized by drug researchers and law enforcement officials as well as respected public figures, it raises the question: why does the war continue? Also, why do those who study it, as well as those who enforce it, condemn it so harshly? Here, we look briefly at these questions.

Why Certain Drugs Are Prohibited

Who's the enemy in this war on drugs? It's a set of prohibited or "illicit" drugs along with those who possess or sell them. The federal Controlled Substances Act (1970) distinguished five categories or "schedules" of drugs based on their alleged susceptibility to abuse and their medical usefulness.[1]

A schedule I drug is defined as both dangerous and lacking any medical benefit. Drugs in this category cannot be possessed or sold legally and cannot even be prescribed by physicians. Examples are marijuana, heroin, LSD, and ecstasy.

A schedule II drug allegedly has a high potential for abuse but has some recognized medical value and can therefore be prescribed. Examples include cocaine, morphine, and methamphetamine.

The remaining categories include medically useful substances that are defined as decreasingly dangerous. For example, schedule III includes amphetamines and codeine, schedule IV Valium and Darvon, and schedule V other medicines containing narcotics.

Illicit drugs include all of those in schedule I along with the substances in the other four categories when used or sold outside of medical channels. The severest criminal penalties are applied to the possession or distribution of the drugs in schedules I and II.

Who decides which drug belongs in which schedule? You might think it would be the Federal Drug Administration (FDA) or the Surgeon General. Not so. It's the responsibility of the U.S. Drug Enforcement Administration (DEA) of the U.S. Department of Justice to make recommendations.[2] The Attorney General makes the final decision, one of many indications that drug abuse is considered a legal rather than a medical problem in the United States.

All the illicit drugs have two things in common—they are psychoactive (mood altering) and they give pleasure to the consumer. According to the National Survey on Drug Use and Health, in 2005, approximately 8.1 percent of Americans over the age of twelve (19.7 million) were "current users" of illicit drugs, that is, they had used an illicit drug in the month prior to the interview. Six percent of Americans over twelve were current users of marijuana in 2005 (14.6 million); 1.0 percent (2.4 million) used cocaine; 0.3 percent (0.72 million) crack; 0.1 percent (0.24 million) heroin; and 0.2 percent (0.48 million) methamphetamine.[3]

We are so often reminded of the harmful effects of these drugs, we can forget that people take them for a reason. Here I describe some of the pleasurable sensations people report along with some of the dangers.

Marijuana smokers report that they experience relaxation, euphoria, laughter, amusing distortions of space and time, heightened sensitivity to colors and sounds, increased sociability, and an enhanced enjoyment of music and sex.[4] *The Merck Manual of Medical Information* refers to "the sense of exaltation, excitement, and inner joyousness" that the smoker often experiences. Not everyone enjoys marijuana, however. Many try it a few times and stop. One common negative reaction is a feeling of paranoia. A major complaint, often made by parents, is that users lose the drive to achieve in school or work.[5] (We explore this in chapter 10.)

A laboratory study involving hypothetical choices among drugs by heroin addicts found that marijuana and heroin are "substitutes," that is, a rise in the price of one causes an increase in the consumption of the other.[6] This result probably reflects the fact that the high from heroin is similar to the intoxication marijuana smokers experience.[7] The heroin high is a warm, drowsy, and euphoric state that lasts four or five hours.[8] For those who inject the drug, the high is preceded by a "rush," which lasts only a few minutes. The rush has been likened to a sexual orgasm, and is described as a feeling of "great relief." Given the myths about heroin, I was shocked to learn that, unlike alcohol or cocaine, it does not cause organic damage even to those who have become dependent, as long as they don't overdose. As *The Merck Manual* put it, "People who have developed tolerance [to heroin] may show few signs of drug use and function normally in their usual activities as long as they have access to drugs."[9] Many of the complications of heroin dependence are due to unsanitary conditions in the black market. But, the drug is physically addictive and carries the danger of overdosing, which can be life threatening.[10]

While marijuana depresses brain activity[11] and heroin is a depressant to the central nervous system,[12] cocaine is a stimulant, with effects similar to those produced by caffeine and amphetamine.[13] At moderate doses, users typically report that the drug combats fatigue, boosts energy, increases sociability, enhances sexual arousal, and creates feelings of euphoria and competence.[14] If the drug is injected or smoked, rather than inhaled, it produces a rush similar to heroin, followed by a high, which lasts less than a half an hour. High doses can lead to nervousness and agitation. Chronic users often suffer severe depression if they try to stop. Dependence on cocaine can develop rapidly if the drug is used frequently. Those who become dependent on it often suffer from "degeneration of the nasal mucous membranes ... digestive disorders, nausea, loss of appetite, weight loss, tooth erosion, brain abscess, stroke, cardiac irregularities, occasional convulsions, and sometimes paranoid psychoses and delusions of persecution."[15] Since the drug raises blood pressure, it can be lethal for someone with heart problems.[16]

Unlike marijuana, heroin and cocaine, amphetamines are not plant based. They were first synthesized in Germany in the 1880s. Among the drugs classified as amphetamines are ecstasy (MDMA) and methamphetamine (speed).[17]

Ecstasy is a mood elevator, which produces feelings of empathy, euphoria, and sociability, lasting three to six hours.[18] Users take the drug at "rave" dances, which often last all night. Ecstasy is not highly addictive and few deaths are associated with it (nine in 1998).[19] Some of those deaths are related to overheating, which is preventable if water is available at rave dances along with rooms where people can rest. Ecstasy raises the blood pressure and the heart rate. At high doses the drug can be dangerous, causing a large increase in body temperature that may result in muscle breakdown, kidney failure, and lethal cardiovascular effects in people who have heart disease.[20] Recent research has found a positive association between heavy use of MDMA and decreased performance in memory tasks and other cognitive functions.[21] It was made a schedule I drug in 1985.[22]

Methamphetamine, developed in Japan in 1919, has become the most frequently abused amphetamine in the United States.[23] Meth is a powerful stimulant, creating a rush of energy. Users report that it makes them "feel like Superman."[24] The drug can be eaten, snorted, injected, or smoked. When it's injected or smoked, it can, like cocaine, give the user a highly pleasurable rush that lasts a few minutes, followed by a euphoric high. As *The Merck Manual* puts it, "Amphetamines increase alertness (reduce fatigue), heighten concentration, decrease the appetite, and enhance physical performance. They may induce a feeling of well-being or euphoria."[25] Amphetamines temporarily relieve depression, improve athletic performance in the short run, help long-distance truck drivers stay awake, and bolster students putting in an all-nighter studying for exams.[26] From Vietnam up through Desert Storm, the Air Force has provided amphetamines to pilots.[27] Meth is prescribed on a limited basis for narcolepsy and attention-deficit hyperactivity disorder.[28] While the drug is rarely fatal, even small amounts can have potentially lethal effects, such as strokes, respiratory problems, cardiovascular collapse, anorexia, hyperthermia, convulsions, Parkinson-type diseases, insomnia, paranoia, and depression.[29]

It's widely believed that stimulants such as cocaine and the amphetamines are instantly addictive. Not true; but any substance that causes euphoria also creates a potential for abuse. As a highly respected psychopharmacology text put it: "Despite the popular view that drugs like cocaine and heroin are instantly and automatically addictive, that is not the case."[30] Drug researchers at the Duke University Medical School sum up the issue this way: "There are thousands of people, ranging from children with ADHD to truck drivers, who regularly use psychomotor stimulants but never develop a compulsive pattern of use ... yet we know that the drive to use cocaine or amphetamine is considerably stronger than that for any of the other addictive drugs."[31]

Meth labs have been spreading rapidly in the rural areas of the Southeast.[32] Labs are found in homes, cheap hotel rooms, and backyards, and on deserted roadways. The drug can be cooked up in a few hours with a potentially explosive cocktail of household ingredients, such as farm fertilizer, anhydrous ammonia, lithium from car batteries, and pseudoephedrine from cold tablets. The waste from these meth labs is hazardous for humans and the environment.[33]

LSD is a hallucinogen, which induces the sensation of floating, along with visual and auditory distortions.[34] The user often experiences "sensory crossovers," that is, hearing colors, tasting sounds, and seeing music in colors. The LSD "trip" usually lasts six to twelve hours. It can be good or bad depending on the person's mood and the setting in which the drug is taken. A bad trip can cause anxiety and panic. A danger of using the drug is impaired judgment. For example, the user may believe they can fly and may try to do so. Chronic users may experience recurring hallucinations, called flashbacks, which usually disappear within a year after the last use, but may recur occasionally for up to five years. The existing data suggest that bad trips and flashbacks are rare.[35] There are no withdrawal symptoms and I found no reports of deaths from the drug. Recreational use of LSD was banned in the United States in 1967.

Getting back to the question of why these drugs are prohibited, we might ask whether heroin, cocaine, and amphetamines are more life threatening than tobacco and alcohol. The answer is no. Tobacco and alcohol are more dangerous by far.[36] Together, they kill over a half million people a year: in 2000, tobacco was responsible for 435,000 deaths, and alcohol for 85,000 deaths.[37] The deaths per 100,000 users per year has been estimated at 650 for tobacco and 150 for alcohol.[38] In 2000, the consumption of *all* illicit drugs contributed to the deaths of around 17,000 people.[39] The deaths per 100,000 users per year have been estimated at eighty for heroin and four for cocaine.[40] Most of these deaths are due to contamination by black market suppliers and the government's restrictions on clean needles for drug injectors.[41] No death has ever been reported for marijuana.[42] According to a recent report by the European Monitoring Centre for Drugs and Drug Addiction, "Acute deaths related solely to cocaine, amphetamines or ecstasy are unusual despite the publicity they recjeive."[43]

A recent annual survey of hospitals and medical examiners conducted by the National Institute on Drug Abuse (NIDA), called DAWN (Drug Abuse

Warning Network), found that the emergency room visits involving the so-called club drugs—which include methamphetamine, LSD and ecstasy—are "relatively rare," constituting 4 percent of drug-related emergencies. Some of these visits are caused by multiple drug use. Combinations involving alcohol are especially risky.[44]

Are the banned drugs the most addictive? No again. Legal drugs such as nicotine and alcohol have a higher addictive potential than many illicit drugs.[45] Ironically, except for heroin, the schedule I drugs—marijuana, LSD and ecstasy—are, according to studies, less likely to hook you than nicotine, alcohol, or even caffeine. In a National Survey on Drug Abuse, nicotine was found to be most addictive, with less than 20 percent of tobacco users managing to avoid getting hooked.[46] You may be surprised to learn that most heroin users consume only intermittently and do not become heavy users.[47] Of those who use cocaine, around 20 percent are dependent.[48] And about 10 percent of those who use marijuana smoke it daily.[49] In one survey, where 746 drug abuse researchers were asked to rank commonly used drugs on how addictive they were, nicotine and heroin ranked as the most addictive, followed in descending order by crack, meth, cocaine, alcohol, amphetamine, caffeine, marijuana, LSD and ecstasy.[50] Contrary to conventional wisdom, most consumers of the prohibited drugs use them casually, suffer little harm, and stop within five years without coercion or treatment.[51]

Many people believe that the rationale for prohibiting certain drugs is that they induce violence, an accusation often leveled at crack in particular. The truth is that crack is not in the same league as alcohol in the violence department.[52] As we'll see in chapter 3, it's the drug war, along with alcohol, not the consumption of illicit drugs, that is responsible for most drug-related violence.[53]

As David Musto, an historian of American drug policy put it, "The history of drug laws in the United States shows that the degree to which a drug has been outlawed or curbed has no direct relation to its inherent danger."[54] So, how can we explain why certain drugs are prohibited while more dangerous ones are not? Researchers suggest that illicit drugs are associated in the minds of many with groups that are feared or hated, such as immigrants, African Americans, criminals, and rebellious young people.[55] The history of United States' drug policy illustrates how the criminalization of drug users has been fueled by racial, ethnic, and economic antagonisms (see chapter 2). Nineteenth-century anti-opium laws were aimed at Chinese laborers who were in competition with American workers and whose opium dens were an attraction to American youth. Marijuana first came to be seen as a problem in the early twentieth century, when it was the drug of choice of Mexican farm laborers who were thought to be taking scarce jobs away from Americans. Marijuana was further stigmatized by its connection with antiwar and anti-establishment protests during the Vietnam War. Cocaine and heroin came to be perceived as a danger to society as they were associated with blacks, juvenile gangs, and prostitutes.[56] The drug scene is frightening to mainstream society because it's seen as a cause of violence, disease, and social disorder.[57]

Those who study the drug war often claim that it's "rooted in a puritanical strain in American culture."[58] The strongest opponents of decriminalizing drugs appear to be evangelical Christians, many of whom see drug use as sinful because they believe it's a threat to the authority of parents, the nation, and the social order. For example, S. K. Oberdeck claimed in a 1971 *National Review* article that marijuana represents a lifestyle that threatens to "bring down 'ordered life as we know it.'"[59]

Other researchers of the drug war argue that psychoactive drugs are perceived as a danger to our capitalistic economic system. The historian H. Wayne Morgan observed that illicit drugs produced an "indolence and reverie" that "seemed especially unsuitable to a modernizing industrial society whose success depended on hard work, rationality, and the mastery of complex facts."[60]

In sum: America's war on drugs is not driven by objective information concerning the effects of illicit drugs or the repercussions of the drug laws, but rather by emotional factors: racism, xenophobia, a fear of social disorder and disease, a perceived threat to the success of the economic system, and a religious crusade against "vice." As a result, the mainstream public and the government tune out overwhelming evidence that the drug war is causing irreparable damage to our society. As economist Thomas Sowell has written, "Policies are judged by their consequences, but crusades are judged by how good they make the crusaders feel."[61] The drug war is clearly a crusade.

Attitudes toward Drug Law Violators

Some of the statements made by public figures about drug law violators are more suggestive of a religious crusade than a law enforcement issue. Consider a few examples.

Nancy Reagan has gone beyond "just say no"; she has stated that "The casual drug user cannot morally escape responsibility for the actions of drug traffickers and dealers. I am saying that if you are a casual drug user, you are an accomplice to murder."[62]

On September 5, 1990, the Los Angeles police chief Daryl Gates testified before the Senate Judiciary Committee that casual drug users "ought to be taken out and shot."[63] (That would polish off a third of our tenth and twelfth graders.)[64]

In August 1996, former House Speaker Newt Gingrich, while campaigning for presidential candidate and former Senator Robert Dole, told a crowd that drug dealers should be executed. (Even a high-school student selling pot to his friends?)[65]

In November, 1999, at a literary luncheon in Brisbane, Australia, "Judge Judy" suggested that, instead of attempting to control AIDS and hepatitis by providing clean needles to drug addicts, we should "give them all dirty needles and let them die."[66] (This pretty much reflects government policy.)

Drug czar William Bennett told a national radio audience that it was "morally" OK to behead drug traffickers.[67]

According to former Senator Paula Hawkins (R., FL), "Drug traffickers are mass murderers."[68]

The United States agreed to support Colombia and Peru in a policy to shoot down planes that were even suspected of carrying illegal drugs. In April 2001, a Peruvian jet fighter mistakenly shot down a private plane carrying American missionaries.[69]

Hardly a critical eyebrow was raised when the distinguished liberal Justice Thurgood Marshall told *Life* magazine, "If it's a dope case, I won't even read the petition. I ain't giving no break to no drug dealer."[70]

In a 1989 White House document, called the *National Drug Control Strategy*, drug czar William Bennett argued that casual users were more dangerous than hard-core users:

> The non-addicted casual or regular user ... is likely to have a still-intact family, social, and work life. He is likely still to "enjoy" his drug for the pleasure it offers. And he is thus much more willing and able to proselytize his drug use—by action or example—among his remaining non-user peers, friends, and acquaintances. A non-addict's drug use, in other words, is *highly* contagious.[71]

Under Bennett's reign as drug czar there was a dramatic increase in drug-related arrests and an accelerated expansion in the prison system.[72]

The loathing expressed for drug law violators seems out of all proportion to their crimes. The drug war appears to give people a license to say things about illicit drug users that they would never be allowed to say about the groups whom they associate with these drugs: African Americans, Latinos, and rebellious young people.

Punishments for Drug Law Violators

Given these powerful emotions about drug law violators, it's not surprising that the punishments imposed on them often rival those for murder and rape. In our criminal justice system, the federal courts are designed to deal with the larger and more serious cases, such as interstate drug trafficking, while the state courts typically handle the less complicated street crimes.

Many drug offenses involve mandatory minimum sentences. For example, under federal law, a dealer, convicted for the first time of selling 5 grams of crack (a weight about equal to that of a quarter), will serve a minimum of five years in prison. A first-time peddler of powder cocaine would have to sell 500 grams to receive the same sentence.[73] This 100 to 1 punishment disparity between two forms of the same substance is widely seen as racist, since most crack dealers are African American, while peddlers of powder cocaine are usually white. The average federal sentence for a first-time, low-level crack dealer is 128 months, longer than the average term for rape (79 months) or for weapons offenses (91 months). The average sentence for murder is 153 months.[74]

Under federal law, as well as the laws of various states, drug offenders who have served their prison sentences can be denied public housing, college loans, food stamps, and welfare benefits, often for life.[75] Armed robbers, rapists, and even murderers, once out of prison, are still eligible for these benefits.[76]

State drug laws vary enormously. In many cases they are even harsher than the federal law. In Oklahoma, for a first-time offender, a conviction for the possession of any amount of cocaine less than 1 ounce leads to a minimum of two years in prison, while the possession of 1 ounce or more requires incarceration for ten years to life.[77] In Louisiana, being convicted of possessing 1 ounce of cocaine mandates imprisonment for a minimum of ten years and a maximum of sixty.[78]

While eleven states have decriminalized marijuana, most states, as well as the federal government, still have severe laws against the drug.[79] In Louisiana, the sale of 1 ounce of marijuana can lead to incarceration for twenty years. in Washington state, selling almost any amount results in a recommended prison sentence of five years.

Under New York's Rockefeller drug laws, enacted in 1973, the possession of 4 ounces or the sale of 2 ounces of a narcotic substance carries a mandatory penalty of fifteen years to life. This is as harsh as the sentence for murderers and kidnappers, and harsher than the penalty for rapists and arsonists. Here are a couple of examples.

- Amy Fisher was to serve four years and ten months for shooting a woman in the head, and Robert Chambers was serving five years for a Central Park strangling, while Lawrence V. Cipolione, Jr., was sentenced to fifteen years to life for selling $2^1/_3$ ounces of cocaine to an undercover officer.[80]
- Andre Neverson shot his girlfriend's uncle five times. The uncle lived and Neverson served five years in prison. Kenia Tatis was convicted of possessing 20 ounces of cocaine and is serving a mandatory sentence of fifteen years to life in a state prison. She had never been in trouble with the law before and no drugs were found on her. She was convicted by the testimony of a woman who in return received a lighter sentence for herself.[81]

In spite of widespread opposition to the Rockefeller drug laws, the politicians have so far not been able to agree on an overhaul. However, the law has been increasingly circumvented over the years to reduce some of its harshness.[82] Prosecutors have started to divert addicts into treatment programs instead of prison. Also, the governor and the legislature have agreed to allow convicted felons with no history of violence to earn reductions in their sentences with good behavior. Still, there are currently about 16,500 drug offenders incarcerated in the state of New York.

The drug war has led to an overcrowding of our prisons. As a result of the mandatory minimums, it has become routine for wardens to grant early releases to violent criminals to make room for nonviolent drug violators who must serve out their full sentences.[83]

The Goal of a Drug-Free America

The stated goal of the war against drugs is to eliminate the consumption of these illicit substances—it's called zero tolerance. The phrase "drug-free America" pops up frequently. It was the title given to a White House conference in 1986, and showed up in legislation of that year which declared that it was the "policy of the United States Government to create a Drug-Free America by 1995."[84]

When 1995 rolled around, President Clinton's drug czar Lee Brown concluded that not only had America not been freed of drugs but that "drugs are readily available to anyone who wants to buy them. Cocaine and heroin street prices are low and purity is high—making use more feasible and affordable than ever."[85]

Facts notwithstanding, many of our political leaders still assert that zero tolerance is achievable if we just try harder. In 1998 House Speaker Dennis Hastert coauthored a plan to "help create a drug-free America by the year 2002."[86] The year 2002 was a reprise of 1995.

To state the obvious—that zero tolerance is an impossible dream—would be politically hazardous for any politician. Even examining the pros and cons of the drug war is dangerous territory. In December 1993, Bill Clinton's Surgeon General Jocelyn Elders said, "I do feel that we would markedly reduce our crime rate if drugs were legalized. But I don't know all the ramifications of this. I do feel that we need to do some studies."[87] She observed that in countries that had legalized drugs "there had been a reduction in the crime rate and there has been no increase in their drug use rate."[88] Her remarks caused a storm of protest. Eighty-seven Republican members of the House sent a letter to the president demanding that she be fired. Former drug czar William Bennett labeled her "nutty, just plain nutty." Elders continued to argue that the drug war should at least be studied. The White House sided with her critics! Press secretary Dee Dee Myers said, "The president is against legalizing drugs, and he's not interested in studying the issue."[89] President Clinton fired Elders in December 1994.

The Drug War Is a Mission Impossible

It's no secret that we're losing the drug war. It's been raging for over eighty years with no end in sight. No political leader has explained how we would know that an armistice had arrived. Over the past twenty-five years, our government has dramatically accelerated spending on the war. Enormous quantities of contraband have been confiscated and our prison population has exploded, but the street prices of cocaine and heroin have declined,[90] and the consumption of illicit drugs by our teenagers is higher in 2005 than it was in the early 1990s.[91]

Listen to Joseph D. McNamara, the former police chief of both San Jose, California, and Kansas City, Missouri: "It was my own experience as a policeman trying to enforce the laws against drugs that led me to change my attitude about drug-control policy ... I was a willing foot soldier at the start of the modern drug war, pounding a beat in Harlem. ... We made many arrests but it did not take long before cops realized that arrests did not lessen drug selling or drug use."[92]

Scholars overwhelmingly agree with McNamara that Washington's war on drugs is a mission impossible. The reason? The laws of supply and demand, which even the most powerful government on the planet cannot repeal. There are two mechanisms at the heart of these laws. One is the *lure of profits*. Suppliers respond to profits like bees to honey, and the underground market for illegal drugs generates enormous profits. According to the United Nations, in 2001 a kilogram of heroin in Pakistan cost about $300 and sold on the streets of the United States for about $290,000, while a kilogram of coca base in Colombia cost about $400–600 and sold in the United States for about $110,000.[93] How could law enforcement stand up to a market with such a tax-free profit margin?![94]

The other mechanism is called the "balloon" (or "hydra," or "push–down–pop–up") effect; namely, whenever law enforcement cracks down on the production or distribution of illicit drugs in one area, these substances pop up in another.[95] For example, in 1989 the voters of Jackson County, Missouri (containing most of Kansas City), imposed a ¼ percent sales tax on themselves to be given to law enforcement to fight the war on drugs.[96] Fifteen months after the tax went into effect, the head of the Street Narcotics Unit of the Kansas City Police Department reported that the police were "holding even" and that, "At best, we may move [dealers] a few blocks."[97] Albert Riederer, the Jackson County Prosecuting Attorney, who had proposed and campaigned for the sales tax, said a few years later, "I got caught up in it [the idea that the police can stamp out drugs] and I probably believed it. It isn't true."[98]

As we'll document in chapter 7, the billions we spend attempting to eradicate marijuana plants, coca plants, and opium poppies is money poured down a rat hole. The acreage required to satisfy demand is an infinitesimal fraction of that suitable for growing these crops.[99] When eradication reduces production in one area, new suppliers inevitably pop up elsewhere. In addition, our eradication campaign is inflicting economic, political, and health damage on the citizens of the countries that grow these plants.

We are also spending billions trying to prevent illicit substances from entering the country. Making even a dent in the inflow of these drugs is impossible.[100] Around 8 million shipping containers enter U.S. ports every year and our customs check only about 2 percent. The United States has 5,500 miles of coastline and 7,000 miles of shared borders with Canada and Mexico.[101] There's no way to search the bowels of the millions of cars, planes, trains, buses, boats, and passengers that enter the country every day.[102] Even President Ronald Reagan admitted the futility of stopping drugs from coming into the country, and he likened interdiction to "carrying water in a sieve." But he concluded that it was important to keep trying.[103]

Using law enforcement to eliminate the domestic distribution of illicit drugs is also a hopeless undertaking. Since the transactions are between willing buyers and sellers, there's no injured party to bring charges. To convict someone, law enforcement agents have to go undercover to set up an illegal buy. Consequently, the likelihood of being convicted for drug peddling is very small. There is a much higher probability that the undercover police will be corrupted or injured or killed in performing this dangerous, futile, and expensive task. When one drug pusher is taken off the streets, another is waiting in line to take his place. Selling illicit drugs promises quick profits, and it costs very little for a new peddler to set up shop.[104]

Damage Caused by the Drug War

Study the drug war from any perspective—economic, public health, civil liberties, violence, corruption—and you get a different dimension of the enormous damage caused by this crusade.

- **Violence** Since drug lords operate outside the law, they cannot appeal to the legal system to resolve disputes.[105] They're forced to take the law into their own hands. According to the FBI Uniform Crime Reports, the most violent episodes in the twentieth century coincided with the prohibition of alcohol and the escalation of the modern-day war on drugs.[106]
- **Drug contamination** When the government outlaws a drug, it surrenders the authority to regulate its quality. Consequently, black market drugs are frequently contaminated, sometimes with toxic substances. Most overdoses are a result of contaminants and ignorance about potency. Both would occur far less in a legal and regulated market.[107]
- **Property crimes** Drug prices are far higher in a black market than they would be in a legal market. In order to pay these artificially elevated prices, drug addicts commit property crimes to finance their habit. A study of prison inmates by the Bureau of Justice Statistics revealed that one in three robbers and burglars had committed their crimes to obtain money for drugs.[108]
- **Corruption** There is voluminous evidence that profits from the black market have corrupted many law enforcement officials. Corruption is inevitable where large amounts of cash are available to bribe low-paid police to look the other way in an undercover operation.[109] Judge James Gray observed that "Almost everyone in the legal profession knows

someone who has succumbed to the temptation of large amounts of 'easy' drug money."[110] According to the FBI, over half of the police convicted of corruption between 1993 and 1997 were involved in drug-related offenses.[111]

- **The Fourth Amendment** The United States Constitution guarantees against "unreasonable searches and seizures." This protection has been gutted by the drug war. For example, police can get search warrants on the word of an anonymous informant and often don't even bother with a warrant. International travelers can be strip searched and held incommunicado without reasonable suspicion or probable cause.[112]
- **Asset-forfeiture** The drug laws have allowed, and in fact encouraged, state and federal law enforcement to seize and keep real and financial property, often without even bringing charges. In 2000, the federal law was finally changed so that asset forfeiture could occur only if evidence existed that the person was involved in a drug crime. But property can still be permanently confiscated under federal law without a conviction.[113]
- **Drug McCarthyism** Project DARE is an anti-drug program taught by police officers in the school systems of 5,000 communities. Every study evaluating this program has concluded that it's ineffective, yet it continues.[114] In a number of cases, the program has resulted in students snitching on their parents, with serious legal consequences.[115] Drug czar William Bennett told middle-school students that exposing drug-using parents "isn't snitching ... It's an act of true loyalty—of friendship."[116] Sergeant Robert Gates, DARE's national coordinator, defended snitching on parents, saying that "an arrest is the best thing that could ever happen to that parent ... What may turn out to be negative for the parent is positive for society."[117]
- **The AIDS epidemic** Drug prohibition has made heroin more expensive, inducing addicts to get a bigger bang for the buck by injecting. Our government has refused to support the provision of clean needles, even though injection with dirty needles has been estimated by the Centers for Disease Control to be responsible for more than 250,000 HIV infections and more than half of the pediatric AIDS cases in the United States.[118] Numerous scientific studies, many funded by the government, have shown that providing clean needles would both save lives and, by bringing drug injectors into contact with the health care system, reduce drug addiction.[119] Needle exchange is strongly recommended by many organizations, including the National Academy of Science, the National Institutes of Health, and the American Medical Association.
- **Incarceration** We punish illicit drug users with prison, even though numerous studies have found that the "the perceived certainty and severity of punishment are insignificant factors in deterring use."[120] What is worse, the prison environment may actually encourage drug use. Drugs are readily available in most prisons. A federal survey found that, of those inmates who had regularly used hard drugs, three-fifths had not done so until after they were first incarcerated.[121]

Benefits of the Drug War?

If the United States abandoned this war, would the consumption of illicit drugs increase, perhaps even skyrocket? That's the fear many people have. The outcome would depend on how the country regulated, controlled, and taxed the different drugs, and I will examine this question in chapters 13 and 14.

Has government spending on the drug war reduced the rate of consumption of illicit drugs? Not according to the data. Federal spending on domestic law enforcement, interdiction, and eradication rose from $7.8 billion in 1994 to $12.9 billion in 2003, while, over the same time period, the percentage of Americans over twelve who had consumed illicit drugs in the month prior to the survey increased from 6.0 percent to 7.1 percent in 2001 and to 8.0 percent in 2003.[122] (Note: The increase from 2001 to 2003 may have been a result of a change in survey procedures, especially initiating federal payments in 2002 to those responding to the survey. The changes in the consumption rate of illicit drugs between 2002 and 2005 were insignificant. Also in 2003, the federal drug control budget was altered so that the data in subsequent years could no longer be compared with those of previous years. See chapter 7 for more on this.)

Regardless of how successful criminal penalties might be in reducing drug consumption, treatment has been shown to be far more effective. RAND Corporation researchers undertook a study funded by the U.S. Army to compare the effectiveness of prison versus treatment. RAND concluded that one dollar spent on treatment was equivalent to seven dollars put into the "most successful law-enforcement efforts to curb the use of cocaine."[123]

Plan of the Book

The focus of this book will be on the social costs and benefits of the drug war, along with alternatives to our current law enforcement approach. By now, you've undoubtedly guessed that I join those who see recourse to the criminal justice system to prohibit the use of certain drugs as an unmitigated disaster. I intend to spell out this disaster. I also examine different ways that the government could regulate the production and distribution of drugs if the war were abandoned.

In the next chapter, I look briefly at the way we were when all drugs were legal and how the drug war came into being.

2   The Birth of the Drug War

Then and Now

Cocaine

Dr. William Stewart Halsted (1852–1922) was a brilliant surgeon and a founder of Johns Hopkins Medical School. He was also a cocaine addict, and it almost destroyed him. He ultimately "cured" his abuse of cocaine by switching to another addictive substance, morphine, which allowed him to proceed with one of the most distinguished careers in American medicine.[1] Today, if law enforcement were to discover Halsted's drug use, he would be deemed a felon and incarcerated.

In 1993, Kay Tanner, aged fifty-six, was convicted of conspiracy to distribute cocaine, and was sentenced to ten years in prison without parole.[2] Tanner, a published writer, a mother of two, and a grandmother of two, had never been arrested and was convicted on hearsay evidence by government witnesses who earned reduced sentences for their testimony. There are many thousands of cases like Tanner's. See, for example, the many portraits of drug war victims in the book *Shattered Lives*.[3]

Hemp

In colonial America, the hemp plant, known as *Cannabis sativa*, was cultivated in all the colonies. Both George Washington and Thomas Jefferson grew it on their plantations.[4] Unlike most plants that provide drugs, hemp is the raw material for many other products as well. The stalk of the plant yields rope, cloth and paper, which, by the way, do not contain significant amounts of THC, the main psychoactive ingredient in marijuana. Most of the clothing of the colonists contained hemp fiber. The Constitution and the Declaration of Independence were originally written on hemp.[5] By the middle of the nineteenth century hemp was America's third largest crop, exceeded only by tobacco and cotton.[6]

Both marijuana and hashish are derivatives of the hemp plant. Marijuana is composed of hemp's flowers and dried leaves, and hashish is the resinous extract.[7] By the mid-1800s, hemp was also widely used recreationally. Hashish clubs for the well-to-do existed in every major city.

The 1937 Marijuana Tax Act was not a revenue-raising measure. Its real objective was to prohibit the use of marijuana for any purpose. It accomplished this by imposing a nominal tax, along with a "maze of affidavits, depositions, sworn statements and constant Treasury Department police inspection" on every medical and other licensed transaction involving hemp.[8] Failure to pay the tax immediately would make the physician and the patient liable to five years' imprisonment, a $2,000 fine, or both. In addition there was a prohibitive tax of $100 per ounce for unlicensed transactions, with similar penalties for tax evasion. The effect of the Act was to prohibit the production of hemp.[9]

During World War II hemp from the Philippines and jute (an alternative source of fiber) from India were cut off by the Japanese, and the American army was running short of rope and cloth. Restrictions on the production of hemp were eliminated. In fact, growing hemp now became a patriotic duty, essential for the war effort.[10] The government produced a film entitled *Hemp for Victory*, which extolled cannabis, and featured American flags waving and the strains of "My Old Kentucky Home". After the war, growing hemp in the United States was again prohibited.

Today, if you're a first-time, non-violent offender and are convicted in a federal court of growing 100 or more marijuana plants for any reason, you will serve five years or more in a federal prison without parole. According the U.S. Penal Code you could be imprisoned for up to a year for possession of one marijuana cigarette and up to five years for growing one marijuana plant.[11]

Opium

In the summer of 1789, the 83-year-old Benjamin Franklin wrote to a friend who had inquired about his health, "I have a long time been afflicted with almost constant and grievous pain, to combat which I have been obliged to have recourse to opium, which indeed has afforded me some ease from time to time, but then it has taken away my appetite and so impeded my digestion that I am become totally emaciated, and little remains of me but a skeleton covered with a skin."[12] Pain or no pain, Benjamin Franklin, at age eighty-three or twenty-three, would be guilty of a felony in the present-day United States were he "to have recourse to opium." Even physicians in America are prohibited from prescribing opium or its derivative heroin, although other opiates, such as morphine or fentanyl, are allowed. If you're a first-time, non-violent offender convicted in a federal court of possessing 3½ ounces or more of heroin, you will serve five years or more in a federal prison without parole.

The Good Old Days

There were no federal laws restricting the use or sale of narcotics, cocaine, or cannabis until the twentieth century. Toward the end of the 1800s a few states attempted to ban opium and cocaine, but these restrictions were unsuccessful, since the drugs could easily be smuggled from one state to another and the states lacked resources for effective enforcement.[13]

From the colonial period until World War I, Americans were legally able to buy and sell any drugs they wanted. They could purchase opiates, cocaine, and marijuana from pharmacists, physicians, drug stores, street vendors, and mail-order catalogs. Often, these substances were contained in patent medicines. As the historian David Musto observed, "Opiates and cocaine became popular—if unrecognized—items in the everyday life of Americans."[14]

In colonial America, opium was a highly popular medicine. Its therapeutic use had been "passed down to American physicians as an ancient and honorable practice, sanctioned by the greatest medical authorities over many centuries."[15] Its popularity with physicians did not rest on its ability to cure, but rather on its pain-relieving properties. It was prescribed for practically everything because it could make anyone feel better. As the historian David Courtwright describes it: "During the eighteenth century the drug was given to dull pain, induce sleep, control insanity, alleviate cough, check diarrhea, and treat a wide range of communicable diseases, including malaria, smallpox, syphilis, and tuberculosis."[16] When Alexander Hamilton lay dying with a shattered spine, it was a liquid potion called laudanum (a tincture of opium) that his physician gave him to alleviate the pain.[17] Laudanum was even used to quiet crying infants, as was another potion containing opium, called Godfrey's Cordial.[18] Many referred to opium as "God's Own Medicine".[19] Between 1830 and 1860 there was a growing concern about addiction to opium, probably a result of its use during the dysentery and cholera epidemics that struck the country during this period.[20]

When hypodermic medication became available in the 1860s and 1870s, morphine, derived from opium, replaced it as the medicine of choice. Like opium, morphine was seen as a panacea and used for practically everything, such as neuralgia, headache, painful menstruation, hangovers, rheumatism, insomnia, anxiety, and fatigue. It was also prescribed for chronic respiratory disorders such as bronchitis and tuberculosis, as well as for chronic infectious diseases such as malaria and syphilis.[21]

Physicians became so enamored of their magic needle they often caused addiction in their patients. If they didn't directly cause the addiction themselves, the patients or their families did, since the morphine and syringe were frequently left with the family with instructions to resort to it in case of pain.[22] This widespread use of opiates continued until the late 1890s, even though frequent warnings from doctors about addiction started to appear after 1870.

Heroin, derived from morphine, appeared in 1898. Like opium and morphine, it was also employed as a therapeutic agent. But unlike the other opiates, it was used mostly for respiratory complaints rather than as an all-purpose pain reliever, even though it was at least as potent an analgesic as morphine. Consequently, physicians caused far fewer patients to be addicted to heroin than the other opiates.[23]

Between 1890 and 1905, cocaine was extremely popular in the United States. It was believed to be effective in treating numerous health problems, including hay fever, sinusitis, fatigue, and drug addiction.[24] Even the scientific journals recommended it, as did Sigmund Freud, who used it and praised it, until he recognized its dangers as an addictive and potentially destructive drug. Cocaine was included in medicines, soft drinks, liquor, ointments, and sprays. One widely used drink was Vin Mariani, a coca wine, taken and praised by Thomas Edison and president William McKinley.[25] The Parke Davis Company sold coca-leaf cigarettes, coca cheroots, and an alcohol mixture called Coca Cordial.[26] Coca-Cola contained cocaine until 1903, when a substitute stimulant, caffeine, replaced it.[27]

After 1895 doctors became less liberal in dispensing opiates and were less likely to create addicted patients. This change was partly due to the warnings about addiction, but it also resulted from advances in medical knowledge and treatment, which provided alternatives. There was a growing acceptance of the germ theory of disease, and bacteriology became the model for the medical profession. Public health measures focusing on sanitation and hygiene reduced the incidence of diarrhea and dysentery. Vaccination began to be used against typhoid fever in 1896.[28] The pain-relieving qualities of aspirin were discovered in 1899. The German bacteriologist Paul Erlich developed the first successful drug against syphilis in 1909.[29] Developments such as these kept many people from being dosed with morphine. The use of opiates as a feel-good drug began to appear unprofessional and unscientific as well as dangerous.[30]

Drug War Rumblings

The state laws that intended to ban opium, cocaine, and marijuana prior to federal prohibition revealed a pattern that has characterized U.S. drug policy to the present day: the use of the drug laws to repress and punish minorities that are feared and hated. In the nineteenth and early twentieth centuries, three of these minorities were the Chinese, the African Americans, and the Mexicans. Each of these groups was associated with the use of a particular drug.

- San Francisco passed an ordinance in 1875 penalizing opium smoking, which was practiced by Chinese immigrants. The police raids were aimed at the dens in Chinatown, especially those patronized by whites. The nightmarish image that precipitated this legislation was described by a San Francisco physician, Winslow Anderson, who wrote of the "sickening sight of young white girls of sixteen to twenty years of age lying half-undressed on the floor or couches, smoking with their 'lovers'. Men and women, Chinese and white people, mix in Chinatown smoking houses."[31]

- In the last decade of the nineteenth century, states were enacting laws against the use of cocaine, which was especially feared in the South, because of the belief that the drug would spur blacks to violence against whites.[32] This fear coincided with lynching, legal segregation, and restrictive voting laws. There were rumors of superhuman strength exhibited by blacks high on cocaine. There was even the myth that cocaine made blacks unaffected by .32 caliber bullets, which caused the police to switch to .38 caliber revolvers. The fact that cocaine may not have been widespread among blacks did little to allay white panic. As the historian of cocaine Joseph F. Spillane put it: "The extent to which blacks were actually overrepresented in the cocaine-using population, however, is still an open question."[33]
- Mexican immigration into the United States soared during the first thirty years of the twentieth century. Most remained in Texas but the others fanned out into the Rocky Mountain area.[34] They were mostly farm laborers and tended to use marijuana as their drug of entertainment. While employers were happy to have them, the Mexicans were intensely feared, and so was their drug of choice. There were reports of violent crimes, which were attributed to their use of marijuana. Consequently, during this period almost every state west of the Mississippi passed legislation against marijuana, beginning with California and Utah in 1915. When the anti-marijuana bill came before the Montana legislature in 1929, Dr. Fred Fulsher got a laugh and instant recommendation for passage after saying, "When some beet field peon takes a few rares of this stuff, he thinks he has just been elected president of Mexico so he starts out to execute all his political enemies."[35]

Opening Shots

Fearing that it would be struck down as unconstitutional, Congress presented the Harrison Narcotic Act of 1914 as a revenue-raising measure, but its real purpose was to medicalize the distribution of opiates and cocaine. The Act limited the sale of these drugs to physicians and pharmacists, who were required to register with the United States Treasury, pay a nominal tax, and keep records. The Act turned out to be a time bomb.

The key issue was whether it was legitimate medical practice for a doctor to prescribe drugs to maintain an addict. The Act was ambiguous on this point, saying merely that doctors could prescribe drugs, but only "in good faith and in the course of ... professional practice."[36] Law enforcement officials argued that addict maintenance violated "good faith" and "professional practice," and they started to bring indictments against physicians, pharmacists, and addicts.[37] The Supreme Court rejected the government's argument in 1916.[38] But three years later, in *Webb* v. *United States*, the court emphatically reversed itself, saying that the notion that it was legitimate medical practice to provide opiates to keep an addict "comfortable" and maintain "his customary use" was a "perversion" of the law.[39]

On January 1, 1920, the Narcotic Division of the Treasury Department was created by the federal government to enforce the Harrison Act. As the law closed in on physicians and pharmacists, addicts flooded into hospitals, into police stations, and into the streets seeking help. Between 1919 and 1921, an estimated forty-four heroin maintenance clinics opened up in the nation's cities to help out.[40] But the Narcotic Division closed them all down.[41] Street sellers and buyers were arrested and jailed. (Even though the Supreme Court reversed its Webb ruling in 1925, in Linder v. *United States*, the punitive approach of the Treasury Department was so entrenched by then that the court's reversal had little effect on enforcement practices!)[42] Major targets of the Narcotic Division were physicians and pharmacists.[43] Thousands were threatened, and in 1921 over 1,500 were convicted. As a result many doctors refused to prescribe opiates and cocaine.[44] Soon, federal prisons were flooded with drug law violators, and wardens complained of overcrowding and the difficulty of dealing with addicted prisoners.[45]

The drug war had begun.

Causes of the War

A major cause of the war was a transformation in society's perception of addicts. In the latter part of the nineteenth century the main cause of opiate addiction was the excessive administration of the drug by physicians.[46] The typical opiate addict was a chronically ailing middle- or upper-class woman who had been addicted by her doctor. A literary example is Mary Tyrone, in Eugene O'Neill's play *Long Day's Journey into Night* (modeled after O'Neill's own mother). The typical cocaine addict in this period was a professional male in his early thirties who had been using the drug for medical purposes. Most of these addicts were physicians.[47] Addiction in those days was seen as a bad habit, indulged in by people who were mentally disturbed or weak-willed.[48] Addicts might be pitied or even scorned, but they were not seen as evil and dangerous. There was no possibility that a Mary Tyrone or her physician would wind up in a federal penitentiary.

In his study of opiate addiction in the United States, the historian David Courtwright showed that between 1895 and 1915 the composition of the addict population was transformed, and so was the attitude toward addicts.[49] Opiate addiction began to appear less frequently among middle- and upper-class white women and more frequently among lower-class urban men, often operating in the underworld. By 1915 this trend was well under way, with the typical addict seen more and more as a dangerous criminal rather than as a pitiful recluse. As Courtwright put it, "It could be plausibly argued that the high-strung matron or exhausted clerk addicted to opium was basically neurasthenic [nervous and exhausted], or that the invalid morphine addict was only the normal person in pain; but when the young tough snorting heroin on the street corner was perceived as the dominant addict type, new and more radical theories of addiction were in order."[50] Cocaine also became identified with criminals.[51]

Addiction came to be regarded with fear and loathing, and addicts were increasingly seen as a danger that needed to be eliminated from society. Respectable journalists, doctors, and politicians believed that opiates and cocaine led to insanity and crime. These substances became widely associated with foreigners and blacks, even though the police and physicians rarely mentioned blacks as users.[52] As David Musto put it, "Cocaine raised the specter of the wild Negro, opium the devious Chinese, morphine the tramps in the slums."[53]

This fear of drugs and addicts was amplified by the national threat posed by World War I.[54] Addiction was perceived as a danger to the war effort. People were frightened that our fighting men would get hooked. Rumors abounded that the communists, the anarchists and German immigrants were using drugs as well as bombs to destroy us. The Bolshevik success in Russia in 1919 intensified fears that the communists would take over here. Reports in the press alleged that German agents were trying to make our school children addicted to cocaine.[55] In 1919 the mayor of New York set up a committee to investigate what many believed was a link between heroin addiction and bombings by revolutionaries. The Attorney General A. Mitchell Palmer, ignoring free speech and assembly, rounded up anarchists and Bolsheviks, with no evidence ever being found to justify these unconstitutional raids.[56] In such a rabid atmosphere, popular support for addict maintenance was inconceivable.

This hysteria helps us understand why the Supreme Court radically reversed its initial interpretation of the Harrison Act. Earlier, in 1916, Oliver Wendell Holmes, Jr., speaking for a seven-man majority, had rebuked the government for interpreting a revenue measure as prohibition. But, in the Webb decision of 1919, the court unanimously condemned addict maintenance—saying that it was "so plain a perversion of meaning that no discussion of the subject is required."[57]

By denying addict maintenance the Court gave birth to the drug war.

Part II

Damage from the Drug War

Introduction

In August of 1976, Ron and Marsha "Keith" Schuchard held a birthday party for their thirteen-year-old daughter Ashley in their backyard.[1] Both Schuchards were English professors in Atlanta, self-described liberal Democrats, living in a comfortable suburban neighborhood. They had been worried about a personality change in their daughter. She had become moody and apathetic, had given up tennis, and only wanted to hang out with her friends. When she asked for a birthday party, her parents were encouraged.

The party took place at night and festive lanterns illuminated much of the backyard. Many of Ashley's friends were unknown to the Schuchards, who retired into the house so the kids could enjoy themselves. One red-eyed girl came inside and tried to use the phone but had trouble dialing. Peering out the window they could see that the hamburgers were not being eaten and that the kids had retreated to the darkened far corners of the yard, where lights were flickering.

After everyone had left, about 1 a.m., Ron and Keith went into the yard to survey the mess. The found malt liquor cans, and wine bottles, and were shocked to also discover marijuana butts and roach clips. They had no idea that children of twelve and thirteen smoked marijuana. They didn't use it, and in fact had had a bad experience years before when someone had served marijuana-laced brownies without telling them. At last they felt they had discovered the reason for their daughter's frightening personality change. It wasn't the growing pains of adolescence; it wasn't the malt liquor or the wine; *it was pot*!

This realization marks the moment when a powerful new force entered the war on drugs: parents panicking over drug use by their kids. Reacting to the discovery of marijuana in her own backyard, Keith Schuchard observed, "We had a sense of something invading our families, of being taken over by a culture that was very dangerous, very menacing."[2] She contacted the parents of her daughter's friends asking for a meeting to discuss what happened and see what could be done. Some thirty showed up but many were defensive and hostile. Nevertheless, she persuaded many of them to meet again in three days after getting more information.

What they learned appalled them. The police didn't think it was worth their time. The school principal denied there was a problem. The local merchants knew the kids were hanging out in their parking lots smoking pot. The school counselor told them not to worry and so did the experts. But the parents could see that drugs were harming their kids.[3] They also began to notice how pervasive the drug culture was. They looked more carefully at the posters, magazines, and albums in their kids' bedrooms. They realized that the smelly pieces of plastic lying around the house were pipes for smoking pot. It even seemed that TV shows sent a message that getting high was cool. Keith Schuchard went to see the Cheech and Chong movies that were so popular with the young, only to be outraged that it was considered funny to see people debilitated by drugs. By the time the parents met again, they were mad as hell. They set down rules for their kids, and began to chaperone or shadow them wherever they went. Schuchards group was called the Nosy Parents Association by the kids.

Susan Rusche lived across the street from the Schuchards. She was a homemaker, with two sons, aged seven and eight. One day in 1977 she took the boys to a store to buy a *Star Wars* record and was stunned to find display cases filled with drug paraphernalia, clearly aimed at young kids, such as bongs looking like space guns and pot pipes in the shape of frisbees. The magazine *High Times* was lying on the counter. It was also filled with come-ons to children, with advice on ordering LSD through the mail and ads featuring bongs for "Tots who Toke."[4] She and Keith Schuchard drove to several stores in Atlanta and found they were all selling the same kind of items. They felt this was powerful evidence that the drug culture was attempting to recruit young people, and they began to lecture about their concerns at PTA meetings, hoping to mobilize parents. In 1980, the DEA, with the help of Susan Rusche, drafted a drug paraphernalia law which banned not only their manufacture and sale but also their advertising. The White House funded the circulation of this model law to every state legislature.[5]

Keith Schuchard founded a national organization called PRIDE (Parents Research Institute for Drug Education), whose purpose was to educate and empower parents to assert proper parental control. It held annual conferences, and by 1981 it was attracting some five hundred people from thirty-four states.[6] There was great excitement that year because of the election of a sympathetic president, Ronald Reagan. In Keith Schuchard's address to the conference, she sounded a call to battle: "The dream we dared to speak of rather timidly three years ago in this auditorium seems well on its way to realization—that is, the growth of the parents' movement for drug-free youth ... to a powerful national movement."[7] She was right. PRIDE had been noticed and approved by the White House. The following year Nancy Reagan made the keynote speech at the annual PRIDE convention, saying, "I'm happy to be here among all of you concerned parents, because, while drugs have cast a dark shadow in recent years, the parent movement has been a light in the window."[8]

Good intentions, such as the understandable passion of parents to protect their young, do not necessarily lead to benign results for society. As I'll
document in this part of the book, the escalation of the drug war, fueled
partly by the parents' movement, is causing enormous damage to our
society, including our children.

The first casualty of any war is the truth, or so the saying goes, and the
truth certainly has been a casualty of the war on drugs. Consider the first
prime-time television address to the nation of President George H. W. Bush
on September 5, 1989.[9] He announced a plan to achieve "victory over
drugs" by drastically escalating the war. He held up a plastic bag of crack
labeled "EVIDENCE," and announced that it had been "seized a few days
ago by Drug Enforcement agents in a park across the street from the White
House." The next morning newspapers all over the country showed the
president holding up the bag. Surely the nation was in grave danger if crack
pushers were plying their trade right outside the White House.

Within a few weeks, the truth was discovered by the *Washington Post*
and widely broadcast by the media. The Attorney General had asked DEA
agents to find crack peddlers around the White House but they were unable
to do so. The pushers operated in the poor African-American neighborhoods several blocks away. An undercover DEA agent located an eighteen-
year-old high-school senior, Keith Jackson, who seemed willing to sell
crack. To comply with the president's wishes, the agent tried to entice
Jackson to come to Lafayette Park for the sale. According to the agent,
Jackson was confused by the request. He had never heard of Lafayette Park.
"It's across from the White House," the agent told him. "Where the fuck is
the White House?," Jackson asked, and then said, "Oh yeah, where Reagan
lives."[10] But Jackson didn't show up. The next day the agent called him and
had him driven to Lafayette Park, where they paid him $2,400 for the bag.
Jackson was arrested but the result was a hung jury. The jury foreman told
reporters, "The majority of the jurors felt it was a setup. People felt as
though because it was the president saying 'get me something to show on
TV', the government agents were pressured to go out and say, 'get any-
body.'"[11] A few months later, Jackson was convicted of selling drugs and
sentenced to ten years in prison.[12]

Truths about the drug war are not often so dramatically discovered and
publicized as in this case. Many of us remain ignorant of key facts about our
government's drug control policy. When I've told people that an anonymous
tip could result in their property being confiscated permanently without drug
charges ever being brought, they were incredulous.[13] And they were stunned
to learn that over 600,000 people are being arrested every year for simply
possessing marijuana.[14] They were appalled to discover that a first-time,
non-violent offender convicted of possessing less than 2 ounces of any substance containing cocaine powder would be sentenced to five years or more
in a federal prison without the possibility of parole.[15] With all the publicity
about AIDS, few realized that a major factor causing the epidemic in the

United States is the refusal of the federal and most state governments to fund the distribution of clean needles to intravenous drug users.[16]

Shocking facts such as these are just the tip of the iceberg. The never-ending drug war is damaging our society with no discernible benefits. Many of the harmful consequences of the war are unintended and unrecognized. In this part of the book I examine the devastation resulting from this crusade. Specifically, I show that the war causes:

- violence and property crime;
- a public health hazard;
- an erosion in our civil liberties;
- racial and class divisions in our society; and
- an enormous waste of our tax dollars.

3   Crime

Violence

It was no accident that the bag that President George H. W. Bush held up in his 1989 TV address to the nation held crack. He knew that crack was a terrifying specter to many Americans. It still is, and no wonder. The media have reported hundreds of stories claiming that the drug spurs all types of violence, along with a host of other horrors.[1] It has been billed as a major cause of the blight and violence plaguing America's inner cities.

This notion was heavily promoted by CBS and NBC in widely seen documentaries. In 1986, CBS presented "48 Hours on Crack Street," which Dan Rather previewed on his evening news program by saying, "Tonight, CBS News takes you to the streets, to the war zone, for an unusual two hours of hands-on horror."[2] The documentary featured the then New York Senator Alphonse D'Amato and the then U.S. Attorney Rudolf Guiliani in disguise purchasing crack on an inner-city street corner. Media reports such as these were the basis on which the Reagan and Bush administrations accelerated the war on drugs. "By the late 1980s ... cocaine in the form of crack was stimulating a major violent crime wave"—so claimed a 1996 book coauthored by William Bennett and John Walters, drug czars under presidents Bush senior and junior, respectively.[3]

President Clinton had a similar view of crack. He rejected the U.S. Sentencing Commission's recommendation to equalize the penalties for crack and powder cocaine, even though the disparity was widely seen as racist. His spokesman Mike McCurry explained why, asserting that crack and powder cocaine are "two different drugs" and that "crack cocaine is associated with much more violent, much more dangerous, much more anti-social behavior."[4] In fact, crack and powder cocaine are not two different drugs. The powder can easily be converted into the smokeable rocks called crack by being heated in baking soda and water.[5] Moreover, as we'll see, the violent and anti-social behavior associated with crack is rarely caused by the drug itself, but is rather a result of the economic and social conditions of the users and U.S. drug control policy.

It's true that crack and violence are related. In fact, there is a strong link between illicit drugs and violence, with the exception of marijuana.[6] But there is confusion among politicians, pundits, and much of the American public about the nature of this relationship. What causes what? Consider homicide. Fieldwork by drug researchers has focused on the extent to which drug-related murders are caused by the state of mind induced by consuming illicit drugs, warfare between black market suppliers, or addicts killing for drug money. This research analyzed the 414 murders which took place in New York City between March and October in 1988, of which 218 (53 percent) were classified by the police as drug related.[7] Of these 218 murders, 162 (74 percent) were caused by fighting among drug gangs, eight (3.7 percent) were killings to obtain money for drugs, and twenty-three (10.6 percent) were deemed to be the result of the consumption of alcohol, two of which also involved cocaine. Only three of the 218 drug-related homicides involved crack alone. Of these three murders, two had been precipitated by threatening behavior from the victim, one of whom was "reportedly high on crack and acting irrationally."[8] Unlike crime in the age of Al Capone, there were no gang killings over alcohol. Legal drugs don't spawn violent drug cartels or addicts desperate for a fix.

In sum, this research found that drug-related homicides have been overwhelmingly caused by the drug war, mainly turf battles between illegal drug cartels, and only to a very minor extent by the consumption of crack. (Keep in mind that those who are murdered by gang warfare are not only drug traffickers. The police are also victims, as are innocent bystanders caught in the crossfire.)

Crack is a more significant factor when considering all violent crimes rather than just homicides.[9] However, it's not crack itself that causes violence. As researchers John Morgan and Lynn Zimmer put it, "No drug *directly causes* violence simply through its pharmacological action ... Among people predisposed to behave violently, cocaine may increase the likelihood of their involvement in violent episodes" (emphasis in the original).[10] According to a panel of experts studying drug-related violence for the National Academy of Sciences, "Most of the violence associated with cocaine and narcotic drugs results from the business of supplying, dealing and acquiring these substances, not from the direct neurobiologic actions of these drugs."[11] Studies from the Netherlands, Canada, Australia, and the United States have found that crack users who engage in violence are "overwhelmingly concentrated among the most impoverished and vulnerable segments of their populations."[12] None of the gainfully employed crack users who were examined had committed violent acts or other street crimes.

There is additional evidence that alcohol consumption is a much bigger factor in violent crimes than crack. A study conducted at Columbia University found that, among violent felons in state prisons, 21 percent had committed their crimes while under the influence of alcohol alone, while only 3 percent had been on crack or powder cocaine alone, and only 1 percent had been using only heroin.[13]

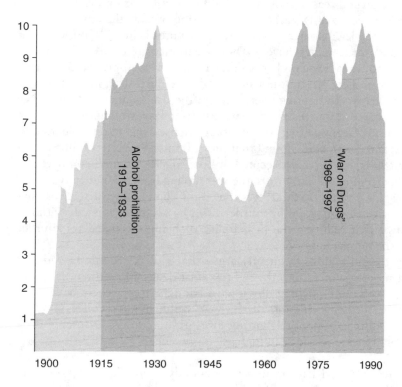

Figure 3.1 Murder in America: Homicides per 100,000 population 1900–7.

Other research also points to the drug war as a major cause of violent crime. Consider figure 3.1, which shows the homicide rate in America from 1900 to 1997.[14] The association of alcohol prohibition and the current war on drugs with the U.S. murder rate jumps out at you. The most violent episodes coincide with the prohibition of alcohol (1920–33) and the escalation in the drug war, which began in the late 1960s.

As the late Nobel Prize-winning economist Milton Friedman put it: "I believe that no one who looks at the evidence can doubt that ending [alcohol] prohibition had a significant and prompt effect on the homicide rate. Homicides ... rose very rapidly after Nixon introduced his drug war." Friedman estimated that, "if drugs were decriminalized, the homicide rate would fall sharply ... saving in excess of 10,000 lives a year!" (exclamation point in the original).[15]

In a rigorous statistical study, the economist Jeffrey Miron found that "the enforcement of alcohol and drug prohibition has been strongly associated with higher homicide rates," even after controlling for other variables that could cause homicide.[16]

There are several reasons why we would expect a war on drugs to cause violent crimes. Since drug pushers are operating outside the law, they have no access to the legal system to settle their disputes.[17] In addition, in going underground, drug gangs have to buy weaponry to protect themselves against the police and each other, so they're already well primed for battle; and, of course, there are enormous profits in the illicit drug market, which makes the turf worth fighting over. Finally, the drug war forces the police to devote scarce resources to nonviolent drug law violations.[18] Getting tough on drugs means getting soft on other offenses, including violent ones. A *Los Angeles Times* study found that only about 47 percent of murders in the early 1990s were even prosecuted in Los Angeles County, compared to about 80 percent in the late 1960s, the war having been dramatically revved up during this period. By the 1990s the county had so few detectives covering homicide that most of the murder cases had to be dismissed.[19] Studies have shown that reducing the probability of being convicted for murder increases the homicide rate.[20]

Politicians and pundits frequently argue that violence would be reduced if we put more resources into the fight against drugs. How often have you heard that we're not cracking down hard enough? Researchers have studied whether further escalation of the war would reduce violence. What they've found is the opposite! Putting more resources into enforcing drug prohibition appears to cause an increase in violence.[21]

- Harvard's Mark Kleiman, in a classic study of a police crackdown in Lawrence, Massachusetts, found an upsurge in violent crime, but no decline in drug use.[22]
- The Rand Corporation analyzed the results of a 1986 intensification of the drug war in Washington, D.C. The crackdown resulted in almost thirty thousand arrests in the first seventeen months, but as soon as the police turned off the pressure the drug markets were back to business as usual, except that drug-related murders had increased.[23]
- In July, 2004, all patrolling police in Newark, New Jersey, were ordered for the first time to wear bulletproof vests. The reason was a rash of violence against law enforcement. Four officers had been shot in July. According to the police chief, Irving Bradley, Jr., and the local political leaders, the violence was a reaction by drug gangs to an escalation in the war against the drug dealers. As Bradley put it: "We found a lot of areas where the drug dealers had a comfort zone. So what we did was add an additional hundred officers out there. Now, they're rebelling against the change."[24]

One outcome of a police crackdown, which displaces a drug gang, is that other gangs are motivated to battle each other for control of the area. An example occurred in late 1992 on 110th Street and Lexington in East Harlem, New York city.[25] It was a profitable drug market, taking in an estimated $6 million a year. The police had been routinely rounding up and arresting drug peddlers but came to realize the futility of doing so. As Captain Robert Curley, commanding officer of the 23rd Precinct, explained it: "They're all addicted, all selling just to get by. A high percentage of them are HIV-positive. They're in very, very bad shape. And they're easily replaced."[26] In light of this realization, the police decided to go after the top of the drug chain.

The organization that controlled drugs on 110th street was structured like an army; it had sergeants, lieutenants, and privates. It maintained control by the use of ruthless enforcers. Its commanding officer was a 32-year-old Dominican nicknamed Flaco. Going after the top of this organization was difficult, since Flaco and the other brass rarely got close to their products. Nevertheless, the police went all out. They borrowed specially trained agents from the ATF to help and consulted with a DEA task force. After several months of intensive and costly undercover operations they felt they had accumulated enough evidence to hold up in court. So they arrested fourteen members of the gang, Flaco among them. Federal charges were brought against them and it was expected that half of them would be behind bars for life.

Captain Ronald Welsh, the head of the narcotics unit that conducted the investigation, said that this was a "big case" and was the most successful that his unit had ever carried out. Welsh soon realized, however, that his work had been in vain. "There's still heroin on that corner," he said. As soon as Flaco's organization had been eliminated, "other guys moved right in picking up the slack."[27] Welsh was unable to do much against these new "guys" since he had busted his budget on the big case. To make matters worse, there were now several organizations fighting each other to gain control of this area. The crackdown had failed to stop heroin on that corner but had succeeded in bringing about an increase in violence!

What about a different way of cracking down? Why not simply lengthen the prison sentences for drug pushers? In the 2000 senate race in North Carolina, Elizabeth Dole advocated boosting the severity of the punishment for selling cocaine. Would such a policy shrink the number of drug peddlers? Not according to those likely to know. Listen to Dino, who managed a drug market at 109th and Lexington: "We know a lot of users willing to work. They're constantly hanging around the area, waiting to make a fast buck."[28] Michael Massing, author of *The Fix*, who did much of his research on the streets, observed that "the pool of potential pitchers [pushers] seemed bottomless."[29] Ironically, Senator Dole's recommendation would likely increase the dangers faced by law officers as well as the rest of us. As the punishment for drug law violations is increased *relative to* the punishment for violence, a drug trafficker facing arrest would have a greater incentive to shoot his way out in order to escape the harsher drug sentence.[30]

To sum up: The major cause of drug-related violence is turf warfare among drug gangs. Violence caused by addicts needing a fix is a small part of the picture. Contrary to conventional wisdom, the consumption of illicit drugs, such as crack or heroin, is a minor contributor to violence as compared to the consumption of alcohol. Police crackdowns and harsher punishments for drug traffickers are likely to have the unintended consequence of increasing violence without making a dent in the army of peddlers.

What are the policy implications of this research? It's almost certainly the case that violence would be reduced if the government took control of the prohibited drugs away from the underworld. If these drugs were accessible in some way to adults, and regulated by our governments, the enormous black market profits that nourish the drug cartels would be eliminated. In 1933, when alcohol prohibition was repealed, the states took control of the alcohol market, leading to the downfall of mobsters such as Al Capone along with a sharp drop in violence. Since then, the only contact we've had with turf warfare between bootleggers has been in the movies. I'll examine how governments might regulate the currently illicit drugs in chapters 13 and 14.

Property Crime

Black market cocaine and heroin are so expensive that many addicts resort to property crimes to feed their habit.[31] (Were these drugs legal and not taxed, their prices would be 10 to 15 percent of the black market prices.) In Michael Massing's four-year research project on drug addicts in Spanish Harlem, described in his book *The Fix*, he obtained much of his information by accompanying the operators of a small agency called Hot Line Cares, which helped addicts locate hospital beds, treatment centers, places to live, and jobs. As Massing put it, "Hot Line was one of the few places in the area where addicts could simply walk in off the street and get immediate help."[32]

Of the many addicts Massing interviewed, the one he was able to follow most closely was Yvonne Hamilton (not her real name). She was a "big woman, about five-ten and 170 pounds, with broad shoulders and large hands."[33] When Massing met her she had been addicted to crack for about seven years, smoking as much as two hundred dollars-worth a day. She had two children, who were being looked after by others.[34] Feeding her habit was all she thought about. Her mother was her main victim. She would snatch anything from her mother's apartment "that wasn't nailed down—TV, radios, cameras, fur coats, watches, a VCR, even her mother's wedding ring"—peddle them on the street, and then rush to her favorite corner to buy crack.[35] When her mother's apartment was stripped, Yvonne would prey on the community. She would shoplift clothes from places such as Lord & Taylor and the Gap, grab steaks and canned fish from supermarkets, and lift wallets from drunken patrons at bars. She also used her size to advantage by physically attacking likely targets on the street. As Massing put it, "She robbed widows and pensioners, the sick and disabled. She even went after 'Blind Lee', an elderly blind man who lived in her building, shaking him down several times in the elevator."[36]

Surprisingly, Yvonne spent no time in prison during this seven-year crime spree. Finally, out of detox for the nth time, and exhausted, she agreed, with the help of Hot Line Cares, to enter a drug treatment center called New Hope Manor, located in the wooded Delaware Water Gap on the New York–Pennsylvania border. It was a residential program for women, run by nuns that stressed education, and reputedly worked well for hard-core addicts.[37] It worked for Yvonne. After three months her craving for crack subsided and she began paying attention to the program. After six months the program's teachings began to sink in.[38] As she put it after being there for eight months, "Today, I realize that New Hope Manor is my focal point ... I choose no longer to be defiant."[39] She remained there for thirteen months,[40] then worked for several months at the Salvation Army,[41] and eventually obtained a job at a home for the disabled where she could earn a living wage. She moved into a five-bedroom house with her family in Chestnut Ridge near Spring Valley, and remained drug free for six years after her entry into New Hope Manor. She became a law-abiding citizen.[42]

Yvonne's life of crime is typical of drug addicts; they commit a staggering number of property crimes. One study of 237 Baltimore narcotic addicts found that they had committed over 500,000 property crimes over the average of the eleven years they had been on the street, an average of 192 crimes per person per year.[43] Another study found that heroin users in Miami had committed an average of 332 property crimes per person each year. Drug researcher James Inciardi reported that, "of 611 adolescent drug users (primarily crack) in Miami, 59 percent had participated in over 6000 robberies during the one year period prior to interview."[44] In spite of the enormous number of offenses, Inciardi found that the arrest rate was "almost insignificant," with less than 1 percent of the offenses leading to an arrest.[45]

One explanation for this insignificant arrest rate is the fact that police resources are stretched so thin prosecuting drug law violators that robbery gets short shrift. Judge James Gray reports that in some communities, on account of the prosecution of drug crimes, even "911 calls reporting household burglaries are not answered for hours, *if at all*" (emphasis in the original).[46]

A number of these property crimes would undoubtedly have taken place without the drug war. Many addicts had been committing crimes before they ever started using drugs.[47] But the evidence is overwhelming that the inflated black market price of drugs causes addicts to mug and rob to satisfy their habit. A survey of inmates by the Bureau of Justice Statistics found that one in three robbers committed their crime to get drug money.[48] Researchers also observe that when addicts are on methadone maintenance they commit fewer crimes.[49] Statistical research finds that when the prices of heroin or cocaine go up, so do property crimes.[50]

By causing these crimes, the war on drugs imposes a cost on all of us, even those of us who have not been directly victimized. A larger police force is necessary. Property insurance rates go up. We feel impelled to improve the security of our homes and cars, or even to move into a gated community. These findings suggest that, if drug addicts had safe and inexpensive access to the drugs they needed, property crimes would decline. Several programs have provided drugs to addicts with the cooperation of health professionals, for example, in Switzerland, the Netherlands, Liverpool, and Vancouver.[51] In the early 1970s, the United States set up government-sponsored treatment centers for addicts on a large scale, but only for a brief period.[52] The results of all these programs have been astonishing: the health of the addicts improved, their employment increased, they engaged in less crime, and a growing number opted to kick their habit. I'll examine these programs in chapter 14.

4 Public Health

While drug abuse is a danger to public health, prohibition is a far greater danger. Most of the diseases and deaths attributed to cocaine and heroin are a product of the drug war, not of the drugs themselves.

Black Market Dangers

Anarchy reigns in underground markets.[1] Consumers of black market drugs are often ignorant as to what they're getting. The Food and Drug Administration obviously cannot regulate drug quality in illegal markets. The Federal Trade Commission cannot prevent false advertising. Rather than build a reputation for quality, drug traffickers hide their identities to avoid the police.[2] Unlike cigarette and alcohol packages, heroin and cocaine carry no information or warning labels.

Pharmacology professors Avram Goldstein and Harold Kalant have pointed out that black market drugs, including marijuana, may contain "adulterants," "toxic byproducts," and "bacterial or viral contamination."[3] Snorting, eating, or injecting these drugs could cause such diseases as hepatitis, tetanus, malaria, and pulmonary infections. Were these drugs regulated by the government, contamination would be far less of a danger.

Consumers also risk fatal overdoses from black market heroin, because they don't know how potent the drug is. As Ethan Nadelmann put it, "People overdose [on heroin] because ... they don't know if the heroin is 1 percent or 40 percent ... Just imagine if every time you picked up a bottle of wine, you didn't know whether it was 8 percent alcohol or 80 percent alcohol [or] if every time you took an aspirin, you didn't know if it was 5 milligrams or 500 milligrams."[4] If the government regulated the currently illicit drugs, packages would contain information and warning labels. Drug prohibition has even increased the risk of legal drugs, by preventing appropriate warnings on them. It's well known that alcohol, barbiturates, and many other drugs combined with heroin or cocaine can kill, but you'd never learn that from the packaging on alcohol or prescription drugs.[5]

AIDS

The greatest health hazard stemming from the drug war is HIV/AIDS.[6] A major cause of the disease is the sharing of needles by heroin and cocaine injectors. According to the Centers for Disease Control and Prevention, contaminated needles resulting from needle sharing have been responsible for about one-fifth of HIV infections and most hepatitis C infections in the United States.[7] By the end of 2005 dirty needles had been responsible for ever 9,000 cases of AIDS among U.S. children under the age of thirteen.[8] Of the 984, 155 cases of reported AIDS in the United States at the end of 2005, 241, 364 (24.5 percent) were reported to have been the result of injection drug use.[9]

The war against drugs has stimulated intravenous injecting at the expense of less efficient and less dangerous modes of ingesting, such as drinking, smoking, snorting, or eating. Inflated black market prices create the incentive to inject, since injecting gives the greatest intoxication per dose.[10]

The drug war is also the prime cause of needle sharing. Even though almost all states now allow access to syringes without a prescription, illicit drug injectors continue to face a variety of barriers to obtaining clean needles:

- Most states have drug paraphernalia laws which make it a crime to possess any item that may be used to consume illegal drugs, including syringes. So the drug injector is in a catch-22—he may be able to buy clean needles legally, but possessing them may land him in jail![11]
- Even when states such as New York and Connecticut make an exception to their drug paraphernalia laws by legalizing the possession of syringes, it is often ignored by officers on the street.[12] For example, in Connecticut a class action suit in Federal District Court maintains that the Bridgeport police are harassing and arresting people for possessing injection equipment. In June, 2006, US District Court Judge Janet Hall ordered the police to stop, but the practice continued. The judge complained that "My order may well have been written in invisible ink."[13] She subsequently issued a second order chastising the police department.
- In forty-seven jurisdictions, drug possession laws can be applied to trace amounts of illegal drugs if they are found in used syringes. As one drug injector put it, "They'd [the police] catch you with a dirty syringe and you'd go to jail for [drug] possession."[14]
- Since syringes are usually sold in pharmacies, pharmacy regulations, such as requiring drug injectors to show ID or prove medical need, may deter people from even trying to purchase a syringe.[15]

Surveys of drug injectors have repeatedly found that they avoid carrying sterile injection equipment for fear of being arrested.[16] One heroin addict told interviewers, "I would rather get AIDS than go to jail."[17] Only a small percentage of addicts who inject possess sterile needles.[18] Most inject clandestinely, scrounging up syringes wherever they can. The result is a sharing of needles, leading to the spread of the HIV virus.[19]

According to federal law, national needle exchange programs could be funded if the secretary of health and human services determined that such a program would reduce the spread of HIV and not encourage illegal drug use. In April 1998, Secretary Donna Shalala made that determination, saying, "A meticulous scientific review has now proven that needle exchange programs can reduce the transmission of HIV and save lives without losing ground in the battle against illegal drugs."[20] Her conclusion was unanimously supported by seven major government-funded studies between 1991 and 1997.[21]

In 1998, Dr. Harold Varmus, Nobel Prize laureate in physiology and medicine, and then director of the National Institutes of Health, made the following announcement: "An exhaustive review of the science in this area indicates that needle exchange programs can be an effective component in the global effort to end the epidemic of HIV disease."[22]

In March of 2000, David Satcher, the surgeon general of the United States, stated that, "After reviewing the research to date, the senior scientists of the department and I have unanimously agreed that there is conclusive scientific evidence that syringe exchange programs, as part of a comprehensive strategy, are an effective public health intervention that reduces the transmission of HIV and does not encourage the use of illegal drugs."[23]

In 2004, the World Health Organization of the United Nations evaluated some two hundred studies on the effects of syringe exchange programs. Their report concluded that "There is compelling evidence that increasing the availability and utilization of sterile injecting equipment by IDUs [injecting drug users] reduces HIV infection substantially." They also found that "There is no convincing evidence of any major, unintended negative consequences" and that "paraphernalia legislation is a barrier to effective HIV control among IDUs."[24]

Numerous prestigious organizations have recommended the distribution of clean needles, including the National Commissions on AIDS of both presidents George H. W. Bush and Bill Clinton, the National Academy of Science, the National Institutes of Health, the Centers for Disease Control and Prevention, the American Medical Association, and the World Health Organization.[25] Most countries in Western Europe, along with Canada and Australia, authorize needle exchange as a major component of AIDS prevention. Hawaii is a dramatic example of the success of needle exchange programs. The state authorized such a program in 1990, and since 1996 there have been no cases of HIV infection among drug injectors.[26] In Hong Kong, in 1987, where needles were available and cheap, there was no drug-related AIDS.[27]

But, *this overwhelming scientific evidence in favor of needle exchange programs is no match for America's holy war.* The White House and Congress have continued to block funding for needle exchange.

Robert Martinez, President George H. W. Bush's drug czar in the final year of his administration, explained that distributing clean needles "undercuts the credibility of society's message that drug use is illegal and morally wrong. We must not lose sight of the fact that illegal drugs still pose a serious threat to our nation. Nor can we allow our concern for AIDS to undermine our determination to win the war on drugs."[28] But the National Commission on AIDS appointed by Martinez's boss disagreed:

> National drug policy must recognize the success of outreach programs which link needle exchange ... with drug treatment. ... These programs have demonstrated the ability to get substance users to change injection practices. Most significantly, these programs, rather than encouraging substance use, lead substantial numbers of substance users to seek treatment.[29]

As Ethan Nadelmann has pointed out, needle exchange programs "bring hard-to-reach drug users into contact with health care systems, and inform addicts about treatment programs."[30]

In 2003, President George W. Bush's attorney general, John Ashcroft, instituted a nationwide crackdown on sellers of drug paraphernalia.[31] In February, a hundred homes and businesses throughout the nation were raided. The inventories of forty-five drug paraphernalia businesses were seized, several internet sites were closed down, and fifty-five people were indicted. Defendants were charged with breaking the law against selling such items. One of those arrested was Tommy Chong of "Cheech and Chong" fame. He pleaded guilty on behalf of his bong and pipe business. Facing a maximum of three years in prison and $250,000 in fines, Chong pleaded for leniency and was sentenced to nine months in prison and a fine of $123,000.[32]

In September, 2006, a resolution calling for universal access to treatment for HIV/AIDS had to be withdrawn from the World Health Organization's Asia-Pacific conference because the United States objected to the recommendation for needle exchange programs. The New Zealand health minister, Pete Hodgson, who chaired the conference, said that the U.S. "position is that if they have needle exchanges then people will use needles more and use intravenous drugs more. I think it is demonstrably wrong. New Zealand has had needle swaps for 20 years—it has been an amazing success."[33]

Sending people to prison is another way the drug war has promoted the spread of the HIV virus. The United States imprisons about 450,000 nonviolent drug law violators.[34] Prison is a well-known incubator of AIDS as well as of drug abuse.[35] According to the Bureau of Justice Statistics, the prevalence of AIDS cases in prisons is three times higher than in the general population.[36] While sexual activity in prisons may not be as rampant as on the HBO series Oz, sex does occur. Shockingly, the distribution of condoms is prohibited in most prisons, making sex between inmates a possible death sentence.[37]

There is also little consideration of the public health danger that inmates pose when they're released. Dr. Robert Fullilove, dean of public health at Columbia University, observed that "The war on drugs took the group that was at greatest risk for HIV infection and made sure that they would be locked up, without ever considering what to do when they got out."[38] Dr. David Wohl, an infectious disease specialist at the University of North Carolina, Chapel Hill, who regularly sees current and former inmates in his clinical practice, describes what prisoners do when they get out: "Many inmates who have been locked up for a while want two things when they come out. One of them is a Big Mac. The other is sex. If you're going to get to them with condoms or health messages, you have to be quick."[39]

Not only are we not quick, federal and state laws make it difficult for many felons who have served their sentences to reenter society by denying them and their families public housing, college loans, public assistance, and other benefits, often for life.[40] The 1996 federal welfare reform law denies TANF (Temporary Assistance for Needy Families) or food stamps to anyone convicted of a drug offense even after completing their sentence.

By federal law, the rules for voting are set by the states. As a result, former prisoners can vote in some states and not in others. As I write (spring 2007), two states, Kentucky and Virginia, permanently ban felons from voting no matter how long ago the offense occurred. In nine other states, selected groups of felons are banned from voting for life. Only two states, Maine and Vermont, have no restrictions, even allowing inmates to vote. Most states do not allow inmates or parolees to vote. According to a report issued in October 2006 by the nonprofit Sentencing Project, legislatures in sixteen states have loosened voting restrictions on felons over the past decade, restoring rights to more that 600,000 people. Still, some 5.3 million Americans are denied the right to vote because of prior criminal behavior.[41]

Since a large fraction of felonies are nonviolent drug convictions, a major cause of voter disenfranchisement is the war on drugs. As pointed out by Thomas Clodfelter, a former felon with HIV, who now counsels other ex-convicts in Greensboro, North Carolina, these obstacles to felons reentering society often push them into dangerous social as well as sexual behavior.[42]

These public health dangers of imprisoning nonviolent drug law violators are no secret to our government officials, but you would never know it when you hear them extolling the war on drugs. For example, the book *Body Count*, written jointly by ex-drug czar William Bennett and the current drug czar, John Walters, preaches the virtues of incarcerating drug law violators. They refer to these prisoners as "felons who are very dangerous."[43] As they put it, "It is simply a (deadly) myth that our prison cells are filled with people who don't belong there, or that we would somehow be safer if fewer people were in prison."[44] So, the drug czars want us to believe that all those who consume illicit drugs are dangerous felons. That includes the more than 100,000 unfortunates who are behind bars for being caught possessing the wrong substance.[45] Logically, the czars' view also implies that the 112 million Americans who have used illicit drugs, as of 2005, but have escaped incarceration, are dangerous felons on the loose.[46] There's not a single mention in their book about any connections between the drug war, drug abuse, needle sharing, sex, prison, and AIDS. (More on the czars in chapters 8 and 9.)

The drug czars are not the only ones who see nonviolent drug law violators as felons. In my state of North Carolina, the state Supreme Court in June of 2004 clarified confusion in a 1979 law about whether cocaine possession was a misdemeanor or a felony. The court unanimously declared the behavior a felony, which mandated longer prison time than a misdemeanor. Attorney General Roy Cooper reacted to the decision by saying, "This ruling is critical to our fight against drugs and crime, because it allows for longer sentences and gives prosecutors the opportunity to use cocaine-possession charges to keep habitual felons off the street."[47] The defense attorney Daniel Shatz argued that the "system needs some overhauling" and that "What you get is essentially a lot of people who are drug addicts or have substance-abuse problems who are being warehoused in the prison system instead of getting treatment."[48]

When George W. Bush was running for governor of Texas in 1994, he harshly criticized a program initiated by the late Ann Richards, who was then governor, which provided long-term treatment and education to drug offenders prior to release from prison and a fifteen-month follow up "continuum-of-care program."[49] As candidate Bush saw it, "So long as we've got an epidemic of crime I think we ought to forget about rehabilitation and worry about incarceration ... I believe that most adult criminals are, sad to say, beyond much chance of rehabilitation."[50] When he became governor in 1995, he gutted Richards's program.

Prohibition and Potency

Drug prohibition often causes both suppliers and consumers to switch to drugs that are more potent.[51] Penalties depend on weight, not potency. For example, 1 gram of 90 percent pure cocaine brings the same punishment as 1 gram of 10 percent pure cocaine. Black market sellers respond to these punitive incentives by diminishing bulk and increasing potency. Consumers have a similar reaction. They switch to more potent psychoactives, which are also easier to conceal. As a result of the intensified drug enforcement of recent decades, heroin and cocaine have become more potent, and traffickers have favored heroin and cocaine over the more bulky and odorous marijuana.

During alcohol prohibition, smugglers and drinkers turned from beer to hard liquor for the same reasons. Beer was too bulky for the bootleggers to bother with, while with whiskey, a lot of alcohol could be packed into a small amount. When repeal came, the consumption of hard liquor declined by two-thirds, and consumers switched back to beer.[52]

The emergence of crack is another consequence of our drug control policy. By keeping the price of cocaine powder artificially elevated, dealers have an incentive to reach lower income consumers by developing and peddling a cheaper and more potent form of cocaine. As Steven Duke and Albert Gross put it, "The invention of crack is to the drug business what the development of the Ford assembly line was to the automobile business. Crack's discovery was breakthrough technology; it made mass marketing of cocaine economically feasible."[53]

The drug war also creates an incentive to use illicit drugs less often but more intensively (that is, a large dose consumed all at once).[54] More intensive use increases the chance of overdosing or becoming addicted. When a drug is prohibited, consuming it frequently raises the risk of being detected by law enforcement. Prior to 1914, when cocaine and opiates were legal, most users consumed them throughout the day in small doses, usually in pills or in highly diluted liquid solutions, such as Coca-Cola. They were incorporated into our everyday lives much like cigarettes and caffeine are today.[55] After 1914, people turned from the weaker and bulkier opium to the more potent and easier-to-hide heroin. The illegal status of heroin and cocaine caused consumers to use them less frequently but more intensively. People switched from pills and liquids to snorting and injecting.

Economists Daniel Benjamin and Roger Leroy Miller argue that the same pattern may exist today for teenagers who drink alcohol illegally, namely, drinking less often but binging more than people who are of legal age. As they put it, "Just as teenagers are prone to 'chug' illegally obtained beer to dispose of the evidence quickly, users of illegal drugs have an incentive to snort, smoke, or otherwise ingest their psychoactives intensively."[56]

In recent years, the trend has been the opposite for legal psychoactives, where both consumption and potency have been decreasing. This decline may be due to the growing emphasis on health and the dissemination of credible information about the dangers of these drugs. Millions of Americans, including teenagers, have quit smoking, and others have switched to cigarettes with lower nicotine and tar. People are consuming less alcohol and have turned from hard liquor to beer and wine. There has even been a decline in the use of caffeine in coffee and in sodas. Interestingly, in the years prior to the passage of the Harrison Act of 1914, there was a decline in the consumption of opiates.[57] No one argues that the trend is always downward for legal psychoactives, but it does seem clear that prohibition causes some people to switch to more potent drugs and to consume them in more dangerous ways.[58]

Ecstasy

In 1986, MDMA (or ecstasy) was declared a Schedule I drug, stamping it as having a potential for abuse and no medical value. A first-time offender selling more than 200 grams would serve at least fifteen to twenty-one months in prison.[59] Then, horror stories about the drug began to emerge from scientific research conducted at Johns Hopkins University. Government-funded studies led by Dr. George Ricaurte and his colleagues seemed to show that ecstasy caused irreversible brain damage and Parkinson's disease when injected into monkeys and baboons.[60] While many scientists disagreed with Ricaurte's conclusions, the media and the DEA regularly disseminated these frightening reports.[61] In 2000, Congress reacted by instructing the U.S. Sentencing Commission to increase the severity of the penalties for selling ecstasy. A key factor in the commission's deliberations appeared to have been Ricaurte's research, even though several other scientists harshly criticized it during the hearings. As the commission put it, "Dr. Ricaurte's work has appeared in peer-reviewed scientific journals of excellent reputation. The method of peer-review and dissemination lends credence to his work."[62] Harsher sentences were duly recommended and legislated. Currently, a first-time offender selling more than 200 grams of ecstasy would serve at least sixty-three to seventy-eight months in prison.

The end of this tale is a shocker. The findings in Dr. Ricaurte's studies turned out to be false. He published a retraction in *Science* magazine on September 12, 2003, claiming that the vials used to inject the drug had been mislabeled: methamphetamine had been used rather than ecstasy.[63] This error has stimulated accusations that government-funded research on illicit drugs is biased.[64] One of Ricaurte's team, Una McCann, said she regretted the role these erroneous results played in the deliberations of Congress over how to deal with ecstasy.[65] But the punishments based on these false results are still entrenched in the law.

Recent data for the United States show that ecstasy has been involved in thirty to forty deaths per year. According to Dr. Charles Grob of the UCLA School of Medicine, these deaths were "for the most part preventable."[66] The drug raises body temperature, which can be lethal in hot environments where there is vigorous dancing and a lack of water.[67] The war against drugs increases the danger of ecstasy, by discouraging safety measures at "raves," such as testing the pills, and ensuring that there are supplies of water and rooms where people can rest. As Dr. Grob put it, "To a regrettable degree, official drug policy has gone far beyond resisting harm reduction alternatives to a de facto maximization of the potential harm likely to be incurred through recreational Ecstasy use."[68] To make matters worse, the drug war has created an underground market. Surveys of the black market ecstasy sold to young people showed that samples contained a variety of foreign substances, ranging from the benign to the dangerous.

The Dutch have significantly reduced illness and mortality at raves by their harm reduction efforts. In the Netherlands, there has been an average of only one death a year involving ecstasy, even though much of the world's supply passes through that country. It's not even clear that ecstasy was a factor in these deaths.[69]

Studies of heavy use of ecstasy strongly suggest the existence of cognitive problems (mainly, loss of memory) as well as brain damage. Psychopharmacologists recommend that regular use of ecstasy be avoided.[70]

Medical Marijuana

There is overwhelming evidence that marijuana reduces pain, nausea, vomiting, and loss of appetite associated with AIDS and cancer, and that it lessens uncontrollable body movements resulting from multiple sclerosis.[71] Research also suggests that it may help control asthma, insomnia, and anxiety.[72] Marijuana is less addictive than caffeine, is incapable of causing an overdose, and has never caused a death.[73] (See chapter 3.)

Numerous organizations have endorsed medical access to marijuana, including the American Academy of Family Physicians, the American Public Health Association, the British Medical Association, the New England Journal of Medicine, and the National Academy of Sciences, which is authorized by Congress to advise the federal government on scientific matters.[74] The Institute of Medicine, established by the National Academy of Sciences, has issued a report saying, "there are some limited circumstances in which we recommend smoking marijuana for medical uses."[75] In 2002, the federal government's General Accountability Office (GAO) issued a report on how medical marijuana was working in Alaska, California, Hawaii, and Oregon. The GAO researchers were told by law enforcement that the programs were working well, and had not been taken advantage of by adolescents. The study found that most patients were using the drug for chronic pain and/or multiple sclerosis.[76]

A heavy majority of the American public favor legalizing medical marijuana. In a *Time*/CNN poll conducted in October, 2002, 80 percent of Americans believed that people should be "allowed to legally use marijuana for medical purposes if their doctor prescribes it."[77] In spite of this overwhelming public and scientific support, federal law prohibits physicians from prescribing marijuana, even though they can prescribe cocaine, morphine, and methamphetamine. The schedule I status of marijuana even prevents American researchers from investigating its medical properties.[78]

Currently (summer of 2008), thirteen states, including California, have legalized marijuana for medical purposes, which place these state laws in opposition to federal law.[79] In July, 2004, the United States House of Representatives reaffirmed the illicit status of medical marijuana by refusing to pass a law that would have prevented the federal government from arresting patients and doctors in states where physicians can legally prescribe the drug. The legislation gathered 148 votes, seventy short of passage. The House had turned down similar legislation in 2003.[80]

While marijuana has proven to be an effective antidote to the nausea, vomiting, and weight loss experienced by cancer and AIDS patients, there is a legal alternative, namely, dronabinol (brand name, Marinol). This medication is a synthetic version of THC, the psychoactive ingredient in marijuana. Dronabinol also decreases nausea and increases appetite, but many chemotherapy patients prefer smoked marijuana to dronabinol pills for several reasons:[81]

- Swallowing pills is difficult and sometimes impossible for patients who are nauseated and vomiting.
- Dronabinol acts more slowly than marijuana.
- Many patients who find dronabinol ineffective obtain relief with marijuana.
- Marijuana contains a component, cannabidiol, which has anti-anxiety effects that patients find helpful. This ingredient is not found in dronabinol.
- Adjusting the dose is easier when puffing than when taking pills.
- Dronabinol is expensive, costing from $600 to $1,000 a month.[82] A comparable dose of marijuana would cost about one-hundredth as much.[83]

In a survey conducted by the Kennedy School of Government, 75 percent of the oncologists who responded considered marijuana superior to dronabinol at preventing nausea and vomiting, with 48 percent saying they would prescribe marijuana if it were legal.[84] In a study published in the *New York State Journal of Medicine*, 29 percent of the cancer patients whose nausea and vomiting were not relieved by dronabinol did obtain relief from smoking marijuana.[85]

Relieving vomiting and nausea may sound like a relatively minor matter to those of us unfamiliar with the side effects of chemotherapy drugs. But, listen to Harvard Medical School professors Lester Grinspoon and James Bakalar: "Retching (dry heaves) may last for hours or even days after each treatment, followed by days and even weeks of nausea. Patients may break bones or rupture the esophagus while vomiting ... Furthermore, many patients eat almost nothing because they cannot stand the sight or smell of food. As they lose weight and strength, they find it more and more difficult to sustain the will to live."[86]

There are innumerable testimonies praising marijuana from people who have cancer, AIDS, and other diseases where conventional treatments had been ineffective.[87] Michael Ferruci, fifty-one, who runs a music store in Livermore, California, is afflicted with lung and testicular cancer. He claimed the drug has saved his life, and that he has suffered from its illegal status. Mr. Ferruci said, "it has been far more beneficial to me than other medications they have recommended to me, including powerful narcotics like morphine, Demerol and codeine."[88]

A woman from Santa Barbara, California, who underwent chemotherapy for ovarian cancer, said that the prescribed medications didn't work and she was forced to try marijuana, which she had never used before. She said, "Before marijuana, I'd become dangerously dehydrated. I would use enough [marijuana] so that I could finally sleep a few hours. Previously, I'd been awake nonstop and so miserable I wished I'd just die. Unlike with the doctor's pharmaceuticals, there were no side effects—like dopey drowsiness, constipation or depression."[89]

Carter Singleton, sixty-five, was diagnosed with non-Hodgkin's malignant lymphoma in 2001. Unable to eat, he lost 80 pounds in five months. "I was starving to death," he said.[90] Desperate, he followed a friend's advice and tried marijuana, which helped him get his appetite back. He was growing the plants in his basement because it was too expensive for him to buy. The plants were discovered when a neighbor who misinterpreted a flickering light called in firefighters. Marijuana is illegal under Ohio state law, and a county grand jury indicted Singleton in October of 2003. Hamilton county prosecutor Michael Allen said he had no choice but to prosecute. The judge could have sentenced Singleton to prison for up to five years, but in May 2004 he placed him on probation for three years with the proviso that he rely only on prescription drugs in the future. Singleton promised he would never do anything illegal again. What legal recourse he would have if he were once again unable to eat was apparently not of concern to the laws of his state, or his country.

When George W. Bush was running for president, he declared that medical marijuana should be a states' rights issue. He said, "I believe each state can choose that decision as they so choose."[91] This position put him at odds with most Republicans as well as with President Bill Clinton, who believed cannabis should be illegal in all the states. Since becoming president, George W. Bush has altered his position. Following a directive from the White House, Bush's attorney general, John Ashcroft, declared war on medical marijuana. He ordered a string of raids on cannabis clubs in California, clubs that had been established to provide relief for both terminally and chronically ill patients who had been prescribed marijuana by their physicians.

An example was an early morning raid in September, 2002, on a medical marijuana club in Santa Cruz that served the terminally ill.[92] It was a hospice-style, nonprofit organization. Thirty federal DEA agents burst into the place armed with automatic weapons, leveled the pot garden with chain saws and, while holding the patients at gunpoint, confiscated and destroyed 167 marijuana plants. They ordered Suzanne Preil, a paraplegic, to stand up, and when she could not, they handcuffed her to her bed. They arrested the founder, Valerie Corral, and took her away in her pajamas. Corral has been called the Florence Nightingale of the medical marijuana movement. She uses marijuana to control debilitating seizures as a result of a head trauma from an automobile accident. Corral had been operating the hospice under California's medical marijuana law, Proposition 215, as well as a 1992 Santa Cruz county ordinance, which permitted medical marijuana clinics. The place had been run openly and had a cooperative relationship with both state and local authorities.

A lawsuit to stop such raids was filed against Attorney General Ashcroft by Angel Raich of Oakland, California, who uses marijuana to ease her suffering from an inoperable brain cancer, and Diane Monson of Oroville, California, who uses the drug to treat chronic pain. In December, 2003, the U.S. Ninth Circuit Court of Appeals in San Francisco rejected by a two to one decision the government's use of the interstate commerce clause to prosecute people such as Raich and Monson.[93] The court ruled that patients couldn't be prosecuted by the federal government for using marijuana as long as all activity remains within a state that has legalized it. The Bush administration appealed the Raich decision to the U.S. Supreme Court.

In June, 2005, the Supreme Court upheld the right of the federal government to ban the medical use of marijuana even in states where the plant is grown and consumed within the state's borders. The court reasoned that allowing a state to grow marijuana would substantially affect interstate commerce, and the constitution grants Congress the power to regulate interstate commerce. What the ruling means is that users of marijuana as a medical treatment risk legal action by federal agencies and that the state laws provide no defense.[94]

Drug Substitutions

The war on drugs often has the unintended consequence of causing users to switch to more dangerous drugs when the supply of their favorite is disrupted.[95] For example:

- Studies have found marijuana and alcohol to be substitutes in the sense that an increase in the price of one causes an increase in the consumption of the other.[96] Alcohol is a major contributor to violence and traffic accidents, while marijuana is not.[97] Whenever the legal risks of using marijuana increase, there is likely to be more alcohol consumption, with a resulting upsurge in violence and traffic accidents. There is also evidence that marijuana might be a substitute for hard-drug use, suggesting that crackdowns on marijuana may stimulate heroin consumption.[98]
- The discovery in the 1930s of amphetamines, a class of synthetic stimulants, all but eliminated interest in cocaine.[99] Amphetamines had psychoactive effects much like cocaine, but were cheaper, easier to get, and produced a longer lasting high. When the federal control of amphetamines was tightened in the late 1960s, cocaine made a dramatic comeback.[100]
- The war against crack has stimulated the production of methamphetamine, a particularly powerful and dangerous amphetamine derivative, which is more potent and dangerous than crack.[101] Meth can also be readily brewed at home with legally available materials. (See chapter 4.)
- Opiates much more powerful than heroin have been developed by legitimate pharmaceutical manufacturers.[102] Many of these synthetics can also be made in basement laboratories. One of these is fentanyl, which is anywhere from fifty to 500 times more powerful than heroin. Fentanyl is a schedule II drug, which means it can be prescribed. It is

used by anesthesiologists to put patients to sleep; and it's also used in transdermal patches for the purpose of providing long-lasting pain relief. The reason that synthetics such as fentanyl are not commonly used by street addicts is that they cost more than heroin on the black market. Cracking down on heroin could stimulate the illegal distribution of synthetic opiates. The recreational use of such powerful synthetics could be deadly.

As economists Benjamin and Miller summarized it, "ample, low-cost supplies of nature's own raw materials [such as cocaine and heroin] have kept the back-room chemists at bay so far, but any significant disruptions in the existing supply chains will be met with a flood of synthetic substitutes."[103]

5   Civil Liberties

No-Knock Drug Raids

An hour before midnight on August 9, 1999, a police SWAT team of about twenty officers in El Monte, California, searching for drugs under a warrant that covered the neighborhood, blasted their way into the home of Mario Paz, a 64-year-old grandfather. The police referred to the procedure as a "high-risk entry," which involved shooting the locks off of the front and back doors and throwing so-called flash-bang grenades behind the house and into the back bedroom window. The agents burst into the room where Paz and his wife were asleep, and in the melee they shot Paz twice in the back, killing him. The lieutenant explained that the rounds were fired into his back because he "appeared to be reaching for something," a claim disputed by his wife. No drugs were found. Myrna Serrano, a family friend, who lives in a converted garage at the front of the house, said, "I didn't even hear them say they were police. I thought they were thieves coming to rob us. I never dreamed they would be police busting into the house in camouflage and hoods."[1]

At 7.05 a.m. on October 23, 1998, armed with a drug-related arrest warrant, a team of police raided the mobile home of Steve and Pat Eymer in Sallisaw, Oklahoma. As the agents burst in, screaming and waving guns at people, Pat Eymer, thirty-two, who was unarmed, picked up her terrified four-year-old daughter, and was shot by the police at close range in the shoulder by a 45-caliber hollow point bullet, shattering the shoulder bone. Her thirteen-year-old daughter passed out. Her four-month-old infant was just a few feet away. No drugs, or drug-making ingredients, were found.[2]

Horrors like these cannot be shrugged off as isolated incidents (for example, see the dozens of similar cases described at www.injusticeline.com/victims .html). Unannounced drug raids are standard procedure, especially in large cities. Police have no problem getting search warrants, even on the word of an anonymous informant.[3] In many cases they don't even bother to get a warrant, especially if they're breaking into the homes of minorities and the poor. The police defend their methods, claiming that overwhelming force, shock, and surprise are crucial to minimize the destruction of evidence and to reduce the danger to themselves.

In 1995, the U.S. Supreme Court supported these methods by ruling that the police do not have to knock and announce themselves if they have a reasonable suspicion that doing so would expose them to danger or lead to the destruction of evidence.[4] In 2006, the court strengthened the hand of law enforcement further by ruling that drugs seized in a home can be used in a trial even if the police failed to knock and announce their presence.[5]

It would be a mistake to blame law enforcement agents alone for these violations of civil liberties. The drug war burdens them with an impossible job and exposes them to enormous pressures and dangers.[6] They're charged with the task of arresting hundreds of thousands of drug dealers and users and seizing their supplies. It can't be done. Not only are illicit drug transactions ubiquitous and easily concealed, they're also consensual. There are no innocent victims. Neither buyer nor seller is going to report a drug sale to the police. Few witnesses would testify voluntarily for fear of reprisals.

Consequently, law enforcement must use different tactics for the drug war than they use for murder, rape, or robbery, crimes where victims or their families are more willing to press charges. Undercover operations are their main method. The police set up drug deals, use informants, and employ wiretapping. Former police chief Joseph McNamara pointed out that "Drug enforcement often involves questionable ethical behavior by the police."[7] As Judge James Gray put it: "These tactics necessarily result in greater intrusions into people's private lives."[8]

The manifest failure of our drug policy to diminish drug-related violence and drug abuse has resulted in the courts expanding the authority of law enforcement, causing many of our constitutional protections to be whittled away. Scholars routinely allude to this erosion in our civil liberties as the "drug exception" to the Bill of Rights. Some examples of this follow.[9]

The Assault on the Bill of Rights

The **Fourth Amendment** prohibits "unreasonable searches and seizures." The amendment has been torn to shreds by the drug war. Here are some of the ways in which this has happened.

- Anonymous tips alone were previously useless in obtaining a search warrant. That's no longer the case. Any of us could have our home searched simply by an anonymous informant claiming—with no corroborating evidence required!—that illicit drugs would be found there.[10]
- The Supreme Court has allowed the police, when stopping a car for a traffic violation, to order everyone out of the vehicle, to frisk anyone they suspect may be dangerous, and to search the car for illegal drugs if they believe there is probable cause.[11]
- Evidence obtained with an invalid search warrant can now be admitted in court as long as the police acted "in good faith."[12]

- The Supreme Court has held that an international traveler, suspected of balloon swallowing, could be strip-searched and forced to defecate. No search warrant or probable cause is required.[13]
- Lawyers Steven Duke and Albert Gross point out that the necessary "level of suspicion can be achieved by matching up the victim of the search or seizure with a few of the characteristics contained in secret 'drug courier profiles'."[14] As circuit judge Warren Ferguson observed: these profiles have a "chameleon-like way of adapting to any particular set of observations."[15] In other words, just about any international traveler can be searched if the magic word "drugs" is invoked.
- Informing on others has become a lucrative industry. In 1985 the federal government paid $25 million to informers, which a decade later had grown to $100 million. Eric Schlosser reports that "in major drug cases an informer can earn a million dollars or more" by being awarded a share of the assets confiscated as a result of their testimony.[16] Informants can obtain legal as well as monetary rewards. Providing useful information to a prosecutor can help a defendant avoid a lengthy mandatory minimum sentence. These benefits for informing create an incentive to provide false information, and many informers have been caught framing innocent people. Judge James Gray is not alone in saying that our "criminal justice system has been crippled and discredited by the large-scale use of 'snitches'."[17] U.S. District Judge Marvin Shoob of Atlanta says that the informants are often worse criminals than those on trial.[18]
- People living in mountainous areas frequently endure police helicopters flying over their homes at low altitudes searching for marijuana fields. "It's noisy, it's scary, there's dust flying," said one resident describing this novel form of an unreasonable search.[19]
- The Bill of Rights provides little protection to public school students.[20] The Supreme Court has approved the searches of purses, lockers, and college dorm rooms. Students have also been subjected to strip searches. The authorities simply need to indicate that they suspect drugs will be found.

According to the **Fifth Amendment**, "no person shall be deprived of life, liberty or property without due process of law; nor shall private property be taken for public use, without just compensation."

Federal and state civil forfeiture laws constitute a major encroachment on the protections provided by this amendment. These laws permit state government agencies in most jurisdictions of the country to confiscate personal assets suspected of being involved in a crime (almost always involving drugs) without even requiring that the owner be convicted.[21] According to Judge James Gray, this "statutory scheme ... is unprecedented in U.S. legal history."[22] One study found that, in 80 percent of the cases where property was seized and never returned, the owner was not even charged with a crime.[23] Cash, houses, cars, boats, planes, apartment buildings, and even ranches are among the assets that have been seized. Often, the burden is on the owner to prove in a court of law, at their own expense, that their property was *not* involved in a drug law violation.

The reason that governments can confiscate assets without convicting the owner or even bringing charges is that these forfeiture proceedings are civil and not criminal actions, therefore constitutional protections do not apply; that is, these laws operate under the bizarre rationale that the action is being brought against the property, not the individual. It's the property that's suspected of a crime, not the owner. Here are a couple of examples.

- In 1987, Ruth Allen of Mississippi loaned her car to her boyfriend, who used it to sell cocaine. The court approved the confiscation of her car even though the judge acknowledged that she "was unaware of and uninvolved in" the illegal act.[24] No criminal charges against her were necessary. Ruth Allen wasn't guilty, her car was!
- In Connecticut, Leslie C. Ohta, a federal prosecutor, seized the house of Paul and Ruth Derbacher, whose 22-year-old grandson was arrested for selling marijuana. They Derbachers were in their eighties and had owned the house for forty years. They had no idea their grandson kept illegal drugs in the house. Prosecutor Ohta insisted upon forfeiture of the house, arguing that people should know what's going on in their own home. A state judge told the Derbachers, "You are probably only guilty of being too tolerant of a criminal grandson." Not long after, Prosecutor Ohta's eighteen-year-old son was arrested for selling LSD from his mother's car; it had also been alleged that he had been selling marijuana from her house. Ohta was transferred out of the U.S. attorney's forfeiture unit, but neither her car nor her house were confiscated by the government.[25]

As Representative Henry Hyde (R-IL), former chairman of the House Judiciary Committee, put it, "Unfortunately, I think I can say that our civil asset forfeiture laws are being used in terribly unjust ways, and are depriving innocent citizens of their property with nothing that can be called due process. This is wrong and it must be stopped."[26]

Forfeited assets often fatten budgets of state and local police departments, which can receive up to 80 percent of forfeited assets when federal agents are involved. In a U.S. Department of Justice study, it was estimated that from 1986 to 1998 the federal government received $5.5 billion of assets from forfeiture cases involving federal agents, with almost $1.9 billion being distributed to state and local law enforcement agencies.[27] As Judge James Gray put it, "We certainly must fund our law enforcement agencies appropriately; but to allow them a share of the booty is an invitation to abuse."[28] A study published in the *University of Chicago Law Review* concluded that the ability of law enforcement to benefit from forfeited assets has caused a targeting of "assets rather than crime."[29] Former officials of the Justice Department have acknowledged that many forfeitures have been motivated by budgetary considerations.[30]

A blatant example of how the drug forfeiture law corrupts law enforcement is what happened to Donald P. Scott, the millionaire owner of a 200-acre ranch in Malibu.[31] A brigade of twenty-seven state and federal agents carried out a commando-style raid on his home on the morning of October 2, 1992. When Scott was awakened by the yelling of the agents and the screaming of his wife, he reached for a handgun on his nightstand, pointed it at the officers, and was killed. No marijuana was found. The warrant was based on the sworn statement of a DEA agent that he had observed fifty marijuana plants as he flew over Scott's ranch at an elevation of 1,000 feet. The ranch had already been entered and searched by the U.S. Border Patrol, who did not find any marijuana. It had also been photographed from the air by the California National Guard without confirming the presence of marijuana. Ventura County District Attorney Michael Bradbury conducted a six-month investigation into Donald Scott's death. He concluded that part of the motivation for the raid was the acquisition through forfeiture of Scott's $5 million ranch.[32] The government officials had appraised it before the raid.

Donald Scott's case is far from unique. In San Diego, government agents, acting on the tip of a paid informant, used a battering ram and flash-bang grenades to break into the home of Donald Carlson, who was shot and seriously injured. No drugs were found and Carlson was declared by the U.S. attorney in San Diego to be "wholly innocent." The government paid him $2.75 million for having destroyed one-quarter of his lung capacity.[33] The information that led to the break-in came from an informant who stood to make hundreds of thousands of dollars by receiving a bonus or a piece of the confiscated property.

In recent years, the federal government and several states have curbed some of the abuses in their asset forfeiture laws.[34] In April of 2000 federal law was finally modified, obliging the federal government to establish by a "preponderance of evidence" (that is, "it's more likely than not") that a property was involved in a crime before that property can be confiscated; but forfeiture can still occur without a conviction. Reforms in state laws vary, but do include such welcome provisions as requiring that an owner be convicted of a crime before the property can be forfeited, that innocent co-owners be protected, and that the proceeds of confiscated assets be redirected from police budgets to other programs.

In spite of these improvements, civil asset forfeiture laws still constitute an assault on our rights under the Fifth Amendment. It remains true in most jurisdictions that state government agents can confiscate property on the mere suspicion that it was involved in a drug crime and use the proceeds for law enforcement budgets without ever having to convict the owner of a crime or even to bring charges.

The **Sixth Amendment** is also a victim of the war on drugs. This amendment guarantees that in "all criminal prosecutions" the accused shall have "the Assistance of Counsel for his Defense." But the attitude in the United States is that almost any trial is too good for a drug law violator. As a result, the definition of the enemy in the drug war has been expanded to include even the attorney defending the accused.[35] Here are some of the ways that our protections under the Sixth Amendment have been eroded.

- Prosecutors have engaged in searching the offices and bugging the phones of attorneys who are defending clients in drug cases. The courts have approved of these practices, which increase the ability of the prosecutors to extract guilty pleas from those accused of violating the drug laws.[36]
- The Supreme Court has held that the government can confiscate the assets of an accused drug law violator, depriving the defendant of money to pay for a lawyer.[37] Court-appointed defense lawyers are notoriously underpaid and all too often incompetent.
- The long-standing tradition that conversations between lawyer and client are confidential appears to be at an end. Courts have concocted the bizarre rule that, if someone has eavesdropped upon a conversation in a prison between an attorney and a client, it follows that the client has given implicit consent to have the conversation monitored! This rationale was applied to the imprisoned drug lord Manuel Ortega, whose phone calls with his lawyer were taped. A federal court found that he waived any attorney–client privilege by speaking to his lawyer over the phone.[38]
- Defense attorneys in drug cases who are under some legal cloud, or who may just be unscrupulous, have been induced by some prosecutors to wear bugging devices to obtain incriminating statements against their own clients. As law professor Steven Duke put it, "The conduct of the government and the defense lawyers in ... [these] cases is not only outrageous, it is a felonious criminal conspiracy, yet I have never heard of a case like ... [these] where *any* proceedings of any kind were brought against the prosecutors. In most cases, nothing whatever is done" (emphasis in the original).[39]

According to the **First Amendment**, "Congress shall make no law ... abridging the freedom of speech." This amendment has protected radical and even hateful speech, including that of neo-Nazis and other racists, but has been challenged again and again by government officials attempting to limit the freedom to discuss illicit drugs.[40]

In 1996, California voters approved a medical marijuana initiative. The Clinton administration warned physicians that recommending marijuana "will lead to administrative action by the Drug Enforcement Administration to revoke the practitioner's registration."[41] This was a serious threat, for if doctors lose their license to prescribe drugs they would be out of business. In response, a group of doctors and patients filed a lawsuit in 1997. In October of 2002, the United States Court of Appeals for the Ninth Circuit ruled that doctors couldn't be punished for discussing marijuana with their patients. In its appeal to the Supreme Court, the Bush administration argued that the ruling of the federal appeals court was "an unprecedented judicial intrusion on the executive branch's investigatory authority."[42] On October 14, 2003, the Supreme Court upheld the ruling of the Ninth Circuit. Physicians can now discuss marijuana with their patients, but they still can't prescribe it.[43]

Another area where First Amendment rights are being attacked by Congress and the White House is the freedom of citizens to advertise their opposition to the drug laws on public buses and trains.[44] Buried in the 2004 omnibus spending bill was an amendment by Representative Ernest Istook (R-OK) that directed Congress to deny federal funds to local transit authorities that displayed advertisements promoting "the legalization or medical use of any substance listed in Schedule I ... of the Controlled Substances Act" – which includes marijuana. Congress and President George W. Bush approved the Istook amendment. The financial threat was a lethal one, for without federal subsidies many transit systems would go out of business.[45] So, if you wanted to place a paid advertisement on your local public buses or subways that conveyed scientific information about medical marijuana, you would most likely be turned down as a result of this law. Not surprisingly, this limit on free speech doesn't apply to the government. The 2004 spending bill provided the federal government with $145 million to advertise its war against drugs. Government ads promoting the war, especially focusing on marijuana, appear on public transport systems all over the country.

In February 2004, with more than $85 million of federal funding on the line, the Washington Metropolitan Area Transit Authority rejected an advertisement criticizing the marijuana laws. The ad was submitted as a test case by a coalition of drug policy reform groups. It shows a random selection of Americans behind bars, with the caption "Marijuana laws waste billions of taxpayer dollars to lock up non-violent Americans."[46] The ad's small print describes the barriers to reentering society after completing a drug-related prison sentence. The American Civil Liberties Union, along with other groups, sued the government and the Metropolitan Area Transit Authority. The lawsuit, *ACLU* v. *Mineta*, asked the court to declare the Istook amendment unconstitutional. As Steve Fox of the Marijuana Policy Project put it, "For the government to advertise one view while banning ads expressing differing opinions in the same forum is viewpoint discrimination and a clear violation of the First Amendment."[47]

In June, 2004, Judge Paul L. Friedman of the U.S. District Court for the District of Columbia ruled the Istook amendment unconstitutional. He stated that "there is a clear public interest in preventing the chilling of speech on the basis of viewpoint," and that "the government articulated no legitimate state interest in suppression of this particular speech other than the fact that it disproves of the message, an illegitimate and constitutionally impermissible reason."[48] The government is appealing the decision.

Believe it or not, Congress has even tried to prevent the results of a ballot measure on medical marijuana from being tallied.[49] In November 1998, Initiative 59 was put before the voters of Washington, D.C., asking them to answer yes or no as to whether marijuana should be legalized for medical use, if recommended by a physician, to alleviate serious illnesses such as AIDS, cancer, and glaucoma. A congressional measure introduced by Bob Barr (R-GA) prohibited the district government from spending money to count the results. This attempt to hide the outcome of the vote was struck down by Federal Judge Emmet G. Sullivan, who ruled that "There can be no doubt that the Barr Amendment restricts plaintiffs' First Amendment right to engage in political speech."[50] Barr accused the court of ignoring the "constitutional right and responsibility of Congress to pass laws protecting citizens from dangerous and addictive narcotics."[51] Sixty nine percent of D.C. voters approved the legalization of medical marijuana.

Mandatory Minimum Sentences

The **Eighth Amendment** prohibits the infliction of "cruel and unusual punishments." What constitutes "cruel and unusual" is of course a subjective matter, but many judges, including two Supreme Court justices, have complained about the punishments required by our drug laws. In the mid-1980s, Congress adopted sentencing guidelines to make criminal punishments in federal cases more uniform. Mandatory minimum sentences were also adopted, especially in drug cases. As a result, judges have often felt pressure to hand out longer sentences than they otherwise would, since these laws limited their authority to take into account the circumstances of the offense or the nature of the accused. Harsh sentences have frequently been imposed on nonviolent offenders.[52] Here are some examples, which, unfortunately, have been typical.

- Brenda Valencia, nineteen, drove her aunt to the home of a drug dealer in Florida. She was arrested, convicted, and sentenced to more than twelve years in prison without parole, even though she had no prior convictions and there was no evidence that she was involved in the sale of drugs. The federal district judge Jose Gonzales, Jr., who was required to give her that sentence, called it "an outrage."[53]
- U.S. District Judge Richard A. Gadbois had to sentence a low-income mother of four to a mandatory ten-year prison sentence. She had been paid $52 to mail a package, which contained crack. There was no evidence that she knew what the package contained. The judge said, "This woman does not belong in prison for 10 years. That's just crazy."[54]

- Zodenta McCarter, an elderly woman, first-time offender, poor and illiterate, was sentenced to eight years in federal prison for selling ditch weed, a strain of marijuana that is rarely psychoactive.[55]

Federal District Court Judge J. Lawrence Irving quit the bench over mandatory minimum drug laws. He said, "You've got murderers who get out sooner than some kid who did some stupid thing with drugs … These sentences are Draconian. It's a tragedy."[56] Judge John Martin, Jr., appointed by the first President Bush, has left the federal bench rather than be a part of "a sentencing system that is unnecessarily cruel and rigid."[57]

Mandatory minimums transfer power from judges to prosecutors. Except in special cases (mentioned below), judges have been required by law to abide by the sentencing guidelines. Prosecutors, on the other hand, can decide whether to bring charges, what charges to bring, and thus whether a mandatory minimum should apply. Particularly important, prosecutors can reward a defendant's assistance with a reduced charge. The resulting punishments have often conflicted with the principle that the longest sentences be imposed on the most dangerous drug law violators. The higher-ups in the drug cartel are the ones most likely to have information of value to the prosecutors, while low-level peddlers usually have little to offer.[58] A good illustration of the advantage of being a kingpin rather than a mule is the following report of an actual case before a federal judge in the Northern District of California. The judge said that the situation was typical:

> The accused, a low-level "runner" for a drug operation, knew only a very few people in the operation. Therefore, he had nothing to "bargain" in terms of giving information to the prosecutors. He was sentenced to a minimum of 20 years in prison. In the same courtroom, same judge, same drug operation, a drug dealer very high up in the organizational structure could and did name over a dozen people around and below him. For his "cooperation with the prosecution" he received a reduced sentence of only two years in prison.[59]

Mandatory minimum sentences have been opposed by the American Bar Association, by the U.S. Sentencing Commission, and by 92 percent of U.S. federal judges. Former Attorney General Janet Reno was also critical and called for an evaluation by the Department of Justice.[60]

The harshness of our drug laws has been increasingly challenged. Supreme Court Justice Anthony Kennedy, a Reagan appointee, argued that the sentencing guidelines should be "revised downward." Kennedy said on August 9, 2003, in an address to the American Bar Association, "Our resources are misspent, our punishments too severe, our sentences too long. I can accept neither the necessity nor the wisdom of federal mandatory minimum sentences. In all too many cases, mandatory minimum sentences are unjust."[61] Kennedy asked the lawyers to think about the consequences of our drug laws, including the "remarkable scale" of 2.1 million people behind bars, with 40 percent of the prison population black. The justice urged the ABA to lobby Congress and the lawyers applauded enthusiastically.

Judges still retained the discretion to impose sentences below the mandatory minimums if certain "safety valve" provisions applied, namely, if the defendant was a first-time offender, provided the government with accurate information, and was not violent or armed or a higher-up in a drug cartel.[62] But even this limited judicial discretion has been under attack. In April, 2003, Congress passed the PROTECT Act (popularly known as Amber Alert), which created a national notification system for child kidnappings.[63] While the bill was pending, representative Tom Feeney (R-FL) attached an amendment, which required that downward departures from the mandatory minimums by judges be reported to the Justice Department. As a result of the law, former Attorney General John Ashcroft directed federal prosecutors to report judges who issue sentences lighter than the guidelines. Critics are calling Ashcroft's plan to track individual judges a judicial blacklist.[64] The Feeney amendment and the attorney general's heightened scrutiny of judges' sentencing decisions has created a hostile atmosphere in which judges may have been reluctant to grant downward departures to the mandatory minimums even when the safety valve provisions applied.

The late Chief Justice William Rehnquist headed a group of twenty-seven judges calling for repeal of the Feeney amendment. He said the amendment could appear to be "an unwarranted and ill-considered effort to intimidate individual judges in the performance of their judicial duties."[65]

Lawyers and judges are not the only ones that have condemned mandatory prison sentences for drug abusers. Dr. Stanley Yolles, director of the National Institute of Mental Health, has testified:

> This type of law has no place in a system devised to control an illness … it should not apply to people who are sick … It destroys hope on the part of the person sentenced … A prison experience is often psychologically shattering … He may for the first time in his life learn criminal ways. Such mandatory sentences *destroy* the prospects of rehabilitation (emphasis in the original).[66]

One feature of mandatory minimums that has been particularly outrageous is the linking of the penalty to the *gross weight* of the drugs.[67] This means that the penalty depends on the weight of the mixture that contains the drug, not on the weight of the drug itself. For example, a first-time offender in possession of a mixture of 5.1 grams containing crack would be sentenced to a minimum of five years in prison. But, if this mixture weighed only 5.0 grams, the sentence would be at most one year. The difference between the weights could be the result of some harmless and legal ingredient rather than the drug. Judge Richard A. Posner, of the United States Seventh Circuit Court of Appeals, labeled this law "crazy," and said, "To base punishments on the weight of the carrier medium makes about as much sense as basing punishment on the weight of the defendant!"[68]

Here is a case reported by Judge Clay M. Smith of Orange County, California, where an infinitesimal amount of gross weight made all the difference in the life of a twenty-year-old man. Police in a routine traffic stop had stopped him. His car was searched and a small bag of marijuana was found, weighing 28.5 grams, just a shade under an ounce. The weight was crucial, because if it was under an ounce the result was a misdemeanor, involving a penalty of $100. If it was over an ounce, the result was a felony, punishable by a long prison term. The police took the man to the Orange County jail to be booked. A body search discovered another small bag of marijuana, one weighing only 2 grams. Adding the two weights together came to about a gram over an ounce, namely 1.035 ounces. As Judge Smith puts it, "Imagine the consequences! That extra smidgen of dope increased the defendant's exposure from a $100.00 fine to life in prison [under the Three Strikes Law]."[69]

In January, 2005, the Supreme Court struck down the mandatory federal sentencing guidelines, effectively freeing judges to use their discretion in imposing prison terms. But, there's a loophole. The court ruled that the guidelines were unconstitutional because they violated the defendant's Sixth Amendment right to trial by a jury. The court was reacting to the fact that the guidelines were forcing judges to boost sentences beyond the maximum that the jury's findings would support. But the court did not prohibit mandatory minimum sentencing, and Congress and the White House appear to be moving to institute even tougher mandatory minimums.[70] Attorney General Alberto R. Gonzales has been proclaiming that there is evidence of "a drift toward lesser sentences" since the Supreme Court's decision.[71]

6   Social Cohesion

It's no exaggeration to say that the drug war is tearing our society apart. It's transparently racist in effect and it leads to widespread corruption of our public officials.

Race

The evidence that our drug control policy disproportionately punishes African Americans is overwhelming. It's also been widely publicized, but that doesn't seem to have improved matters. In the past twenty years things have gotten worse.

According to the 2004–5 National Survey on Drug Use and Health, about 2.6 million blacks and 13.6 million whites over the age of twelve had used illicit drugs in the month prior to the survey.[1] Yet, while these numbers show that more than five whites used illicit drugs for each black who did so, there were almost twice the number of blacks than whites in state prisons for drug law violations. Specifically, of the 265,100 drug violators in state prisons in 2004, 126,000 (47.5 percent) were black, while 64,500 (24.32 percent) were white.[2] Whites not only outnumber blacks as consumers of illicit drugs, they also supply most of the peddlers. As DEA chief Robert Bonner put it, it's "probably safe to say whites themselves would be in the majority of traffickers."[3]

Studies by the U.S. Sentencing Commission—established by Congress to reform the drug laws—found that blacks received considerably longer prison sentences than whites for comparable crimes.[4] The commission recommended a substantial reduction in the difference between the sentence for crack cocaine and powder cocaine. To generate a five-year prison term, 500 grams of cocaine powder were required but only 5 grams of crack.[5] This disparity between powder and crack has been widely criticized as racially motivated. More than 90 percent of defendants in crack cases are African American, compared with about 25 percent in cases involving cocaine powder.[6] In 1996, Congress, with the support of President Clinton, rejected the Sentencing Commission's recommendation to diminish the disparity in punishment between these two forms of cocaine. In March 2002 the Bush administration announced that the harsher punishment for crack was justified. Deputy Attorney General Larry Thompson told the Sentencing Commission that it should not change the guidelines, but that if it insisted on doing so it should recommend tougher sentences for cocaine powder.[7]

Here is other evidence suggesting that the drug war disproportionately punishes African Americans.

- According to the Bureau of Justice Statistics, whites convicted of drug felonies in state courts are less likely than blacks to wind up in prison. Thirty-three percent of convicted whites receive a prison sentence, compared to 51% of convicted blacks.[8]
- In 1986 the average federal sentence for a drug offense was 11% higher for blacks than for whites. Four years later, following the mandatory minimum sentences for crack offenses, the average federal drug sentence was 49% higher for blacks than for whites.[9]
- According to a study published in the *New England Journal of Medicine*, black women are ten times more likely to be reported to child welfare agencies than white women for similar illicit drug use during pregnancy.[10]
- From 1990 to 1999, 64,900 blacks and 21,100 whites were sent to state prisons for drug violations.[11] (Recall that about five times as many whites use illicit drugs as blacks and that whites form a majority of traffickers.)

The war on drugs is waged mostly in the inner cities rather than in largely white middle-class neighborhoods. Street sweeps, rounding everyone up for questioning and searches, are common, as are aggressive and often warrantless searches of apartments in public-housing projects. Here is how one agent from the Bureau of Alcohol, Tobacco, and Firearms explained the rationale for a Washington, D.C., street sweep:

> This is definitely not a method you'd want to use in Georgetown or out in the suburbs. But in a neighborhood like this we knew the probability was great that out of every ten people we detained, at least six or seven would be in some kind of trouble with the law. That was our thinking. It was that kind of neighborhood.[12]

Inner cities aren't the only places where the drug war is used as a weapon against racial minorities. Consider what happened in Tulia, a small town of 5,000 people in the Texas Panhandle.[13] On August 22, 2003, Governor Rick Perry of Texas pardoned thirty-five people, thirty-one of whom were black, who had been convicted and imprisoned on drug charges in 1999 on the uncorroborated word of one state narcotics agent, Tom Coleman. Early on the morning of July 23, 1999, Texas police arrested forty-six men and women in the biggest drug bust in Swisher County's history. They had been rousted out of bed, were handcuffed, and were paraded, half-dressed, in front of television cameras, as they were taken into custody. Many were too poor to pay for a lawyer or meet bail.

Coleman's investigatory methods were beyond belief: he acknowledged he wore no recording device, had no video surveillance, asked no one to help, had no fingerprint evidence, jotted all information on his leg, and changed his testimony from one trial to the next. No cash, drugs, drug paraphernalia, or weapons were ever found. Nor was there any evidence of drug dealing.

Yet many of those arrested served years in prison, with sentences of twenty to 341 years! For example, Kizzie White served four years of a twenty-five-year sentence, and Freddie Brookins, Jr., aged twenty-six, served three and a half years of a twenty-year sentence. After he was par-doned, Mr. Brookins said, "What hurt the most was that the people in the courtroom and on the jury knew me and knew I hadn't done it. All of it had to do with race. It's a stupid way to try to get people out of town."[14] One of the harshest punishments, ninety years in prison, went to Joe Moore, aged sixty, a hog farmer, who had lived most of his life in a one-room shack. He had been described by the authorities as the drug kingpin. After he was freed he said, "I didn't even know nothin about a kingpin. I don't even know how a kingpin lives or nothin. But I know they live 30 times better than this. No, a 100 times better than this."[15]

The only way this horror could have happened is if many people went along with it. Coleman was hired by and was under the supervision of a fed-eral government narcotics task force, whose funding depended on the number of drug convictions. They were responsible for his behavior and were alerted to it by the NAACP and others, but did nothing. How the judges and the almost all-white juries could have approved any jail sentences given Coleman's methods is impossible to imagine. In addition, Coleman freely admitted that he routinely used the word "nigger" in front of his supe-rior officers in Tulia. As a reward for his drug bust, he was selected by the attorney general of Texas as the outstanding lawman of the year.

In January, 2005, Coleman was convicted of aggravated perjury. He was sentenced to ten years' probation and ordered to pay $7,500 in restitution to Swisher County.[16]

Corruption

The drug war generates enormous amounts of money, which flows in underground channels between groups of law breakers who are in constant danger of arrest. Police, judges, prosecutors, legislators, DEA agents, and prison guards are among those subject to bribery. Many succumb.[17]

Given the astronomical profits in black market drugs, and the fact that the illegal transactions take place between colluding sellers and buyers, law enforcement officials find themselves in possession of an extremely valuable service—looking the other way. Imagine that you're an undercover officer observing an illicit drug transaction. Who would know if you accepted the dealer's offer to augment your meager salary by just ignoring the whole thing? As a fellow officer told the detective Robert Sobel when he joined the Los Angeles narcotics division, "If you look the other way, I can make you a rich man." Sobel followed the advice, and made $140,000 over two years.[18] The police can sell other services as well: giving dealers information about drug stings or providing favorable testimony at a trial. As Steven Duke and Albert Gross put it "Policemen in virtually every American city are on the payrolls of drug merchants, earning their pay by tipping off drug dealers. Hundreds of law-enforcement officials have been convicted of taking bribes, stealing from drug dealers, even selling their drugs."[19] Judge James Gray reports that "Almost everyone in the legal profession knows someone who has succumbed to the temptation of large amounts of 'easy' drug money."[20]

The corruption of public officials as a result of the drug war has been amply documented. Here are some examples.

- In the late 1960s, the Knapp Commission's investigation into the New York City police department found that about half of the narcotics agents had been indicted or discharged on grounds of corruption. In the New York office of the Federal Bureau of Narcotics and Dangerous Drugs, corruption was so rampant that almost every agent was fired or transferred.[21]
- In the early 1980s, the entire homicide squad of nine detectives in the Metro Dade Police Department in Florida was indicted on federal charges of "racketeering, bribery, extortion and dealing in narcotics." Four of the detectives were convicted.[22]
- In 1994, New York City's Mollen Commission reported that corruption had become more vicious than the bribery scandals of earlier years, with the police now "acting as criminals, especially in connection with the drug trade."[23]
- The number of federal, state and local law enforcement officials in federal prisons for corruption, mostly in connection with illicit drugs, increased from 107 in 1994 to 668 in 2000.[24]
- In 1998, the General Accounting (now called Accountability) Office (GAO)—the investigative arm of Congress—reported that "several studies and investigations of drug-related police corruption found [that] on-duty police officers engaged in serious criminal activities, such as (1) conducting unconstitutional searches and seizures; (2) stealing money and/or drugs from drug dealers; (3) selling stolen drugs; (4) protecting drug operations; (5) providing false testimony; and (6) submitting false crime reports."[25] As one example: From 1995 to 1998, ten police officers in Philadelphia were charged with planting drugs, shaking down drug dealers, and breaking into homes to steal drugs.

Corruption is not limited to the police. Other public officials are also vulnerable.[26] For instance, a few months after the first President Bush expanded the war on drugs in 1989, several agents of the Drug Enforcement Administration were sentenced to prison on corruption charges.[27]

This evidence raises the question of whether honest government and the drug war can coexist. A federal prosecutor who spent months investigating a Los Angeles sheriff had this to say on the question: "I realized how much of the story of police corruption revolved around drugs. The temptation to skim came from the constant contact with outlandish sums of untraceable drug proceeds. ... If you ask enough people—good, bad, or indifferent—to go into a room with a bag of apparently untraceable cash, sooner or later, someone will unzip the bag and take a bundle ... And, regrettably, those are things we must ask some people to do every day."[28] A United Nations report on drugs also commented on this issue: "In systems where a member of the legislature or judiciary, earning only a modest income, can easily gain the equivalent of some 20 months' salary from a trafficker by making one 'favorable' decision, the dangers of corruption are obvious."[29]

This pervasive corruption of public officials is not an aberration; it's intrinsic to the war on drugs, which operates undercover, hence largely free of public scrutiny. There's an unholy alliance between drug agents and drug lords, which is enormously valuable to both parties.[30] That's the reason government crackdowns on corruption connected with illicit drugs have been futile.

7   Your Tax Dollars at Work

America's war on drugs has focused mainly on supply reduction, that is, employing law enforcement and the military to destroy the production capabilities of foreign countries, stopping illicit drugs from being smuggled into the country, and combating domestic production and distribution. Annual federal expenditures for the drug war grew from about $1.5 billion in 1981 to about $19.2 billion in 2003, with the states spending at least that much.[1] About two-thirds of the $19.2 billion of federal spending was devoted to supply reduction, namely, $1.2 billion to combat foreign drug production, $2.3 billion to prevent prohibited drugs from coming into the country, and $9.5 billion on domestic law enforcement. The remaining one-third was spent on demand reduction, namely, treatment and prevention.

In 2004 the Bush administration drastically restructured the federal drug control budget,[2] which no longer includes the cost of housing drug prisoners or the expenditures related to prosecuting drug cases. The revised budget approach also inflates federal spending on treatment by including that for alcohol. The upshot—and presumably the intent—of this number juggling was to eliminate the two-to-one split favoring supply reduction, which has persisted since the early 1980s. Under the new reporting method, the ratio between law enforcement and treatment/prevention is close to even.

How successful has the spending on law enforcement been?

Cocaine and Heroin Prices

The goal of supply reduction is to drive up the price of illicit drugs in order to diminish consumption. But the policy has failed. The street prices of heroin and cocaine have been falling since the early 1980s in spite of the rapid growth in government spending aimed at curtailing supply.[3] Testimony presented to the House Committee on Appropriations revealed that the 1981 price of a pure gram of cocaine was $379, which fell in 1998 to $169. Heroin prices fell from $311 to $180 for 1 pure gram over the same period. The conclusion of this study was that "traffickers are finding it easier to get drugs to our streets, not harder."[4] There are several likely explanations for these price declines, such as the acquisition of experience by smugglers, the increased use of juveniles as cheap labor, higher-yielding crops, and improvements in transportation and communication networks.[5]

As for the consumption of illicit drugs, the rate increased from 1994 to 2003 even though federal spending on supply reduction rose: in 1994, 6 percent of Americans aged over twelve were currently using illicit drugs, while in 2003 this figure had risen to 8.2 percent.[6]

Eradication

"The logic is simple. The cheapest and safest way to eradicate narcotics is to destroy them at their source ... We need to wipe out crops wherever they are grown." So said George H. W. Bush in a 1988 campaign speech.[7] Congress responded to President Bush's "logic" in 1989 by appropriating $2.1 billion for a five-year plan, "the Andean Initiative," to eradicate coca plants in Colombia, Bolivia, and Peru.[8]

The program contained a carrot and a stick. The money would be used to provide support for law enforcement and the military, and to fund projects to develop crops to replace coca. But if the recipient country did not "take adequate steps to prevent narcotic drugs ... from entering the United States unlawfully," financial assistance would be withheld, and the United States would block loans to the offending country from the International Bank for Reconstruction and Development and the International Development Association.[9] Similar commitments had been made by the Nixon and Reagan administrations and would be continued by presidents Bill Clinton and George W. Bush.

In attempting to exterminate the coca plant, the United States has been assaulting an ancient and revered tradition among the Andean Indians, who represent a majority in Bolivia and a near majority in Peru. For them, coca is a precious herb. The leaf of the plant is chewed or sprinkled in tea as a mild stimulant, and it provides the Indians relief from hunger, fatigue, and the cold. Agricultural workers take several breaks a day to rest and chew coca, which plays the same role in the Andes as coffee, cigarettes, and aspirin do in our society.[10]

In 1988, U.S. pressure led the Bolivian Congress to pass a law limiting the legal production of coca to 12,000 hectares (1.2 million acres) of land, which the American government in its wisdom deemed sufficient to meet the domestic needs of Bolivia.[11] Coca production beyond that was declared illegal. Coca farmers (called cocaleros) and other activists have been fighting the 12,000 hectare limit, which has remained unchanged since 1988 despite the growth in the Bolivian population. The U.S.-backed eradication campaign has ignited a firestorm of opposition in Bolivia as well as in the other Andean nations.

It's hard to imagine that U.S. political leaders genuinely believed that coca eradication could ever be successful, since government studies have repeatedly shown that the attempt is futile.

- In 1992, the State Department reported that eradication had had no effect on Andean coca production.[12]
- In 1993, a U.S. embassy official in Peru concluded that our crop-eradication efforts "haven't had any real impact on the drug flow."[13]
- The U.S. General Accountability Office reported in 1999: "Despite 2 years of extensive herbicide spraying, U.S. estimates show there has not been any net reduction in [Colombian] coca cultivation—net coca cultivation actually increased 50 percent."[14]
- In 2002, studies by the government concluded that the U.S. expenditure of $50 million to induce Colombian farmers to replace coca with legal crops had not worked. Coca cultivation in Colombia surged by 25 percent from 2000 to 2001 despite intensive fumigation, military assistance, and the crop substitution program.[15]
- The U.S. Department of Agriculture has estimated that, out of two and half million square miles in South America where the coca plant can be grown, a mere 700 square miles are currently being used.[16] There's clearly no shortage of land to grow coca.

As Ethan Nadelmann expressed it, "Even where eradication efforts prove relatively successful in one country, the 'push down–pop up' phenomenon ensures that production will emerge in other countries."[17] A congressional report agreed, concluding that crop eradication in the Andes "helped lead to an ironic and undesirable result: the dispersion of the drug trade to other nations in South America."[18] A Mexican official complained that drug enforcement was "like a water balloon. We squeeze one side and it goes out the other."[19]

A dramatic decline in coca production in Peru and Bolivia in the late 1990s coincided with a huge increase in output in Colombia; and the subsequent massive campaign to wipe out coca in Colombia led to predictions that production would merely shift to Peru and Bolivia.[20] The predictions were right on the mark. A UN report calculated that Peru boosted coca production in 2002 by about 6 percent over the preceding year;[21] and Dr. Francisco Thoumi, a Colombian economist, found that there had been an increase in plantings in Bolivia.[22]

In October, 2003, John Walters, President George W. Bush's drug czar, released a success story to the press, stating that "We have already seen a 15 percent drop in overall coca cultivation in Colombia and an increase in cocaine seizures from South America."[23] A UN study pointed out, however, that cultivation is not production; and that more productive varieties of coca had been developed in the Andes in response to the eradication campaign.[24]

In August, 2004, the drug czar reversed himself.[25] After visiting Colombia, Walters conceded that destroying coca crops, seizing cocaine, and imprisoning Colombian drug traffickers had had little impact on the flow of cocaine into the United States. But he insisted that we must continue with the so-called Plan Colombia, a $3.3 billion, five-year program helping Colombia carry on the war against drugs.

A closer look provides additional insights into the failure of our eradication policy.[26] Colombia's police report that 85 percent of sprayed coca is quickly replanted. In addition, coca farmers have begun planting in national parks, where aircraft are prohibited from fumigating. There is also the problem of security: the U.S. General Accountability Office reported that spray planes in Colombia are being hit by small-arms fire about twenty-six times a month. Two U.S. State Department-contracted pilots have been killed since 2000 and three are being held by drug barons.

Aerial spraying of herbicides harms more than coca. It contaminates food crops, animals, and drinking wells, and it damages the health of humans. According to Elsa Nivia, a Colombian scientist, the herbicide used in Colombia can cause rashes, burning eyes, vomiting, and headaches.[27] Also, the aerial spray drifts with the wind, so it can't be precisely aimed. In 2000, while the late Senator Paul Wellstone was watching a government demonstration of herbicide spraying, the wind shifted and gave him a dose.[28]

Drug traffickers aren't the only ones who resist the U.S. eradication efforts: the Andean countries in South America oppose it because drug trafficking is a major source of income and employment, constituting the livelihood for many peasants. In Bolivia, the drug economy employs 20 percent of the labor force. When Bolivia's President Jaime Paz Zamora met President George H. W. Bush in 1990, he explained that 70 percent of their national income was cocaine related and that half of their imports were paid for by cocaine exports.[29] Bolivia's former finance minister Flavio Machicado said that, if cocaine were to disappear, the country would have "rampant unemployment" and "open protest and violence."[30]

Given the honored role of coca in Andean culture, as well as its economic importance, it's not surprising that the peasants have been militant in defense of the coca trade. For example, in 1982, 200 Bolivian cocaleros attacked narcotics agents, killing seven, and forced the Bolivian government to recall its agents.[31] In 1985, hundreds of Bolivian farmers marched to the American embassy, shouting "Long live coca. Death to the Yankees."[32] Even the Catholic Church in Bolivia has condemned the United States for "imposing a policy to liquidate part of our countryside, where the farmer lives exclusively from his products."[33]

In October, 2003, Bolivian President Gonzalo Sanchez de Lozada was driven into exile by a popular uprising following a month of violent protests.[34] A major problem was resentment over the program to eradicate coca. A year earlier, in a visit to the White House, Sanchez de Lozada had told President George W. Bush that he was worried about the impact eradication would have on farmers, saying prophetically, "I may be back here in a year, this time seeking political asylum."[35] The Bolivian scholar Eduardo Gamarra said that "The U.S. insistence on coca eradication was at the core of Sanchez de Lozada's problem."[36] The economist Jeffrey Sachs, an advisor to the Bolivian government, accused the United States of "making demands on an impoverished country without any sense of reality."[37] According to

Gamarra and others, United States drug policy is causing instability in the region and a build-up of anti-American sentiment. Evo Morales, head of the coca growers' federation, has benefited from this sentiment.[38] He finished second to Carlos Mesa in the 2002 presidential election. During the presidential campaign, Washington made it clear that the election of Morales would be seen as a hostile act and that aid to Bolivia would be terminated. Carlos Mesa has been caught between popular pressure to curtail eradication and losing financial assistance. In 2003, David Greenlee, the American ambassador to Bolivia, announced that coca eradication has been "positive" for the country. "We don't think it is a problem," he added.[39] In December, 2005, Evo Morales was elected president of Bolivia.

Interdiction

The federal government of the United States has recently been spending over $2 billion a year to prevent illicit drugs from being smuggled into the country.[40] It's an impressive effort, involving the DEA, the CIA, the customs service, the Coast Guard, and the U.S. military. The traffickers are up against navy warships, air force fighter planes, helicopters, AWACS, sniffer dogs, and border guards, to name just a few. But the smugglers are equally impressive. They send their drugs into the U.S. by every conceivable conveyance: planes, ships, trains, trucks, cars, animals, mail, and people. Astronomical profits inspire traffickers to find ingenious ways of concealing their contraband: they secrete cocaine and heroin in art objects, baby's diapers, swallowed balloons, cadavers, and even boa constrictors.[41] They also take advantage of the 9 million or so cargo containers that legally enter the country every year.

Cocaine begins its trip to the United States in the Andes Mountains of South America where the coca leaves are grown. Most of the production occurs in Colombia, Bolivia, and Peru.[42] The leaves are carried to jungle refineries, where they are transformed into coca paste. The destination for the paste is Colombia, where it's refined into cocaine. Colombia-based traffickers account for more than 80 percent of the world's production and wholesale distribution of cocaine. Cocaine derived from coca leaves that a peasant farmer sold for $750 would be valued at more than $200,000 on the streets of the United States.[43]

Unlike those for cocaine, the production and distribution networks for opium and heroin cover the globe. The major opium producers are Afghanistan and Burma (now known as Myanmar), with smaller amounts grown in Laos, Pakistan, Colombia, Mexico, and Vietnam.[44] Farmers harvest the opium poppy, make incisions in the seed pod, which is the shape and size of a small egg, and scrape off the brownish-black sap that oozes out. This is raw opium. The farmers carry the opium to local refineries, where it's converted into morphine, which is easier to smuggle than the sticky and smelly opium. The complex process of transforming morphine into heroin occurs at clandestine laboratories, which are widely dispersed around the world. Even though Afghanistan and Myanmar are the leading producers of opium, the DEA estimates that two-thirds of the heroin seized on our streets is currently produced in Colombia, while 29 percent comes from Mexico.[45]

The trafficking networks that bring the heroin into the United States involve elaborate transportation routes, which are quickly redesigned by smugglers when necessary. Here are a couple of examples.

- In 1982, President Reagan created a task force under the direction of Vice President George H. W. Bush to intensify the air and sea efforts to stop heroin and other illicit drugs from entering the United States through south Florida.[46] Smugglers responded by shifting to air drops over the Caribbean Sea to be picked up by boats. When the task force caught on to this maneuver, the traffickers switched to new routes through northern Mexico.
- In the mid-1990s, a crackdown on heroin from Myanmar entering the United States via Thailand stimulated three new routes: through Laos and then southern China, through Cambodia, and through Vietnam. Robert Gelbard, the assistant secretary of state for international narcotics and law enforcement affairs, responded by saying that "Trafficking routes have spread like a cancer to all these countries."[47]

The goal of interdiction is to reduce drug consumption by decreasing supply and thus driving up the street price. But economists have estimated that smuggling costs are only about 1 percent of the retail price.[48] The other 99 percent goes to those who distribute the drug once it's smuggled into the country. So, for example, if the street price was $100, the smuggling part would be only one dollar. If interdiction could even raise the smuggling cost by 100 percent, to $2 (which is a fantasy), the price on the street would still be increased by only a negligible amount.

The federal government has been repeatedly informed that interdiction is a waste. Here is what a senior official in the General Accountability Office testified before the Senate Appropriations Subcommittee in 1993: "Interdiction has not made a difference in terms of the higher goals of deterring smugglers and reducing the flow of cocaine. The portion of the federal drug budget allocated to supply reduction initiatives has almost doubled over the last five years, and funding for Department of Defense's detection and monitoring mission has increased over 400% since 1989. Yet cocaine remains affordable, its purity remains high, and it continues to be readily available on American streets."[49] The Department of Justice agreed with the GAO's evaluation: "Years of experience have shown that this band-aid approach to controlling illegal drugs—stopping them midway along the delivery chain—... will never have any permanent effect on drug traffic."[50]

President Ronald Reagan understood that interdiction was futile. As he put it in a 1981 press conference: "With borders like ours, [interdiction] as the main method of halting the drug problem in America is virtually impossible. It's like carrying water in a sieve." Nevertheless, he concluded that it was important to continue the effort.[51] Continue it has—in fact it has grown! Federal spending on interdiction increased from about $700 million in 1986 to over $2 billion in fiscal year 2003 (about 118 percent increase, adjusting for inflation).[52] A commission to study law enforcement practices, chaired by former director of the FBI William Webster, offered the following assessment of interdiction in 2000: "Despite a record number of seizures and a flood of legislation, the Commission is not aware of any evidence that the flow of narcotics into the United States has been reduced."[53]

Interdiction has had one "success," though. The escalated enforcement in south Florida in the 1980s did diminish the amount of marijuana smuggled into the country, which boosted its street price.[54] There were two consequences, hardly favored by the government, but which were easily predictable. Since marijuana is bulky, hard to conceal, and smelly, the traffickers reacted to the intensified interdiction by switching to the more easily concealed cocaine and heroin, which caused their street prices to decline. The other effect was that the boost in the price of marijuana stimulated domestic production, resulting in the United States becoming one of the world's leaders in producing cannabis.[55]

Domestic Law Enforcement

Three-quarters of the federal budget to reduce the supply of illicit drugs is devoted to tracking down and convicting domestic traffickers, producers, and consumers.[56] Frequently, we read in the newspaper that the police have penetrated a drug gang and seized an enormous quantity of cocaine or some other illicit drug. It would be easy to get the impression from such reports that the war on drugs is being won. But every drug ring, cocaine cache, and meth lab that's busted results in others popping up, making domestic drug law enforcement a Sisyphean task that's dangerous and disheartening for our police officers.

ODALE

The story of ODALE,[57] a short-lived federal strike force created by President Nixon, illustrates the futility of police efforts to curtail illicit drug transactions. ODALE was formed as a temporary supplement to existing drug enforcement agencies.[58] Its first target was Phoenix, Arizona, where the goal was to eliminate every street dealer in the city. After spending an enormous amount of time and money buying drugs undercover, ODALE determined there were seventy-six peddlers operating in Phoenix. In the middle of the night, with the help of local and state police, they arrested all of them. ODALE then moved elsewhere. For a week there were no drugs available on the streets. But new pushers soon appeared, and after a month it was business as usual. The regional director of ODALE, retired U.S. magistrate and judge Volney V. Brown, Jr., summed up the results of the Phoenix operation by saying, "We had spent tens of thousands of federal tax dollars, and sent scores of pushers to prison, but there was no lasting effect on the availability or price of illicit drugs."[59]

ODALE next focused on San Diego. They knew that the street sale of heroin was controlled by one gang. After spending thousands of hours manning tapped phone lines twenty-four hours a day, ODALE obtained enough evidence to arrest and convict every member of the gang. But the outcome was a repeat of Phoenix. After about a month, the street price and availability of heroin returned to their pre-ODALE levels. ODALE director Volney Brown concluded from his experience that "there is no practical level of law enforcement that will prevent people from using the narcotics and dangerous drugs they wish to use. We need to consider alternatives to the mindless repetition of useless and expensive drug law enforcement efforts. I know because I have been there."[60]

Busting Traffickers

Busting drug traffickers is not only futile, it's expensive. A great deal of police time is often required to put a peddler behind bars. The 1989 conviction of Desmond Legister, aged twenty-four, illustrates the point.[61] After a five-week surveillance operation by eight New York City police officers, Legister was apprehended selling cocaine to an undercover agent. When his case came to trial, each of those officers had to spend an average of six days in the courtroom, testifying or waiting to testify. Why did the police have to waste so much time waiting? Because the courts were (and still are) choking on drug cases. As the American Bar Association has reported, our justice system "is on a fast track to collapse" as a result of the flood of drug prosecutions and the severity of sentences for drug violations.[62]

Convicting Legister required a total police commitment of more than 200 working days. He was sentenced to twenty years in the New York State penitentiary. His arrest cost the tax payers of New York $150,000, and keeping him in prison will cost about an additional million. Pushers such as Legister are generally small fry; kingpins rarely hang around street corners peddling their wares. According to the U.S. Sentencing Commission, 53.1 percent of *federal* powder cocaine defendants in fiscal year 2005 were low-level dealers (mules) while 12.8 percent were high-level dealers. As for federal crack cocaine defendants, 61.5 percent were low-level dealers and only 8.4 percent were high-level.[63] The ratios for *state* drug defendants would undoubtedly be even more skewed toward the mules, since the federal government concerns itself mainly with serious cases.

Putting a peddler such as Legister behind bars creates a vacancy in the local drug supply business which is quickly filled. It doesn't cost much to become a pusher and the job promises quick profits. Little education is required and all that's needed is a small loan, a car, and perhaps a gun.[64] The illicit drug business is often the only flourishing industry in the inner cities, and it's an equal opportunity employer, with no barriers to entry as a result of racism or a prison record. As Sergeant Ronald Mejia of Manhattan North Narcotics told the reporter Michael Massing, "Very few times do we lock up the same individual over and over. The people wanting to sell seem to come out of nowhere."[65]

Meth Labs

The rise of methamphetaine, known as the poor man's cocaine, is a relatively recent phenomenon.[66] In the past decade, there's been an explosion in the number of illicit methamphetamine labs, which has placed a heavy and dangerous burden on police, fire fighters, and emergency medical personnel. Meth is easily produced in makeshift labs using a cocktail of readily obtainable products, such as over-the-counter cold medicines, diet pills, hydrogen peroxide, charcoal lighter fluid, sulfuric acid, and the highly toxic chemical anhydrous ammonia, used by farmers as a fertilizer.[67] With less than $400 worth of ingredients, and six to eight hours of time, $4,000 worth of the drug can be cooked up.[68]

When meth is manufactured in homemade labs, volatile chemicals and noxious fumes are produced, presenting health and safety hazards to anyone entering the site.[69] Continued exposure to the sulfurous gases emitted by the labs can burn the lungs and damage the liver and spleen.[70] Children living in homes that have been turned into meth labs are at risk of inhaling or swallowing poisonous substances and of developing learning disabilities.[71] In 2003, about 3,300 children in the United States were removed from meth homes that were saturated with toxic chemicals.[72] Twenty to thirty percent of raided labs are discovered because the ingredients have caused an explosion or a fire.[73] Hazardous waste from the labs is being dumped into sewage systems, streams, and wooded areas, where the chemicals seep into the soil, contaminating water sources.[74] Once a lab is discovered, it must be professionally dismantled and cleaned up at an average cost of $3,000, with larger labs costing as much as $100,000. The federal government spent about $24 million closing down meth labs in 2002.[75]

In fiscal year 2002 there were over 9,000 lab raids in the United States, as compared to around 800 in 1995.[76] In spite of the rapidly increasing number of raids, labs continue to sprout up all over the country. Eradication seems impossible, since the labs are small, easy to conceal, and can be dismantled and relocated rapidly. Police initially found them only in trailers and cheap motel rooms, but they are now finding them in middle-class homes as well as in such places as the trunks of cars, storage lockers, campgrounds, abandoned dumps, houseboats, and restrooms.[77]

Reports from those on the front lines typically see the raids as a hopeless effort. Here are a few examples.

- Dwayne Nichols currently administers the federal money to combat drug activity in the state of Missouri. Meth labs "spread like contact dermatitis," he says, "It's like trying to fight a water balloon—you fight it and it goes somewhere else."[78]
- Sheriff Fred Newman of Washington County, Virginia, complained that, whenever the police cracked down on meth traffickers coming in from out of state, local labs sprang up. "I think there's more people getting into the homemade methamphetamine," Newman said. "The chemicals to make it are so accessible."[79]
- Richard Stallard, the coordinator for the Southwest Virginia regional drug task force, said, "Our investigations now are showing that a lot of meth is coming in from out the area. As we've had luck in getting rid of these [local] cookers, people have been turning to people from outside these counties and out of state."[80]
- Detective Travis Blankenship of the police department in Franklin County, Missouri, said that meth has ensnared entire families, and that "It used to be big news to find a meth cook. Now everybody is cooking meth."[81]

Concluding Remarks

The failure of ODALE, the conviction of Legister, and the spread of meth labs illustrate the futility and danger of the attempts to stamp out the production and sale of drugs desired by the public. *Domestic drug law enforcement is defeated by the same mechanisms that doom eradication and interdiction, namely, the lure of profits and the "push down–pop up" effect.* These mechanisms derive their power from the intense and widespread consumer demand for prohibited drugs. Over 112 million Americans over the age of twelve have used illicit drugs at one time or another, and about 35 million consumed them in 2005.[82]

Empirical evidence supports the conclusion that the drug war is unwinnable. As pointed out at the beginning of this chapter, over the past two decades expenditures on the war have been rising, but so has the percentage of Americans who use illicit drugs.[83] The goal of drug law enforcement is to reduce consumption by raising the cost of the prohibited drugs, but the trend of street prices of heroin and cocaine since 1980 has been downward.[84]

So, why does the United States continue to wage this hopeless, costly, and endless war, with all the attendant damages it's inflicting on the country? A major part of the answer, I believe, is that the war is only masquerading as an effort to combat drug abuse. In reality, the drug laws are a tool to control and punish groups which are hated and feared, as well as being a cash cow for numerous government agencies and private groups. If America's drug control policy were genuinely aimed at reducing drug dependence, it would make treatment available to those who need it but can't afford it, instead of criminalizing users and putting them in prisons that are awash in hard drugs. More generally, if the federal and state governments were to assume control of the production and distribution of all currently illicit drugs and make them accessible to the adult public, much as we've done with alcohol, the drug lords would be put out of business, and many of the harms resulting from the drug war would be eliminated. I examine alternatives to the drug war in part IV.

Part III
The Federal Government's Case for the Drug War

Just as cost–benefit analysis would not have stopped the inquisitors from tracking down and punishing heretics in the Middle Ages, crime and AIDS "body counts" do not stop modern drug warriors from crusading against drugs. They are not deterred by the sight of prohibition-caused street violence because they believe that such costs, to the extent they even acknowledge their existence, are trivial in comparison with the ultimate value of achieving a "drug-free" America. . . . Cost–benefit arguments simply do not register with [the] millions of Americans who view the war on drugs as akin to a religious war.[1]

8 The Perception of the Drug Czars

As we've seen, the drug war has caused incalculable damage to the country—spawning homicides and property crimes, damaging public health, eroding civil liberties, corrupting public officials, and wasting billions of tax dollars. Nor is there evidence that the war has diminished—or is capable of diminishing—the consumption or abuse of illicit drugs. The horrors it has inflicted and the futility of its efforts have barely registered with the American people, but they're shared by the overwhelming majority of scholars who have studied America's drug control policy. Ironically, the federal government has also known that its never-ending war against drugs has been a failure and that it's causing harm.

So, how does the government justify such a policy? A valuable source of insight into this question is in a book called *Body Count* (1996), written jointly by two of the drug czars, William Bennett, who served under the first President Bush, and John Walters, appointed by President George W. Bush.[1] Unlike the usual dry government documents, *Body Count* throbs with passion and anger, and gives the reader a rare glimpse into the psyche of drug warriors. The authors are deeply disturbed by trends they perceive in American society:

> America is now home to thickening ranks of juvenile "super-predators"—radically impulsive, brutally remorseless youngsters, including ever more preteenage boys, who murder, assault, rape, rob, burglarize, deal deadly drugs, join gun-toting gangs, and create serious communal disorders.[2]

The czars disagree "strongly" with the premise that they say has "emasculated the criminal justice system," namely, that the goal of punishment is rehabilitation. For them, the purpose is a *"moral"* one, namely, "to exact a price for transgressing the rights of others"[3] (emphasis in the original). They acknowledge that studies have shown that criminals tend to be concentrated in disadvantaged neighborhoods and that public investment in high-risk youths can help bring down crime. But they reject these studies by arguing that, "despite increased government spending on many types of social programs, and despite overall economic prosperity, in the 1960s crime rates soared."[4] They attribute the cause to the crumbling of "America's primary socializing institutions—families, schools, churches, and others."[5] The failure of these institutions led to the creation of "moral poverty" in the younger generation,... [which] "makes some young men pull triggers the way old men fire off angry letters."[6] To the czars, the erosion of socializing institutions is not the only cause of moral poverty; drug use is equally responsible. They argue that "only a willful blindness can obscure the fact that drug use fosters moral poverty and remorseless criminality; that drug use destroys character and brutalizes the lives of users and those around them."[7] And they declare that "Drug use is wrong because it degrades human beings ... and leads them to mock the demands of virtue."[8]

Bennett and Walters maintain that to win the drug war it's essential to understand the "roots" of drug abuse. As they see it, "The illegal drug problem in the United States today began as part of the radical political and moral criticism of American culture and the related youthful rebelliousness of the late 1960s and the 1970s."[9] They argue that the way our society dealt with illicit drug use was a "trial of our national character" which demanded "more and more criminal sanctions."[10] These sanctions must also include "casual drug use," because that is the "vector by which drug use spreads."[11]

As drug czars they've been instrumental in putting their punitive agenda into effect. Their views are reflected, for example, in the drug education to which our young have been exposed in high schools. In 1989 the Bush White House initiated a school-based drug prevention program based on zero tolerance, which advocated the punishment of any student who used drugs. The program called for a "firm moral stand that using drugs is wrong."[12] It featured the expulsion from school of any substance-using student. As the White House put it:

> School-based prevention programs should be reinforced by tough, but fair, policies on use, possession, and distribution of drugs ... We can not teach them that drugs are wrong and harmful if we fail to follow up our teaching with real consequences for those who use them. Policies like these have been criticized for adding to the dropout problem. But experience shows that firm policies fairly enforced actually reduce the numbers of students who must be expelled for drug violations; most students choose to alter their behavior rather than risk expulsion.[13]

Numerous studies have found this policy to be ineffectual as well as harmful. For example:[14]

- A 1997 survey of California high-school students found that alcohol and marijuana use is common among adolescents. These results led researchers to conclude that a zero-tolerance policy is bound to fail. A majority of the sixteen-year-olds surveyed had tried illicit drugs in the preceding six months, with more than 40 percent having used marijuana, and 80 percent having used alcohol. Over 80 percent of these sixteen-year-olds found marijuana easy or fairly easy to get—about as easy as it was to obtain alcohol.[15]

- Drug education programs in high schools have failed to reduce drug use and appear to have stimulated it. A nationwide survey of high-school students in 1995 found that drug use by adolescents had been growing rapidly over the past fifteen years, and that the increases were greatest among those youths who had received the most school-based drug education.[16]

- A California study conducted in 1995 found that the drug education programs in high schools "create policies that exclude those whom students themselves recognize as most in need of help; they drive those, who already might be on the margins of the school system, further out."[17] In the same study, thirty-nine out of forty student focus groups described drug policy in their high schools as consisting of "detention, suspension and expulsion."[18]

- Several years after the 1989 program was put into effect, the government indicated that it was aware of a serious problem: too many kids were being dumped on the streets. The U.S. Department of Education reacted by setting up a competition to create model projects to find "meaningful alternative forms of schooling outside the classrooms for children expelled or suspended from school."[19]

Drug education researchers Rodney Skager and Joel Brown observed that most young people felt they were living in a "schizoid society in which alcohol and illicit drug use is condemned and forbidden to them by the official world of laws and authority, but is widely practiced in the culture they join as teenagers."[20] For example, in their 1997 survey of California high-school students, slightly over half of the sixteen-year-olds knew at least one adult who used marijuana at least once a week.[21]

9　The Czars Defend the Drug War

Over the years an enormous volume of research has criticized the war on drugs, including studies that have been carried out by agencies authorized by Congress to evaluate our drug policy, such as the Institute of Medicine and the U.S. Sentencing Commission. The war has been condemned by researchers on a number of grounds: namely, that it's racist, that it incarcerates nonviolent offenders, that it's ineffective in reducing drug use, and that it punishes people for consuming marijuana, which is misrepresented by the federal government as a gateway to hard drugs. It would not be surprising to find the czars being rattled by the avalanche of criticisms leveled at them from the scientific community; and, indeed they appear to be. What follows are the czars' attempts to refute these criticisms leveled at the drug war.

The War is *Not* Racist

Bennett and Walters argue that those who attack the drug war for being racist are wrong. They conclude that "the best available research indicates that race is not a significant variable in determining whether a convicted adult offender is sentenced to probation or prison, the length of the term imposed, or how prisoners are disciplined."[1] But, as documented in chapter 6, the best available research shows just the opposite: the drug war *is* racist. The U.S. Sentencing Commission has found that blacks serve considerably longer prison sentences than whites *for comparable crimes*. Also, even though whites outnumber blacks by five to one in the consumption of illicit drugs, and constitute a majority of drug peddlers, more than twice as many blacks as whites are in prison for violating the drug laws.

Racial bias exists not only in sentencing but also in arrests. Research by Dan Weikel of the *Los Angeles Times* found that "virtually all" white crack offenders were turned over to state courts while crack-offending nonwhites were sent to federal courts. He pointed out that the sentences are far less severe in state courts and that "the difference can be up to eight years for the same offense."[2]

Only Dangerous Felons are in Prison for Drug Offenses

The Czars ask "who really goes to prison?" Their answer: "They are felons who are very dangerous. That's who."[3] They warn us not to be "fooled by so-called experts who claim that prisons are full of misplaced angels who deserve no punishment."[4]

Incarcerated drug law violators many not be angels, but neither can they be described as dangerous felons. According to a 1997 survey by the U.S. Department of Justice, of the over 270,000 drug violators in federal and state prisons, more than 102,000 (38 percent) were behind bars for simply possessing an illicit substance.[5] Many of these drug offenders were serving long mandatory minimum sentences.[6] Classifying these inmates as "dangerous felons" just because they possessed an illegal substance implies that the 112 million Americans who have used illicit drugs are dangerous felons on the loose.[7] Many of those incarcerated for peddling illicit drugs are also nonviolent. The czars brush aside official statistics like these by asserting that imprisoned drug law violators have gotten away with multiple crimes for which they were not convicted. As they put it, "Swept entirely under the rug are all of the more serious crimes that imprisoned drug offenders have plea-bargained away—not to mention all of the wholly undetected, unprosecuted, and unpunished crimes they *may* have done"[8] (emphasis added).

Recall that only a small percentage of federal drug cases involve drug kingpins as opposed to street peddlers; the percentage is undoubtedly smaller in state cases.[9] The big shots are the ones who are most able to lower their sentences by plea bargaining. They are likely to possess information the district attorneys want, and they can usually afford high-priced lawyers. The vast majority of convicted drug offenders are small-fry traffickers or consumers, neither of whom are likely to have much information with which to plea bargain.

Women have become a fast growing segment of the prison population. According to the Bureau of Justice Statistics, from 1990 through 2002 the number of women in state and federal prisons jumped from 44,065 to 97,491, with drug law violations the main cause.[10] A 1999 study by the Justice Policy Institute found that 85 percent of female inmates were nonviolent.[11] According to testimony before Congress by Kathy Hawk Sawyer, the director of the Federal Bureau of Prisons, "70-some percent of our female population are low-level, nonviolent offenders."[12]

The War Has Reduced Illicit Drug Use

Bennett and Walters argue that the "Just say No" campaign of Nancy Reagan in conjunction with anti-drug parent groups brought about dramatic reductions in drug use between 1985 and 1992. They give credit to the "morally serious and tough-minded leadership of Presidents Ronald Reagan and George Bush," which they claim resulted in "the most successful attack on a serious social problem in the last quarter century."[13] They also state that President Clinton's "I didn't inhale message" and his relaxation of the anti-drug effort caused illicit drug use to begin rising in 1992. Again, the evidence gives a different picture.

- The decline in casual illicit drug use—mostly marijuana—started two or three years before President Reagan escalated the war against drugs. This downward trend was already apparent in 1979, during the administration of President Jimmy Carter, who had proposed decriminalizing marijuana possession.[14]
- Heavy use of cocaine continued rising throughout the administrations of both presidents Reagan and George H. W. Bush.[15]
- President Clinton did not cut back on the anti-drug effort. Federal spending aimed at reducing illicit drug supply rose about $2.4 billion during the eight years of Ronald Reagan's administration (1981–8) and by about $3.5 billion during the Clinton years (1991–8). (These budget numbers include domestic law enforcement, international enforcement, and interdiction.)[16]
- America was much tougher on young adults who violated the drug laws during the Clinton administration than during the Reagan administration: in 1986, thirty-one out of every 100,000 young adults were incarcerated for drug offenses, while in 1996, 122 youths per 100,000 were sent to prison for drug violations.[17]
- The upturn in the rate of cannabis use that began in 1992 was not just a United States phenomenon. It also occurred in many countries, such as the Netherlands, Norway, and Canada, despite very different drug policies.[18]

Marijuana is a Gateway Drug

One of the main arguments the White House uses to support marijuana prohibition is the gateway effect, namely, that using marijuana causes a person to go on to hard drugs. President Nixon appears to have escalated the drug war partly as a result of his belief in the gateway effect. On the Nixon audio tapes, the president is heard saying, "On the marijuana thing, I have very strong feelings that ... once you start down that road ... the chances of going further down that road are greater."[19] Bennett and Walters, as well as a 2003 report from Walters's Office of National Drug Control Policy (ONDCP), accept the gateway effect based on data showing that cannabis users are more likely than nonusers to use cocaine or heroin.[20]

This reasoning is faulty. These data do not prove that marijuana *causes* the consumption of harder drugs. People who use cocaine or heroin are likely to have used marijuana first (not to mention milk!) because it's more popular and widespread in our society. Most Americans don't start with harder drugs. As the Institute of Medicine put it: "Because it is the most widely used illicit drug, marijuana is predictably the first illicit drug most people encounter."[21]

Of more relevance to the gateway effect are data showing the magnitude of the association between marijuana and the subsequent use of hard drugs. Of the 72 million Americans who had used marijuana in 1998, only 0.6 million went on to use cocaine regularly.[22] That is, of every 120 people who had smoked marijuana, only one went on to use cocaine once a week or more. In other studies, among those who had used marijuana, about one in 200 reported that they currently used crack, with one in 333 reporting the same for heroin.[23] These associations do not establish that marijuana use has *caused* the subsequent hard-drug use. Other factors may have caused the consumption of both cannabis and hard drugs, such as psychological problems or living in inner-city neighborhoods.[24] What these magnitudes do suggest is that, if there is a gateway effect, it's small.

The data for high-school students also fail to support the gateway hypothesis. From 1992 to 2005, the percentage of seniors who used marijuana daily increased almost every year from 1.9 to 5.0, while the percentage who used cocaine or heroin daily showed no upward trend.[25]

What *could* produce a gateway effect? Specifically, what factors might contribute to the transition from marijuana to cocaine or heroin? One possibility is a physiological mechanism that links cannabis and the hard drugs, "something similar to the way ingesting salt makes people thirsty."[26] Scientific research does not support this idea. The cannabinoids have their own receptors, which do not react directly to heroin and cocaine.[27] Additional evidence against a biological link is found in animal studies, where "rodents exposed to THC do not show a sudden willingness to press levers for other drugs."[28]

There are, however, other possible gateway mechanisms.

- The federal government broadcasts dire warnings that marijuana is a dangerous as well as an illegal drug.[29] So, when young people use cannabis without being harmed or arrested, or hear that others have done so, the government's messages concerning the risks of cocaine and heroin may be discredited.[30]
- Using marijuana could cause people to see themselves as illicit drug users. This identity might increase the likelihood they would consume illicit hard drugs.[31]
- Since marijuana is illegal, purchasing it may bring one into contact with hard-drug sellers. As Earleywine put it, "A [black market] supplier may have a set of marketing strategies for these harder drugs, including strong personal testimony about their quality."[32] The possibility of exposure to sales pitches for the hard drugs convinced the Dutch to decriminalize low-level cannabis sales, so that the markets for the hard and soft drugs would be separated. Evidence indicates that this separation has reduced the use of cocaine in the Netherlands, which has

resulted in a lack of statistical support for the hypothesis that marijuana is a gateway drug.[33]

- Cannabis users could be more likely to be introduced to hard drugs while intoxicated. There is as yet no data which addresses this possibility.[34]
- Pleasurable experience with cannabis could encourage the consumption of harder drugs.[35] Again, there is no evidence supporting this possible link.

Notice that, except for the last two, these potential gateway mechanisms are a result of the war against drugs.

While a gateway effect is a possibility, especially when there is drug prohibition, researchers overwhelmingly agree that there is no convincing scientific evidence that the effect exists.

- A study by the Institute of Medicine found that "There is no conclusive evidence that the drug effects of marijuana are causally linked to the subsequent abuse of other illicit drugs."[36]
- Research published in the *Journal of the American Medical Association* reported that "it is not possible to draw strong causal conclusions" about early cannabis use and subsequent use and abuse of other illicit drugs.[37]
- Investigation by the World Health Organization concluded that the theory that marijuana use by adolescents leads to heroin use is the "least likely of all hypotheses."[38]
- Research published in 2002 by the British government found that "there is very little remaining evidence of any causal gateway effect."[39]
- According to the National Center on Addiction and Substance Abuse at Columbia University, there is no scientific or clinical research establishing causality between marijuana and other drugs.[40]
- Peter Reuter and Robert MacCoun, behavioral scientists at the RAND Drug Policy Research Center, conclude: "We believe that there is little evidence that expanding marijuana use does increase the use of other, more harmful drugs."[41]
- Researcher Mitch Earleywine reports: "The idea that marijuana causes subsequent drug use ... appears unfounded."[42]
- The conclusion of researchers Lynn Zimmer and John Morgan is that "Marijuana does not cause people to use hard drugs. What the gateway theory presents as a causal explanation is a statistical association between common and uncommon drugs ... Most marijuana users never use any other illegal drug."[43]
- Surveys of heroin users reveal that it was their positive experiences with alcohol and barbiturates, and not marijuana, that led them to try heroin.[44]
- Drug researchers at the Duke University Medical Center dismiss the gateway theory by concluding that "the vast majority of people using cigarettes, alcohol, and marijuana never use 'harder' drugs."[45]

10 The White House Versus the Scientists on Marijuana Dangers

A 2003 report by the Office of National Drug Control Policy (ONDCP), headed by the drug czar John Walters, is entitled *What Americans Need to Know about Marijuana*. It purports to explode the "misperception" that marijuana is harmless. The report cites a lengthy list of dangers, such as skyrocketing "emergency room mentions," "changes in the brain," and a reduction in "skills that are necessary for safe driving."[1] It also warns of the risks of cancer, lung infection, emphysema, schizophrenia, disruption of the immune system, suicidal thoughts, depression, delinquency, and poor performance in school.[2] Finally, it asserts that cannabis is "psychologically addictive" and causes violence.[3] The implication of this litany is that marijuana is so dangerous that it should remain prohibited and that we must continue to use the criminal justice system to punish sellers and users. I recently heard Walters refer to marijuana as "poison" and complain that the Canadians were not harsh enough in their punishment of traffickers.

Let's look at the scientific evidence for the claims made by the ONDCP.

Overall Evaluation of Cannabis

According to drug researchers Lester Grinspoon and James Bakalar of the Harvard Medical School, the overall conclusions concerning the harmfulness of recreational use of cannabis are "strikingly reassuring."[4] They report: "After carefully monitoring the literature for more than two decades, we have concluded that ... so far not a single case of lung cancer, emphysema, or other significant pulmonary pathology attributable to cannabis use has been reported in the United States."[5]

Mitch Earleywine, in a survey of the scientific evidence concerning the health effects of marijuana, concluded that, "Compared to other drugs that are currently legal, its impact on health is minimal" [and that] "Chronic cannabis users rarely report the drastic financial, social, and occupational difficulties typical of addiction to alcohol, opiates, or cocaine."[6]

A review of cannabis by the Institute of Medicine of the National Academy of Sciences found there is no evidence that smoking marijuana "exerts a permanently deleterious effect on the normal cardiovascular system." This finding was endorsed by the World Health Organization.[7]

The British medical journal, *The Lancet* concluded that, "On the medical evidence available, moderate indulgence in cannabis has little ill-effect on health,"[8] and *The Merck Manual of Medical Information* stated that "there is still little evidence of biologic damage [from marijuana] even among relatively heavy users."[9]

After extensive research, the DEA's law judge, Francis Young, concluded that "In strict medical terms marijuana is far safer than many foods we commonly consume. For example, eating 10 raw potatoes can result in a toxic response. By comparison, it is physically impossible to eat enough marijuana to induce death. Marijuana in its natural form is one of the safest therapeutically active substances known to man."[10]

A review of the literature published in the journal *Current Opinion in Pharmacology* in 2005 concluded that "the majority of cannabis users, who use the drug occasionally rather than on a daily basis, will not suffer any lasting physical or mental harm. ... Those who consume large doses of the drug on a regular basis are likely to have lower educational achievement and lower income, and may suffer physical damage to the airways. They also run a significant risk of becoming dependent upon continuing use of the drug. There is little evidence, however, that these adverse effects persist after drug use stops or that any direct cause and effect relationships are involved."[11]

Researchers who study marijuana report that there is no evidence that the drug has ever caused an overdose death and that there is no known dose that is fatal to humans.[12] As Earleywine put it, "even the most devoted pot-head with marijuana of legendary strength could not stumble upon a fatal overdose. In contrast, alcohol and aspirin poison thousands of people each year."[13] Grinspoon and Bakalar find that "After five thousand years of cannabis use by hundreds of millions of people throughout the world there is no credible evidence that this drug has ever caused a single overdose death. ... Marihuana in its natural form is possibly the safest therapeutically active substance known."[14] Researchers Lynn Zimmer and John Morgan conclude that, "Because marijuana does not profoundly alter cardiovascular and respiratory functions, no dose of marijuana is fatal to humans."[15]

Critiquing the 2003 ONDCP Report

> Most of the drug treatment for young people in the United States is for marijuana alone ... Marijuana emergency-room mentions have skyrocketed in the past decade.[16]

According to the government's own statistics, the increase in marijuana treatment for adolescents occurred largely because they had been arrested, not because of evidence of increased abuse or dependence.[17] In general, marijuana users constitute about 10 percent of those admitted to treatment for drug abuse, legal coercion being the reason in a great percentage of cases.[18] Many of those arrested are given the choice of prison or treatment.

When a person is treated in an emergency room for a condition that appears to be drug related, the hospital staff typically interviews the patient and composes a list of the drugs that the patient has used recently.[19] Appearance on the list does not mean that any particular drug caused the emergency. Marijuana is mentioned less often than most other illicit drugs, even though it is the one most frequently used. In a 1995 survey of the general population, marijuana represented about 5 percent of drug mentions, compared to 8 percent for aspirin, acetaminophen, and ibuprofen combined. (Heroin accounted for 8 percent of all drug mentions, and cocaine for 15 percent.)[20] Cannabis is rarely listed alone in emergency room visits. Of the alleged drug-abuse episodes in 1994, only 1.6 percent involved marijuana alone.[21]

> Tetrahydrocannabinol (THC), the main active chemical in marijuana, changes the way sensory information gets into and is processed by the part of the brain that is crucial for learning and memory.[22]

A Johns Hopkins study, published in 1999, examined marijuana's effects on cognition. The researchers measured the performance of 1,318 participants over a fifteen-year period, and found "no significant cognitive differences in cognitive decline between heavy users, light users and non users of cannabis."[23] Measures included tests of such functions as memory, intelligence, and problem-solving.

Studies of chronic marijuana use in adults fail to show cannabis-induced changes in brain structure but do show subtle changes in brain functioning.[24] These changes suggest that chronic heavy users may not process information as efficiently as nonusers or ex-users. As Earleywine summarizes these results: "The practical implications of these changes remain unclear. Subtle deviations in brain function have not translated into deficits on meaningful tasks in daily life. Nevertheless, this evidence supports the idea that the drug alters the way people process information."[25]

Little research exists on whether marijuana effects the brain development of adolescent users. However, a recent study does raise a red flag.[26] Employing magnetic resonance imaging, researchers compared the brains of adults who had begun to use marijuana before the age of seventeen with those who had not. Those who used marijuana as adolescents had smaller brains, with a lower percentage of gray matter and a higher percentage of white matter, results suggesting interrupted brain development. This one study is inconclusive, however, because the sample was small (fifty-seven people), other drugs were not controlled for and may have also been used, and (understandably) the participants were not randomly assigned to adolescent marijuana use. Nevertheless, the danger that cannabis use during a critical period of life could retard brain development provides support for the recommendation of the National Organization for the Reform of Marijuana Laws (NORML) that marijuana should not be used until adulthood.[27]

> Using marijuana may promote cancer ... disrupt the immune system ... [and] increase the risk of chronic cough, bronchitis and emphysema.[28]

On the basis of a survey of the current research, Earlywine finds little evidence of cannabis-induced respiratory illnesses.[29] As he put it, "People who smoke marijuana but not cigarettes rarely experience lung problems."[30] In one six-year study involving a large sample of hospital records, daily marijuana smokers were compared with nonsmokers regarding treatment for colds, flu, and bronchitis.[31] The difference between the two groups was insignificant. Nevertheless, there is research that finds that chronic and heavy smoking of marijuana does increase the risk of bronchitis, characterized by chronic cough and phlegm production.[32]

As to emphysema (a chronic obstruction of the lung's small airways, making breathing difficult), the results are mixed. One study compared nonsmokers to those who had smoked two to three marijuana joints a day for fifteen years. There was no difference between the two groups in the extent to which their respiratory tracts were obstructed.[33] Another study of those who averaged one joint per day did find significant lung impairment.[34]

To date, there is no evidence of a relationship between long-term smoking of marijuana and lung cancer, but, after years of study, researchers at UCLA have found precancerous changes in bronchial cells in heavy smokers.[35] In their most recent study, however, presented in May, 2006, these researchers were surprised by their findings that marijuana smoking does not increase a person's risk of developing lung cancer.[36] Grinspoon and Bakalar point out that any risks of lung cancer and other pulmonary pathology would be diminished if the use of "various filtering and vaporizing systems" were not "foolishly discouraged by the law."[37]

Concerning the impact of marijuana on the immune system, Zimmer and Morgan report, "Using the skin reaction tests that physicians commonly employ to assess immune competence in patients, researchers have found no differences between high-dose marijuana users and nonusers."[38] At a 1981 conference sponsored by the World Health Organization and Canada's Addiction Research Foundation, researchers recorded, "There is no conclusive evidence that cannabis predisposes man to immune dysfunction."[39] The FDA reached the same conclusion a few years later. There is laboratory evidence, however, that marijuana can suppress immune function and lower a person's resistance to viral and bacterial infections, but it is not known whether the drug causes an increase in infectious diseases under real-life conditions.[40]

> Marijuana affects "skills that are necessary for safe driving."[41]

It's widely believed that cannabis intoxication contributes to traffic accidents, but, surprisingly, both the studies of automobile accidents and experiments in the laboratory fail to support this conventional wisdom. The findings from accidents were that "those who used only cannabis were responsible for accidents less often than those who used no drugs at all."[42] For example, studies of fatal accidents in Australia, California, and the United States overall showed that cannabis users were 30 to 70 percent less likely to have caused the accidents than were drug-free drivers.[43] The 70 percent estimate came from a study of 1,800 fatal crashes in the United States conducted by the US Department of Transportation, National Highway Traffic Safety Administration.[44]

Controlled experiments came to the same conclusion. In a number of studies, researchers assigned drivers randomly to placebo or marijuana groups. The experiments revealed that those who received cannabis drove more slowly, allowed more distance between cars, and were less aggressive in passing other vehicles. These differences tend to reduce the likelihood of collisions.[45] Results are the opposite for alcohol intoxication, which often leads to an increase in speeding and passing, and a reduction in the distance between cars. One reason that marijuana has a bad reputation for causing accidents is that it's often used with alcohol.

Before you start to smoke marijuana as an aid to safe driving, keep in mind that research by the Institute of Medicine and the National Commission on Marihuana and Drug Abuse revealed that marijuana intoxication interferes with muscular coordination, diminishes psychomotor performance, and induces drowsiness.[46] As a result of its research, the Institute of Medicine warned, "It is, therefore, inadvisable to operate any vehicle or potentially dangerous equipment while under the influence of marijuana, THC, or any cannabinoid drug with comparable effects."[47]

Marijuana users ... [are] more likely to report symptoms of depression ... [and have] an increased risk of developing schizophrenia.[48]

There is no scientific evidence that marijuana causes mental illness in either teenagers or adults.[49] Some users experience panic, anxiety, and paranoia, but these responses are short-lived and usually occur when the drug is eaten rather than smoked. Researchers report that these reactions "respond well to simple reassurance."[50] Many users find that marijuana reduces anxiety.

Grinspoon and Bakalar point out that "the danger of an anxiety or paranoid reaction is magnified when the drug is illegal."[51] They also report that their clinical research as well as that of others leads them to conclude: "There no reason to believe that marijuana causes or contributes to the onset of schizophrenia itself."[52] A recent study of cannabis use and mental health from adolescence to early adulthood in 800 New Zealanders found no relationship between marijuana and either depression or anxiety disorders.[53]

Marijuana use has been associated with poor performance in school.[54]

In spite of the worry of parents and teachers about the effect of marijuana on school performance, more than a half-dozen studies of college students have failed to show any differences between the performance of cannabis users and nonusers.[55] There were no differences in grades, and no changes in majors or colleges, attitudes toward achievement, or extracurricular activities. A few of the studies even found higher grades in marijuana users, which doesn't imply that the drug was the cause. Chronic users tended to take more time off but were also more likely to plan on a graduate degree.

A seminal 1990 study by psychologists Shedler and Block collected evidence from preschool to age eighteen on the relationship between psychological characteristics, high-school performance, and adolescent substance use.[56] They compared the psychological health and school performance of high-school abstainers, occasional users, and heavy users. In summarizing Shedler and Block's results, RAND researchers MacCoun and Reuter report that high-school students who smoked cannabis only occasionally "functioned quite well with respect to schooling and mental health."[57] Adolescents who refrained from experimenting with marijuana functioned less well and were found by Shedler and Block to be "anxious, emotionally constricted, and lacking in social skills."[58] But these psychological characteristics of the abstainers had been apparent long before adolescence.

Numerous studies, including Shedler and Block's, have shown that heavy marijuana users in high school have lower grades, quit school more often, spend less time on homework, and miss more days of school.[59] The nature of the link between heavy marijuana use and failed academic performance became clear when the data were analyzed. Heavy cannabis users in high school had performed poorly in school prior to discovering marijuana, and had also exhibited emotional, behavioral, and social problems long before adolescence.[60]

In sum: both heavy adolescent marijuana use and failed high-school performance appeared to be a result of psychological problems going back to early childhood. As Earlywine put it, "depressed, unmotivated, unconventional adolescents may choose to smoke marijuana, but the drug does not appear to create their deviance."[61]

Marijuana has proven to be a psychologically addictive drug.[62]

A variety of studies carried out over several decades have found that when chronic cannabis users quit they rarely experience withdrawal symptoms, and when these symptoms do occur they are mild and temporary.[63] A leading marijuana researcher reported an experiment in which subjects smoked twenty marijuana cigarettes a day for two or three weeks and then stopped use entirely. The subjects showed no withdrawal problems.[64]

In a study conducted at the Federal Narcotics Hospital in Lexington, Kentucky, ten men were kept high continuously for thirty days and then withdrawn, with no apparent symptoms.[65] Some studies involving high doses of THC have revealed withdrawal symptoms, such as nervousness, sleep disturbances, nausea, decreased appetite, and sweating, which the researchers described as "modest."[66]

A report to Congress by the U.S. Department of Health and Human Services concluded: "Given the large population of marijuana users and the infrequent reports of medical problems from stopping use, tolerance and dependence are not major issues."[67] (Tolerance is the need for larger and larger doses to get the same effect.)

Researchers have also conducted studies comparing various drugs in terms of how easily they hook you (dependence) and how hard it is to quit (withdrawal). In one study of eighteen drugs, experts ranked nicotine first in its ability to cause dependence and withdrawal discomfort; crack cocaine was ranked third, alcohol eighth, heroin ninth, cocaine powder eleventh, caffeine twelfth, and marijuana fourteenth. Only ecstasy, psilocybin mushrooms, LSD, and mescaline ranked lower than marijuana.[68] In another study comparing nicotine, caffeine, heroin, cocaine, alcohol, and marijuana, two pharmacologists ranked marijuana last in its ability to cause dependence and withdrawal discomfort.[69] Notice that, in both studies, marijuana was judged to cause less dependence and withdrawal discomfort than caffeine or alcohol. According to drug researchers at the Duke University Medical Center, "there is little evidence that marijuana is addictive."[70]

Cannabis is not always experienced as harmless, however. In a 1980 study of chronic marijuana smokers followed over a period of five years, approximately 9 percent reported troubles they believed were associated with the drug, such as difficulties controlling use, interpersonal problems, and health problems.[71] But according to the researchers, these possible adverse consequences of dependence appeared to be modest.[72]

The allegation that marijuana is more potent today than thirty years ago is presented as a danger by the ONDCP but is seen as a likely plus by researchers. Studies have found that, when marijuana becomes more potent, smokers tend to cut down their intake, thereby decreasing the risk of lung damage from smoking.[73]

> Research shows a link between frequent marijuana use and increased violent behavior.[74]

To support this reasoning, the ONDCP appeals to a study that shows that "Young people who use marijuana weekly are nearly four times more likely than nonusers to engage in violence."[75] President Clinton's drug czar, Lee Brown, also stressed that there is a "strong link between marijuana use and violence."[76] Because adolescents who used marijuana were more likely than nonusers to engage in violence does not mean that the drug caused the violence. There are a number of other possible explanations for these data. For example, marijuana-using adolescents may consume more alcohol than nonusers, and alcohol is known to contribute to violence.[77]

100 The Federal Government's Case for the Drug War

Numerous government-sponsored scientific panels have invariably concluded that marijuana does not to lead to violence.[78] For example, the National Commission on Marihuana and Drug Abuse, appointed by President Nixon, studied the relationship between marijuana use and violence and concluded, "Rather than inducing violent or aggressive behavior through its purported effects of lowering inhibitions, weakening impulse control and heightening aggressive tendencies, marihuana was usually found to inhibit the expression of aggressive impulses by pacifying the user, interfering with muscular coordination, reducing psychomotor activities, and generally producing states of drowsiness, lethargy, timidity and passivity."[79] Laboratory experiments have borne out this conclusion. By contrast with alcohol, even when subjects are provoked they do not respond aggressively when given THC.

Also, studies have shown that users of marijuana are under-represented among violent criminals.[80] For example, in a study of 268 homicide offenders in New York prisons, only eighteen said that marijuana contributed to their crime. But fifteen of these had also used alcohol or other drugs when they committed the murder. Researchers concluded that in no case had marijuana been a contributor to the crime.[81]

11 The Czars Versus the Scientists on Cocaine and Heroin

The Czars' Pro-Incarceration Outlook

Since the drug czars accuse cannabis of causing everything from schizophrenia to cancer, it's hard to imagine how they could escalate their rhetoric about hard drugs. But they pull it off. They describe cocaine as "a deadly addictive substance [marketed] on a massive scale, with even grade-school children becoming victims ... a cancer of sorts, threatening all segments of society," and they call for "more and more criminal sanctions."[1] In addition, they assert that crack is responsible for "a major violent crime wave."[2]

Bennett and Walters are especially disturbed by the proliferation of drug courts in our state justice systems. As of 2006, all states have operating or planned drug courts; and while there are differences among them, they all offer nonviolent drug addicts community-based treatment in lieu of prison.[3] Offenders who complete treatment typically have the charges against them dropped. In spite of the views of the current drug czar, John Walters, the Republican-controlled Congress, with the approval of the Bush administration, has provided funding for state drug courts in all fifty states.[4] However, a nonviolent drug offender convicted under the *federal* justice system will almost certainly wind up in prison rather than in a treatment program.[5]

The czars see a "central flaw in the rush to embrace drug courts as a major answer to addiction and crime," because "a very large number of addicted offenders are long-term, hard-core addicts who are poorly suited for diversion programs [they mean treatment]. ... [Drug courts] are not a promising source of the close supervision and imposition of sanctions for resorting to drug use."[6] In plain English: addicts can't be cured with treatment, and drug courts can't do a proper job of locking people up and punishing them for their offense of having resorted to drugs. They assert that those "addicted to cocaine and heroin will die of that addiction if treatment alone is the principal vehicle society employs to save them."[7] In addition, the czars condemn "misguided social policies" that have been "championed," namely the "anti-incarceration outlook."[8]

Research Findings Disagree with the Czars

Contradicting the czars' preference for incarceration over treatment, a study published in 2003 by an independent research arm of the New York State court system found that nonviolent drug offenders who completed a court-monitored treatment program were significantly less likely to commit future crimes than those who served prison time and received no treatment.[9] The rearrest rate among 18,000 New York drug court graduates was 13 percent, compared to 47 percent for those committing comparable crimes who were incarcerated.[10] Also, the cost of treatment is a fraction of the cost of prison.[11]

The findings of RAND's Drug Policy Research Center also fail to support the pro-incarceration approach of Bennett and Walters. RAND researchers found that, per dollar spent, incarceration reduces the consumption of cocaine among heavy users less than treatment programs. They estimated that spending an additional million 1992 dollars on incarcerating cocaine dealers would reduce cocaine consumption by over 27 kilograms over a fifteen-year period, while putting the same money into treatment for those dependant on cocaine would reduce consumption by over 100 kilograms over the same period.[12] They also calculated that spending a million dollars on treating heavy users is fifteen times more effective in reducing violent and property crime than spending the same money on incarcerating dealers. Their explanation for this last result is that putting a dealer behind bars simply creates a job opening which will be quickly filled, while reducing the number of heavy cocaine users through treatment shrinks the cocaine market and diminishes the number of addicts who would commit crimes to get money for a fix.

The Institute of Medicine also disagrees with the czars about the benefits of treatment for drug addicts: it reports that the success rate for treating cocaine addiction has been 50 percent to 60 percent and, for heroin addiction, 50 percent to 80 percent.[13] A major study of drug addicts conducted by researchers at UCLA estimated that every dollar spent on treatment saved 12 dollars of social costs, such as health care, lost productivity, and crime. These result would have been even more favorable for treatment if the reduction in AIDS had also been taken into account.[14]

As for incarceration, an investigation by the *New York Times* found that illicit drugs are easily available in prisons, smuggled in by bribed guards and prisoners' relatives.[15] Drugs were so plentiful in one prison they were exported to the outside for sale! Incarceration not only fails to prevent drug abuse, it creates conditions that promote it. One inmate told the reporter Eric Schlosser that pot was available throughout the federal system, "but you've got to walk through the heroin to find it."[16] He was able to continue smoking marijuana even though he was often in isolation.

The czar's assertion that crack is responsible for a "violent crime wave" has been refuted by the research on homicides discussed in chapter 3.[17] Recall that the state of mind resulting from using crack is a negligible cause of homicides. In so far as any drug can be said to be responsible for violence, alcohol is the main culprit.

Cocaine

Contrary to the terrifying images propagated by the media, most consumers of cocaine use the drug only occasionally and experience no negative consequences.[18] At low doses, the physiological effects of the drug are usually not harmful to the individual. Heavy and chronic use, however, can result in severe mental and physical deterioration.[19] A powerful stimulant that rapidly increases the blood pressure, cocaine can cause sudden death in users who suffer from coronary artery disease. As a killer drug, though, cocaine is an amateur compared to alcohol and tobacco. For every cocaine-related death, there are approximately two hundred tobacco-related deaths and at least fifty related to alcohol.[20] Most cocaine-related deaths involve other drugs, so "cocaine-related" does not necessarily mean "cocaine-caused." According to the European Monitoring Centre for Drugs and Drug Addiction, "Deaths related solely to cocaine, amphetamines or ecstasy are unusual, despite the publicity they receive."[21]

Ads by anti-drug groups proclaim that cocaine will inevitably hook you and that crack is instantly addictive. These frightening allegations are contradicted by the results of government surveys. For example, the 2005 National Survey on Drug Use and Health found that, of the 26 million Americans over the age twelve who had tried powder cocaine, only about 1.7 million had used the drug in the month prior to the survey, while of the 8 million who had tried crack, only 0.7 million had used it in the preceding month.[22] Apparently, the vast majority of Americans who have tried cocaine, in either powder or crack form, have not continued to use it. Note that having used a drug in the preceding month is not an indication of dependence. Among those who are regular users of cocaine, the National Survey on Drug Abuse found that about four out of five are not dependent on the drug; they use it only occasionally.[23]

The University of Michigan's High School Senior Survey (called Monitoring the Future) revealed that, among seniors who had tried crack as of 2005, about 29 percent had used the drug in the month prior to the survey. The percentages for powder cocaine were almost identical.[24] (Daily numbers are not reported.) One limitation of the high-school data is that they don't include dropouts. To remedy this, researchers studied 145 street youths, aged twenty-four or under, in Toronto. Results showed that 46 percent had tried crack, with 6 percent of these youths going on to use it daily.[25] So, of the school dropouts who had experimented with the drug, 13 percent wound up using it every day. In another study involving seventy-nine Toronto subjects, aged eighteen and over, who had tried crack, 9 percent went on to become heavy users.[26]

On the basis of studies on the addictiveness of cocaine, researchers have concluded that neither cocaine powder nor crack are necessarily addictive even after they have been used many times.[27] RAND investigators Robert MacCoun and Peter Reuter report that most users of illicit drugs generally "desist on their own, without treatment or coercion, within five years."[28]

Scholars who study drug use have a different perspective on substance abuse than that conveyed by media images.[29] The popular view is that cocaine has the power to enslave users and turn them into addicts. People are seen as helpless victims, passively responding to the dictates of the drug. Researchers do not downplay the power of the drug, but they emphasize that human beings are capable of making choices, and that social support increases people's capacity to resist drug abuse.

Studies of regular cocaine users have found that the ability to regulate drug use in order to avoid addiction depends crucially on how much of a stake the user has in conventional life, namely a job, a career, and family and community responsibilities.[30] Peter Cohen, of the Centre for Drug Research at the University of Amsterdam, studied a group of cocaine users for a period of ten years. At the end of that period, 60 percent had completely stopped using the drug while 40 percent continued as occasional users. His conclusion was that "Most drug users ultimately stop. Drugs no longer fit their lifestyle. They get jobs, they have to get up early, they stop going to the disco, they have kids."[31]

Researchers Sheigla Murphy and Marsha Rosenbaum interviewed two young women over a period of several years who were heavy cocaine users. They were interested in how class, race, and gender influenced the effects of using cocaine.[32] Here, in brief, is the story. "Monique" is an impoverished African American who was living with her mother in a public housing project in San Francisco. She had never met her father. "Becky" is white, middle class, and was living with her mother in a four-bedroom, family-owned home along one of San Francisco's hills. Her parents are both lawyers and are divorced. Becky's parents were able to put her in a private high school and help get her a well-paying job to earn her own spending money. Monique's mother was able to do very little for her. At about fifteen, Monique began to smoke marijuana and to turn tricks to obtain money. She was arrested for prostitution, and since it was her first offense the juvenile authorities wanted to turn her over to her mother. When her mother refused to come for her they put her into a home for troubled teenagers. She was soon using crack, which was being hawked a few feet from where she lived.

Becky was smoking marijuana by the time she was twelve, and soon began using powder cocaine. She had never been exposed to crack. By age fifteen both girls were heavily into drugs. Monique's drug use had been discovered, and she had been through the court system, and been rejected by her mother. Becky, who was even more experienced with drugs, had not been discovered. A big difference was privacy. Becky had her own space both at home and at work, and could do drugs secretly. Monique had no privacy and did drugs on the street. Also, having money, Becky never felt the need, as did Monique, to exchange sexual favors for cocaine. As

Murphy and Rosenbaum observe, "the very different material conditions wrought by their race and class memberships shaped Monique's and Becky's differential ability to camouflage their drug use. This in turn helped Becky maintain a 'normal' nondeviant identity despite her rising drug use, while similar behavior brought Monique both formal and familial stigma and the attendant loss of self-esteem."[33]

In their final interview, both women were twenty-one. Monique was living in a homeless shelter. She had been off of crack for six weeks but was deeply depressed and said she craved it. She was totally impoverished and had no prospects for a job. She had stolen from her boyfriend, which she felt had destroyed their relationship. Her mother had moved to another state with her current boyfriend and refused to give her daughter the address. Monique felt ashamed and stigmatized. She told the interviewers, "It [crack] kills you and it will mess up your life. Stay away from it."[34]

Becky joined her father in Hawaii, seeing it as a chance to get away from her escalating cocaine and alcohol use. At the final interview, she had not used cocaine for a year, had stopped drinking alcohol, and used only small amounts of marijuana. She had just completed her second semester of college with good grades. Becky described her future plans: "I have a feeling that I'll be smoking pot for the rest of my life. ... No coke. ... I want to try to get it together. You know, get a good job in business accounting. But ... then when I think about it, I'd rather open my own business."[35]

Sociologist Craig Reinarman and associates conducted interviews with heavy crack users and freebasers. (Freebasing is the process of cooking cocaine powder down to crystalline form so it can be smoked.) Their results showed that the contrasting experiences of Monique and Becky were typical: middle-class status made people less vulnerable to drug abuse and its disruptive consequences, while permanent unemployment and difficult living conditions made people more vulnerable.[36] They also found that virtually none of the middle-class users of crack committed crimes or became violent and that most progressed in their careers and maintained family and social lives.[37] Research by Canadian, Dutch, and Australian drug scholars also found that "whatever crack problems exist in their societies are overwhelmingly concentrated among the most impoverished and vulnerable segments of their populations."[38]

Heroin

Our images of heroin users come from the media, which focuses on the most visible types, usually found in the most impoverished areas of the city. One familiar figure is the down-and-out junkie, who is either begging or sleeping in alleys, on park benches or in abandoned buildings.[39] Many of these addicts neglect the standard practices for good health, and wind up with such conditions as malnutrition, abscesses, scarred veins, rotten teeth, hepatitis, and AIDS.[40] Also widely portrayed on TV and film is the most common type of heroin addict in the inner city, namely the hustler, who is actively involved in crime—stealing, robbing, pimping, and killing to get his fix and obtain status in the underworld.[41]

If most addicts fit this description, heroin would indeed be a terrifying drug. But very few users follow such a degraded path.[42] Studies find that most regular heroin users are not addicts.[43] They control their use by spacing out their doses, and are called "chippers." Their life is structured around conventional employment and social activities involving heroin.[44] They rarely commit crimes and do not have income levels high enough to support a heavy habit. Typically, they restrict their heroin use to weekends and consume the drug in groups. Since they avoid frequent use and dependence, they rarely require treatment and therefore are visible mainly to researchers who have observed this pattern in numerous studies.[45]

There are also many high income earners who can afford regular heroin and still support their family and adequately perform their jobs.[46] Some British doctors, nurses, and pharmacists fall into this category, since they can easily get pharmaceutical heroin. Others obtain the drug by contact with dealers or, in the UK, by getting a medical prescription. Dr. Tom Carnwath, a psychiatrist working with drug users in Manchester, England, reports that he has legally prescribed heroin "long-term" and "on a regular basis to a number of people who lead stable productive lives, including a prosperous lawyer, a bookshop owner, a boat-builder and a professional cricketer."[47]

History provides numerous examples of opiate addicts who led long and productive lives. Among the well known were Dr. William Halsted, a famous surgeon and founder of Johns Hopkins medical school;[48] Dr. Clive Froggatt, a leading physician in England, and a favorite of prime minister Margaret Thatcher;[49] William Burroughs, author of the famous novel *Naked Lunch*, who died of natural causes at the age of eighty-three;[50] and the English novelist Enid Bagnold, author of *National Velvet*, who lived until the age of ninety-one.[51]

The experience of U.S. soldiers in Vietnam also shows that heavy heroin use is not necessarily incompatible with productive work.[52] Thousands of American soldiers consumed cheap heroin daily, yet virtually all performed their military duties adequately and in some cases with distinction. The widespread heroin addiction went undetected by superiors, and the army had to resort to urine tests to identify users.[53]

We tend to assume that, once a person is hooked on heroin, they are hooked for life. As we pointed out, addiction is rarely permanent. People tend to mature out of heroin dependence even without treatment or coercion.[54] Addicts over the age of forty are rare. We also assume that heroin quickly hooks the user. The fact is that developing a dependence on heroin is a lengthy process. To get hooked on the drug one has to use it many times.[55] U.S. government surveys find that most people who have experimented with heroin do not continue to use it. According to the 2005 National Survey on Drug Use and Health, of the 3.5 million Americans who had tried heroin, 2.9 million (83 percent) had *not* used it in the month prior to the survey.[56] A 1999 National Household Survey on Drug Abuse found that two-thirds of regular heroin users were not dependent on the drug.[57]

Unlike cocaine, heroin is physically addictive. The body develops a tolerance to it, requiring greater and greater doses to achieve the same affect. Yet, you may be shocked to learn (as I was) that, if the drug is freely available from a reliable source, studies fail to find any physical or mental harm resulting from frequent use.[58] Here is what the experts have to say on this point.

- *The Merck Manual of Medical Information*: "People who have developed tolerance [to heroin] may show few signs of drug use and function normally in their usual activities as long as they have access to drugs."[59]
- Dr. Jerome Jaffe, a drug expert who was President Nixon's director of the Office of Drug Abuse Prevention: "The addict who is able to obtain an adequate supply of drugs through legitimate channels and has adequate funds usually dresses properly, maintains his nutrition, and is able to discharge his social and occupational obligations with reasonable efficiency. He usually remains in good health, suffers little inconvenience, and is, in general, difficult to distinguish from other persons."[60]
- Drug researcher James Inciardi, of the Center for Drug and Alcohol Studies, University of Delaware, reports that, "Unlike the situation with many other drugs, chronic heroin use seems to produce little direct or permanent physiological damage."[61]
- According to a review of the evidence in 2000 by Britain's royal colleges of psychiatrists and physicians, "there is little evidence that long-term use of heroin is damaging to health."[62]
- According to Tom Carnwath, a psychiatrist working with drug abusers in Manchester, "Heroin causes little physical harm and may be taken over long periods with safety. ... It is true that many heroin users become ill, but this is usually the result of using contaminated injecting equipment or impure supplies of the drug."[63]

Another myth about heroin is that withdrawal puts addicts through the tortures of hell. The media has projected this nightmarish image in films such as *The Man with the Golden Arm* and television series such as "N.Y.P.D. Blue" and "Law and Order." But researchers and clinicians agree that the symptoms of kicking heroin are about the same as those resulting from a case of the flu—something we've all gone through.[64] As the *Merck Manual* put it, "when the drug is discontinued, the user may have mild withdrawal symptoms, which are scarcely noticed or are described as a case of influenza."[65] But, after these physical symptoms abate, an addict can experience cravings for a fix that lasts for months, which explains why relapse is so common.[66]

As with cocaine, heroin's power to addict depends less on the pharmacology of the drug than on the situation of the user. Consider again our

Vietnam veterans: 15 percent of them regularly used heroin when they were on the battlefield; when they returned home, 90 percent of those kicked the habit.[67] Another example is the medical patient who gets regular doses of morphine to relieve the pain of a temporary medical problem but rarely becomes addicted. The World Health Organization reviewed this issue and concluded that "the medical use of opiates is rarely associated with the development of psychological dependence."[68] (Note that heroin is morphine that has been slightly altered chemically, and once heroin gets into the brain it's converted back to morphine.)[69]

Concluding Comments

In their book *Body Count*, drug czars William Bennett and John Walters make no mention of any of the harms caused by the drug war. Their message is that every banned drug is deadly, and that every illicit drug user is an addict and a dangerous felon deserving punishment by incarceration. Drug war researchers overwhelmingly disagree with this view.

RAND experts Peter Reuter and Robert MacCoun express the consensus view among scientists who study the drug war: "Most who start using illicit drugs desist of their own volition, without treatment or coercion, within five years," and that "most who try [illicit] drugs, even a number of times, do not become dependent users. This represents a very different pattern from that for the legally available psychoactive drugs, alcohol, and cigarettes; most who use alcohol and tobacco even occasionally have lengthy careers, measured in terms of decades."[70]

The czars' penchant for criminalizing drug users is rejected by every scholarly commission that has investigated drug control policy over the past hundred years. As researchers Arnold Trebach and Kevin Zeese put it: "each of the commission reports calls for a gentle, humane approach to dealing with drug users and abusers. None ... call for a war on drugs, on users or on addicts."[71] Sociologists Craig Reinarman and Harry Levine argue that the propaganda disseminated by the czars and other drug warriors is a necessary justification for a punitive drug policy which results in a "financial drain, the deaths of police and civilians, and repressive policies like imprisoning pregnant women and ten-year sentences for teenagers found to have sold tiny amounts of crack."[72]

Part IV
Beyond the Drug War

I do feel that we would markedly reduce our crime rate if drugs were legalized. [In countries that have experimented with some type of legalization] there has been a reduction in their crime rate and there has been no increase in their drug use rate. There are a lot of things that are sensitive subjects but that does not mean that we should ignore them when they are destroying the very fabric of our country.

(Surgeon General Joycelyn Elders, December, 1993)[1]

As a former drugs squad chief, I've seen too many youngsters die. I'm determined my children don't get hooked—which is why I want all drugs legalized. Seven years of my life was spent in Scotland Yard's anti-drugs squad, four as its head. I saw the misery that drug abuse can cause. I saw first-hand the squalor, the wrecked lives, the deaths. And I saw, and arrested when I could, the people who do so well out of drugs, the dealers, the importers, the organizers. I saw the immense profits they were making out of human misery ... We have attempted prohibition. All that happened was that courts became clogged with thousands of cases of small, individual users, and a generation of young people came to think of the police as their enemies. There were no resources left to fight other crime. I say legalize drugs because I want to see less drug abuse, not more. And I say legalize drugs because I want to see the criminals put out of business.

(Edward Ellison, former head of Scotland Yard's Anti-Drug Squad)[2]

12 Harm Reduction Instead of War

The Case for Harm Reduction

America's war on drugs was born in the aftermath of World War I. From the beginning, the war has been a crusade, driven by a harsh moralistic ideology favoring punitive prohibition. Selected drugs have been labeled evil and banned. Consumers, producers, and sellers have been stigmatized as criminals. The hard-line moralists spearheading the war have pushed incarceration as the preferred punishment for drug law violators. Drug czars John Walters and William Bennett have stated that the purpose of imprisonment is "to exact a price for transgressing the rights of others."[1]

As documented in this book, America's drug control policy has been an unmitigated disaster. Scientific studies, many funded by the federal government, have shown that the war has been a major cause of homicide, property crime, the degradation of minorities, the spread of AIDS, the corruption of public officials, the erosion of civil liberties, and the squandering of tax dollars. There is no evidence that the war has reduced the consumption or abuse of the banned drugs. On the contrary, in the face of an acceleration of the war in the past quarter century the rate of consumption of illicit drugs has not only increased but has shifted to more and more dangerous substances.[2] The war has not only failed to protect our youth, it has created a violent and powerful underworld which has enticed and coerced many impoverished, inner-city juveniles to become peddlers as well as users of drugs of unknown potency and risk. The war has also diminished the ability of the police to protect our children from drug pushers because our law enforcement has been overwhelmed with the impossible task of apprehending millions of adult consumers and peddlers.

Many researchers interpret the drug war as a way of taming and marginalizing citizens that are perceived as a threat to the social order, such as minorities, immigrants, and rebellious young people.[3] These scholars argue that punitive prohibition is less about drug abuse and health, and more about repressing "dangerous groups." Punitive prohibition has powerful constituents in addition to the hard-line moralists. The crusade has been a financial bonanza to the police, the military, government agencies, prison officials, and the drug treatment industry, not to mention the drug lords.[4] Frightened parents mistakenly cling to the view that the war can keep their children safe. Americans have been so thoroughly brainwashed by decades of propaganda that many support the war because they believe the nonsense that the illicit hard drugs are instantly addictive and lethal even when used occasionally. The lack of public debate about the pros and cons of the war has contributed to a widespread ignorance about the harms caused by our drug control policy.

Politicians have usually initiated escalated crackdowns on drug law violators during election years as a way of showing voters they are tackling economic and social problems, such as violence, poverty, and drug addiction. If the war really were about these social and human problems there would be public debates about its benefits and costs. But, except for scholars and a few voices in the wilderness, there is an eerie silence about the drug war in the United States. Yes, there is a public struggle over medical marijuana, with several states supporting it and the federal government opposing. But you rarely hear criticism or even doubts about making criminals out of individuals who are caught possessing or selling illicit substances, even if they happen to be addicted, mentally retarded, or poverty stricken. We are bombarded, as we should be, by debates over taxes, Social Security, globalization, and the Iraq war, not to mention sports, murders, sex scandals, and the latest pharmaceutical-drugs-you-should-ask-your-doctor-about, but with rare exceptions you don't hear public officials examining the pros and cons of the drug war. I'm convinced the ideologues and other vested interests don't want an airing of America's longest war, and, so far, they've had their way.

The United States is almost alone among industrial countries in viewing drug control policy as a war. There's an alternative policy, "harm reduction"—a public-health approach aimed at reducing the harms that can be caused by the illicit drugs.[5] Harm reduction has been recommended by every scholarly commission over the past century; none have recommended the current American policy of punitive prohibition.[6] The United States has consistently ignored—and indeed is hostile to—these expert reports.

The Netherlands pioneered harm reduction in the 1970s. According to RAND researchers Peter Reuter and Robert MacCoun, "The Dutch have shown that harm reduction can be used as a principle to guide decisions consistently, and have some successes to show and no disasters to hide."[7] Partly as a result of the Dutch successes, harm reduction has become a significant force in the United Kingdom, Canada, Italy, Spain, Switzerland, Germany, and South Australia.[8] As Paul Flynn, a long-time Labour member of the UK Parliament, put it, "The drug war, in Western Europe at least, is essentially over. Our course is irreversibly moving toward legalized markets in so-called soft drugs, availability of drugs like opiates for those who are addicted through various health systems, and a more pragmatic approach to substance abuse generally throughout Europe."[9]

Harm reduction does not imply legalization, and indeed none of the nations who have departed from the drug war have so far officially legalized the prohibited drugs.[10] Instead, they have focused on reducing the damage caused both by illicit drugs and by prohibitionist policies. The harm reduction approach has led to numerous policy innovations, such as making sterile syringes freely available to prevent the spread of HIV, permitting physicians to provide methadone or heroin to heroin addicts, establishing safe injection rooms for intravenous heroin users, providing drug analysis units to evaluate the safety of ecstasy and other drugs that may be used by patrons at large dance parties, and decriminalizing the possession of small amounts of marijuana—and even in some cases the possession of small quantities of the hard drugs.[11]

Harm Reduction Alone Ignores the Benefits of Illicit Drugs

Harm reduction as the sole basis for guiding drug control policy is incomplete, however. It assumes that the recreational use of prohibited drugs has the potential to cause only harm, ignoring the fact that millions get pleasure from them. Archeological and anthropological research has shown that human beings have a craving for psychoactive substances. This craving extends to all societies, and goes back to prehistoric times.[12] It shows no sign of going away: the researcher Dr. Andrew Weil has argued that "the desire to alter consciousness periodically is an innate, normal drive analogous to hunger or the sexual drive."[13] Consider that more than 112 million American adults have used illicit substances for such purposes as experiencing euphoria, diminishing pain, combating depression, providing stimulation, relieving anxiety, and inducing sleep.[14] Most of us have consumed *legal* psychoactive substances for the same purposes. Accepting this reality about the benefits of psychoactive drugs implies that, *on the basis of a cost–benefit analysis, our governments should respect people's desire for psychoactive drugs while attempting to make drug use as safe as possible.*

Billions of advertising dollars promote the pursuit of pleasure in American society, so it's curious that commentators rarely mention the benefits people get from illicit drugs. Perhaps the silence on this score is due to our having been bombarded for decades with the puritanical views expressed by politicians and political appointees such as the drug czars. As former czar William Bennett put it: "The simple fact is that drug use is wrong. And the moral argument, in the end, is the most compelling argument."[15] Bill Clinton's drug czar, General Barry McCaffrey, argued that "drugs are wrong and dangerous" because "they're destructive of a person's physical, emotional and moral strength."[16]

What Happened to our Inalienable Right to the Pursuit of Happiness?

Even if one agreed with the czars that drug use is "wrong and dangerous," it doesn't follow that people who consume certain substances with no harm to anyone else—and in fact usually with no harm to themselves—should be treated as criminals. Many scholars and public figures have condemned the policy implications of the harsh puritanical views expressed by the drug czars. For example:

- The late Nobel laureate economist Milton Friedman asked, "Can our laws be moral if they have so racist an effect?" Following John Stuart Mill, he argued that the government has no right to use force to prevent responsible adults from using drugs, as long as they don't harm others.[17]
- The late evolutionary biologist Steven Jay Gould questioned how a policy could be defended which labeled one class of substances as a "preeminent scourge," while the two most dangerous substances, alcohol and tobacco, were being "advertised in neon on every street corner in urban America."[18]
- The philosopher Douglas Husak pointed out that, despite allegations that Americans are puritanical, they engage in all kinds of activities mainly because they give pleasure.[19]
- Walter Cronkite made the following statement at the end of a 1995 Discovery Channel broadcast about the drug war: "Just about every American was shocked when Robert McNamara, one of the master architects of the Vietnam war, acknowledged that not only did he believe the war wrong, terribly wrong, but that he thought so at the very time he was helping to wage it. ... we must not blindly add to the body count and the terrible cost of the war on drugs only to learn from another Robert McNamara thirty years from now that what we've been doing is wrong, terribly wrong."[20]
- In 2003 the U.S. Supreme Court overruled by six to three a Texas law prohibiting sex between homosexuals. The majority decision written by Justice Anthony Kennedy seems to me to implicitly challenge the constitutionality of the drug war by basing the court's decision on the American tradition of liberty and freedom, which goes back to the Declaration of Independence. As Justice Kennedy put it: "Liberty protects the person from unwarranted government intrusions into a dwelling or other private places [sic]. In our tradition the state is not omnipresent in the home. And there are other spheres where the state should not be a dominant presence. Freedom extends beyond spatial bounds. Liberty presumes an autonomy of self that includes freedom of thought, belief, expression, and certain intimate conduct."[21]

As they say, democracy is the worst form of government except for all the others. I argue in the next chapter that *government-regulated legalization* is the worst form of drug control policy except for all the others. By legalization, I mean that *adults would be entitled to acquire the currently banned drugs without fear of losing their liberty or property*. A major benefit of regulated legalization, regardless of how it's structured, is that the control of the drugs would be taken over by the various levels of government instead of being left to the drug lords. As we've seen, whenever a popular drug is banned, black market capitalists, seeking profits, will inevitably construct the supply networks necessary to deliver the product to consumers. Note that governments cannot tax or control the quality of a substance which is produced and distributed in underground markets.

The question I focus on is: *how can governments best regulate the production, distribution, and consumption of the various illicit substances?*[22] That's a big question, and it cannot be definitively answered by lone researchers like me sitting at their computers, or even by blue-ribbon commissions. Any drug control system requires periodic adjustments because the types of drugs are endlessly evolving, as are the attitudes and values of society. After the repeal of prohibition it took decades for the federal and state governments to work out systems of regulating alcohol, and they are still being fine-tuned. What scholars can do, however, is to provide the best scientific evidence that is relevant to the question of how governments can regulate the currently illicit drugs so as to minimize damage while permitting adult access. I examine that evidence next.

13 Legalizing Marijuana

Marijuana is the most popular illicit drug by far. Recall that it's classified as a Schedule I drug, which means that it's considered by the federal government to be a) too dangerous to be consumed and b) to have no currently accepted medical value. According to the 2005 National Survey on Drug Use and Health, over 97 million Americans aged twelve or older have tried it. Of the 19.7 million who had consumed an illicit drug in the month prior to the survey, over 14.6 million (74 percent) had smoked marijuana.[1] In 2005, more that 786,000 people in the United States were arrested for violating the ban on marijuana, about 43 percent of all arrests for drug law violations.[2] Over 88 percent of these marijuana arrests were for possession alone. Those arrested, including many teenagers, face the prospect of fines, lawyers fees, court costs, probation, jail time, forfeiture of property, loss of employment, and public humiliation. A 1999 study estimated that around 60,000 marijuana offenders were in prison.[3]

All this, when scientific evidence has shown that cannabis is relatively harmless: it's not a gateway drug; it's about as addictive as caffeine; and it has never caused anyone to die from an overdose.[4] Recall that the *Merck Manual of Medical Information* concluded that there is "little evidence of biologic damage [from marijuana] even among relatively heavy users,"[5] and that the chief administrative law judge of the Drug Enforcement Administration, Francis L. Young, after a four-month review of evidence from around the nation, concluded that cannabis had medical uses and "is far safer than many foods we commonly consume."[6]

In 2005, 36 percent of tenth graders had used marijuana, as had almost 45 percent of twelfth graders.[7] Would legalization increase the rate of cannabis use by young people, or might it decrease it by making the drug less appealing, as has happened in the Netherlands? There are influences in both directions:

- Assuming the drug was not taxed too heavily, legalization would bring down its price, which would have the effect of increasing consumption.
- The illicit status of marijuana gives it a *forbidden fruit effect*, which makes it attractive, especially to young people. As RAND researchers

MacCoun and Reuter put it, "Drug prohibition may actually motivate some drug use through a forbidden fruit mechanism, but the magnitude of such effects is unknown."[8]

- To some people, it's paramount that social order be maintained. They would obey the law even if the probability of sanctions were minuscule. Making marijuana legal could encourage them to use it.[9]

The evidence from empirical studies suggests that marijuana consumption would probably not change much under decriminalization or regulated legalization.

- In the 1970s, eleven states eliminated criminal penalties for possession of small amounts of marijuana. Studies have found that there was no detectable increase in cannabis consumption in these states compared to the states that did not decriminalize. There are similar findings for Australia, Italy, and Spain.[10]
- In 1976, the consumption of cannabis was legalized in the Netherlands. In the following seven years there was no detectable change in consumption.[11] The rate of marijuana use in Holland is less than that in the United States, with Dutch teenagers consuming the drug at half the rate of American teenagers. As the former Dutch drug czar Eddy Engelsman put it: "We succeeded in making pot boring."[12]
- Punitive prohibition has not prevented American high-school students from getting marijuana. In 2005, over 85 percent of high-school seniors said the drug is "fairly easy" or "very easy" to get.[13] Many college students have told me that in high school it was easier for them to get "weed" than beer, because they had to be carded to get beer.
- Government propaganda about the dangers of marijuana and the soaring arrests throughout the last decade and a half have failed to deliver the desired message to high-school students: In 1991, 78.6 percent of seniors perceived that regular marijuana smoking involved "great risk." This percentage trended downward over the next fourteen years and registered 58.0 in 2005.[14]
- Punitive prohibition has not reduced frequent smoking of marijuana by adolescents—on the contrary. In 1991, the percentage of high-school seniors who had smoked marijuana *daily* in the month prior to the interview was 2.0. That number grew over the next fourteen years, reaching 5.0 percent in 2005.[15]

One legalization possibility would be to allow government-regulated sales to people above a certain age at state-licensed package stores like those that sell liquor in many states; or we could follow the Dutch practice of permitting sales in government-licensed coffee shops. People could also be allowed to grow their own. Advertising could be strictly controlled.

A benefit of any legalization system would be the elimination of the flood of arrests and incarcerations for violating marijuana laws. Law enforcement would be freed to deal with real crimes, including protecting children from drug pushers. The government could raise tax revenue from marijuana, as it now does from tobacco and alcohol. Courts would be less overloaded and so would prisons, saving the taxpayer billions.

Marijuana is sold in black markets, and any legalization scheme would dry up the underground supply. One benefit would be an improvement in safety, for even marijuana sometimes contains disease-causing viruses and bacteria.[16] Legalizing the drug could have other benefits as well.

- Young people might switch from beer to marijuana.[17] Unlike alcohol, marijuana is not biologically damaging and, as we saw in chapter 10, does not cause violence and traffic accidents.[18]
- Users of marijuana would have less contact with the drug pushers and thus less exposure to sales pitches for harder drugs.
- Since users would no longer fear arrest, they would be more likely to contact health professionals when they had problems with the drug.
- Hostility for law enforcement would dissipate. Many people, especially the young, have experienced harassment and humiliation at the hands of the police for possession or suspected possession.

14 Reforming the Laws on Hard Drugs

Addicts

Prescribing drugs that would allow addicts to maintain their habit has been illegal in the United States since the beginning of the drug war.[1] Great Britain followed a different course. In 1926, a blue ribbon commission, chaired by the president of the Royal College of Physicians, ruled that drug addiction was a medical problem to be handled by physicians and their patients without interference from the police. As a result, British doctors were able to prescribe opiates to their addicted patients and did so for decades without drug abuse becoming a significant problem.[2] Thousands of addicts were also maintained on legal prescriptions of amphetamine, cocaine, and other non-opiate drugs.[3] As RAND researchers MacCoun and Reuter put it, "the system muddled along for four decades with few problems."[4]

In the 1960s, partly as a result of the emergence of drug-abusing, unemployed, long-haired hippies, the British dropped their policy of maintaining addicts and followed the lead of the United States. Addicts would be given a drug substitute such as methadone *on a decreasing dosage*.[5] The purpose was to wean them off of drugs as quickly as possible. The effects were devastating. Addicts flocked to the underworld for their fix. Violence erupted, incarcerations skyrocketed, and deaths from drug overdoses soared. Britain's experience began to resemble that of the United States.

Meanwhile, in the United States, researchers Vincent Dole and Marie Nyswander were obtaining favorable results administering oral doses of methadone to heroin addicts at the Rockefeller Institute in New York.[6] Patients given methadone withdrew from heroin, worked more, committed less crime, and stayed in treatment longer. No needles were involved; the oral dose was administered only once a day, and was cheaper than heroin. The Dole–Nyswander findings have been corroborated by numerous scientific studies. As the historian of opiate addiction David Courtwright concluded: "Methadone was to [opiate] addiction what insulin was to diabetes, a medically appropriate answer to a genuine disease."[7]

In 1985, health officials in Edinburgh, Scotland, observed that there were an average of 120 new HIV infections a year in Scotland stemming from contaminated needles. Their response was to allow physicians to prescribe oral versions of virtually any drug to addicts at no charge, provided they did not use needles. Patients were encouraged, but not required, to enter treatment programs designed to help them overcome their addiction.[8] By 1992, there were only eight new AIDS cases a year linked to dirty needles. The program was successful in reducing heroin and other drug use. Crime rates dropped. The results validated the view of the health providers that addicts could make responsible decisions about their lives if given information, motivation, and resources.

Some areas in Britain managed to continue drug maintenance after the 1960s. Liverpool was one. In 1982, Dr. John Marks, a psychiatrist certified to prescribe heroin and cocaine, became director of the Liverpool clinic. He disagreed with heroin maintenance but decided to go along with the ongoing program, expecting to demonstrate that it was a bad idea.[9] Addicts were given a prescription for their drug of choice, whether it was heroin, cocaine, or even crack. They could fill the prescription for free at the pharmacy. Interestingly, no one asked for crack.[10] As long as addicts appeared regularly at meetings to show they were healthy and not involved in crime, they were free to live as they chose. If they were ever arrested they were dropped from the program.

The results were so favorable that Dr. Marks became an advocate for drug maintenance:[11] no intravenous users contracted AIDS; most patients were healthy and had jobs; the police estimated that there was a 94 percent decline in theft and burglary in the area; and drug peddlers migrated elsewhere. The program's success attracted the attention of the United States television program *60 Minutes*, which featured it on December 27, 1992.[12] The show focused on the story of Julia Scott who, before entering the program, had been a heroin addict for ten years and had worked as a prostitute to support her habit. During the three years she was on the program, she was employed as a waitress and was able to care for her infant daughter.

Success notwithstanding, the Liverpool program was closed in 1995, and a new organization took over. Its philosophy was in line with United States policy. Dr. Marks had been warned that the U.S. embassy was exerting pressure to shut him down. He believed the cancellation was due to favorable publicity from the *60 Minutes* program.[13] Most of the 450 addicts who had been at the clinic wound up back on the streets or in prison. Within two years, twenty-five of his former patients were dead, including Julia Scott.[14] Dr. Marks defended maintenance by saying that drugs were being provided for addicts from the clinic rather than from the mafia and that, while the program "doesn't get them off drugs. It doesn't prolong their addiction either. But it stops them from offending; it keeps them healthy and it keeps them alive."[15]

Switzerland, which also had a drug problem, heard about Dr. Marks's clinic. Their health officials interviewed the British doctors who ran the Liverpool program, and after much discussion in the media and a summit meeting between the Swiss president and the heads of the cantonal governments, the

Zurich authorities in 1994, with the approval of the public, launched the largest and most carefully designed drug maintenance program ever attempted.[16] A total of 1,146 heroin addicts volunteered. They were required to be at least twenty, to be hard-core addicts, to be afflicted with serious health problems, and to have repeatedly failed other treatment programs. As Judge James Gray pointed out, these are "the kind of people who in the United States are clogging our prisons."[17] Volunteers were offered heroin, morphine, or methadone. They initially opted for heroin. *A crucial decision was made to allow them to adjust their own doses.* They could receive heroin three times a day every day of the year in safe and hygienic environments. The patients self-injected with equipment prepared by the staff, who also provided advice and supervision.

The final report of the Swiss government was issued in July of 1997. Here are the results of the trials.[18]

- Within a month, the patients reached stable and relatively low dosage levels that allowed them to dramatically improve their health and their economic and social functioning.
- No overdoses were reported.
- No heroin was reported to have leaked into the illicit market.
- The percentage of participants engaged in illegal activities dropped from 59 to 10.
- The percentage of the addicts with stable jobs increased from 14 to 32.
- One-third of the participants who had been dependant on care institutions became able to function independently.
- There were no "incidents" that were upsetting to the public.
- Self-reported mental health improved dramatically.
- After a year and a half, about 69 percent of the volunteers were still in the program. Of the 350 who dropped out of heroin maintenance, ninety-two started methadone treatment and eighty-three chose a rehab program that would help them give up drugs altogether. The government report noted that the probability of switching to an abstinence program increased the longer the individual remained in treatment.
- As a result of the program, the Swiss were able to reduce expenditures on medical care, social support, and crime control by almost 50 percent.
- A side benefit of the experiment was a reduction in the use of cocaine, which is a hopeful finding since there is no equivalent to methadone for cocaine users.[19]

Law enforcement and health officials in Switzerland declared the program a success. So did the Swiss population. On September 28, 1997, in a nationwide referendum, 70.6 percent of the voters opposed an initiative that would have ended the program.[20] In October 1998, the Swiss parliament voted overwhelmingly to make the program permanent.[21] The Swiss government agreed to have the program evaluated by the World Health Organization, which found that the experiment demonstrated that heroin maintenance was feasible and brought about improvements in health and social functioning.[22]

As a result of the Swiss trials, twenty of the thrity police chiefs in the major cities of Germany expressed their support for drug maintenance, as did the German minister of health, Andrea Fischer, who planned similar programs for Hamburg and Frankfurt.[23] The Swiss success encouraged the Dutch to launch a similar trial, involving 750 addicts, which tested heroin versus methadone. Interest was also expressed in Australia, Denmark, Luxembourg, Spain, and Canada.[24]

The official reaction of the United States government to the Swiss trials was hostile. This attitude was illustrated in hearings held by a House subcommittee in 1998, where only witnesses who had long records of condemning drug maintenance were called to testify. Swiss officials who were connected with the trials were not invited.[25] Proposals to undertake similar drug maintenance experiments in the United States so the results could be scientifically evaluated have met with outrage. For example, in 1998, Professor David Vlahov of the Johns Hopkins School of Public Health suggested undertaking trials in Baltimore. His suggestion was immediately disapproved and his supporters censured. Maryland's Democratic governor said, "It doesn't make any sense. It sends totally the wrong signal."[26] As RAND drug researchers MacCoun and Reuter put it: "It is striking that this impassioned hostility is engendered not by a policy proposal but simply by a proposal to conduct a demonstration or trial whose results could inform both sides of the debate. ... [The] indignation and the willful misrepresentation of foreign experiences (Britain in the 1970s; Switzerland in the 1990s) are troubling."[27]

Canada has recently shifted its drug control policy from punishment toward harm reduction. The first safe injection site in North America has been set up in Vancouver, British Columbia, allowing addicts to inject safely under medical supervision, instead of winding up in prison or on the streets. Canadian officials had been persuaded by reports from Switzerland and Frankfurt, Germany, that safe injection sites had led to reductions in HIV infections and drug overdoses, and had caused more people to register for treatment programs. Drug czar John Walters reacted angrily to Canada's new policy. He said in a telephone interview, "The very name is a lie. There are not safe injection sites. It can't be made safe."[28]

The United States policy toward addicts is driven by a harsh morality, which demands that they abstain from drugs or be deemed felons. Criminalizing those who are addicted drives them underground, where they may contribute to the AIDS epidemic, die from contaminated drugs, or wind up in drug and disease-infested prisons. In my judgment, the Dole–Nyswander findings, along with programs like those in Switzerland, Scotland, and Liverpool, demonstrate that drug maintenance not only enables many addicts to function as productive citizens but brings them into contact with health professionals, increasing the likelihood they could overcome their addiction. If our federal and state governments were to reach out to drug addicts with programs such as these the benefits to our society would dwarf the costs.

Occasional Users

Contrary to what the government and the media have led most Americans to believe, a heavy majority of those who are currently consuming hard drugs use them only occasionally and are not addicted. According to the *National Household Survey on Drug Use and Health*, two out of three users of heroin, and four out of five cocaine users, are not dependent on these drugs. As for stimulants such as amphetamines, almost nine out of ten users are not addicted.[29] Also, recall that there is little documented injury to health caused by occasional consumption of these drugs, although people with bad hearts should avoid stimulants such as cocaine and amphetamines.[30]

Banning drugs that consumers demand has one effect for sure: the underworld will happily supply it, with the following repercussions (see Part II).

- Billions of dollars are funneled to the drug lords, but no tax dollars to the government.
- Profit-bloated kingpins corrupt public officials and can afford the best technology to outmaneuver our budget-strapped law enforcement.
- Underground markets for illicit hard drugs, spawned by prohibition, are violent, and attempts to police them are futile, expensive, and dangerous.
- Black market drugs are often contaminated and of unknown potency, causing diseases and overdoses.
- Busting street peddlers eats up tax dollars, takes law enforcement away from violent and property crimes, and creates job openings for an army of eager candidates.
- Requiring police to infiltrate underground drug markets to bust transactions between willing buyers and sellers saddles them with a hopeless task, puts them in harm's way, and erodes civil liberties.
- Jailing Americans for illicit drug use, when more than 46 percent of adults (112 million) have indulged, and more than 14 percent (35 million) are consuming yearly, reveals the drug war to be a civil war.[31]
- Imprisoning drug law violators with lengthy sentences results in millions of stigmatized and embittered ex-cons being dumped back on the streets with advanced degrees in crime.
- Our overcrowded prisons are awash in hard drugs and are a breeding ground for drug addiction and AIDS.

I find the scientific evidence to be overwhelming that American society would benefit enormously if the various levels of our government controlled currently illicit drugs instead of continuing to allow the underworld do so. We would deal drug lords a mortal blow by making these drugs accessible in some way to adults and letting the federal and state governments regulate and tax their production and distribution. If drugs were legally available, and not taxed too heavily, black markets would shrivel, along with the harms that result from allowing the underworld to monopolize their sale. Under government-regulated legalization, casual users would have access to drugs of known quality and potency; and if they had problems they could seek medical help without fear of the police. Note that since prohibition was repealed there has been no violence among alcohol suppliers and no deaths from contaminated alcohol.

People worry that if criminal penalties were repealed the use of drugs such as cocaine, crack, heroin, and methamphetamine would skyrocket. While no one can predict with certainty what would happen, and much would depend on exactly how the drugs were legalized, studies suggest (to me) that the consumption rate would not change much if prohibition were replaced with government-regulated legalization.

- Italy has removed criminal sanctions for the possession of small amounts of heroin and cocaine; and Spain has removed all penalties for the possession of these drugs. Studies comparing Italy and Spain with other nations have failed to find that differences in the severity of drug control laws have any impact on drug use or drug deaths.[32]
- Studies have found that alcohol consumption changed little or not at all following the repeal of prohibition. Economists Miron and Zwiebel conclude from this that by that time the illegal supply network had became well enough organized to satisfy demand. They argue the same is true of illicit drugs today.[33] Also, they note that, following repeal, alcohol consumption became safer, since beer drinking increased at the expense of whiskey. Similar incentives would apply to the currently illicit drugs.
- Drug warriors assert that harsh penalties reduce consumption of illicit drugs. But, in spite of such penalties, from 1991 to 2005 there was an increase in the percentage of high-school students who had used cocaine powder, crack cocaine, and heroin, in the month prior to the survey, with no discernible trend in the percentage who were using amphetamines. By contrast, the percentage of high-school students who were consuming alcohol and cigarettes dropped significantly over this period.[34]
- From 1991 to 2005, there was no measurable change in the percentage of high-school seniors who reported *daily* use of powder cocaine, crack cocaine, or heroin. Over the same period there was a small increase in the percentage using amphetamines daily (0.2 to 0.4) and a significant jump in those using marijuana every day (2.0 to 5.0). By contrast, there was a sharp decline in the daily use of cigarettes and a small drop in daily consumption of alcohol.[35]
- The adult consumption of illicit drugs increased from 1994 to 2003 even though federal spending on supply reduction rose from $7.8 billion to $12.9 billion over this period: in 1994, 6 percent of Americans

over twelve were currently using illicit drugs, while in 2003 this figure was 8.2 percent.[36]

- Estimates by RAND researchers found that the United States had less per capita consumption of cocaine and heroin when these drugs were legal: in 1905, the rate of cocaine use was one-tenth to one-fifth the current figure, even though the drug was cheaper then. The rate of heroin consumption a hundred years ago also appears to have been lower than today, and it was declining prior to the Harrison Act of 1914.[37]

How might the drug market be regulated short of prohibition? A frequently mentioned alternative is *decriminalization*, which is often confused with legalization, but is a different option. Decriminalization usually refers to the removal of criminal penalties for possession of small amounts of a drug. But the drug market would remain illegal, so underground organizations would continue to supply illicit drugs, with many of the same resulting harms to society as under prohibition.[38] Another possibility, which also has major drawbacks, would be to turn the supply of recreational drugs over to the medical profession. But, as Steven Duke and Albert Gross put it, such a setup "would make drug dealers out of our health professionals ... and would demoralize if not destroy the [medical] profession."[39]

Most drug researchers who favor legalization recommend the creation of a system of government-licensed and regulated distributors and retailers for psychoactive drugs, along the lines of our current system for alcohol. The licensees would be required to demonstrate good character, financial responsibility, and uncontaminated and properly labeled products. There is ample precedent for governments to oversee the drug market in the public interest as they regulate liquor sales and gambling.[40] A major advantage of a system such as this is that it would destroy the underground market. Economists Daniel Benjamin and Roger Leroy Miller argue that the impact on the black market would be similar to what happened with the ending of the liquor war in 1933: "Within days, the bootleggers and rum-runners were out of business."[41] The ending of alcohol prohibition stopped turf warfare and bathtub gin.[42] We don't have any modern-day Al Capones in the alcohol business. In addition, many of those drawn into producing and distributing alcohol during prohibition abandoned criminal activities altogether following its repeal, because there were no other illegal pursuits any where near as profitable. The same is true of the illicit drug market today. Legalization would likely result in many drug peddlers dropping out of criminal pursuits, people who would not have been drawn into the underground market except for the enormous profits involved.[43]

Controlled legalization could encompass different policies among the states. After all, our nation's solution for alcohol as adopted in the 21st Amendment was to turn the regulatory powers over to the states and to prohibit the federal government from any role. As Ethan Nadelmann put it, "Most states, cities, and other communities might well continue to prohibit the sale and public consumption of most drugs within their jurisdiction as they do now, but would be obliged to acknowledge the basic right of access by mail order as well as the basic right of possession and consumption."[44] There's no reason why we could not legalize in a way that takes into account the sensibilities of those who oppose legalization, for example, by limiting consumption to homes and places of restricted access.[45] Under regulated legalization there would still be important functions for the police, such as enforcing the laws concerning nuisances, access by juveniles, zoning of neighborhoods, driving under the influence, and where drugs could be used.

Scholars overwhelmingly recommend a public health approach to drug use with the goal of harm reduction, as opposed to the current United States policy of zero tolerance enforced by criminal penalties. A public health and community outreach program has a much better chance than punitive prohibition of bringing problem users into contact with health professionals and into treatment programs. Recall that a RAND study funded by the U.S. Army found that treatment was seven times as effective per dollar in reducing cocaine consumption as the most effective type of domestic law enforcement.[46]

The Netherlands employs a public health approach with success measured by drug-related deaths, crime, AIDS, and the costs of drug law enforcement.[47] A United Nations study in 1994 found that drug-related deaths per capita in the Netherlands were one-seventh as large as in the United States.[48] As Bart Majoor, who was trained as a psychologist in Holland, explains it: "to prevent drug-related harm one has to approach the consumer in an attitude of service. When you provide information, materials, and services the consumer really needs, the majority will show responsible behavior and develop their own safe rules for drug taking."[49]

Hard drugs are illegal in the Netherlands, but the Ministry of Justice has instructed the police not to use their powers against the users and sellers unless other laws are violated.[50] The government is persuaded that enforcement would drive the hard-drug market underground and that a health problem would become a crime problem. Indeed, Holland has had very little cocaine-related crime and few deaths. According to Dirk H. van der Woude of the Municipal Health Service, between 1979 and 1994 the percentage of those under twenty-two who used hard drugs declined from 15 percent to 2.5 percent. Data from 1987 found that only 1.7 percent of the adults in Amsterdam had used cocaine in the past year, compared to 6 percent of the adults in New York who had used the drug in the preceding six months.[51]

While powder cocaine is available in the Netherlands, crack is apparently hard to find. The explanation seems clear: powder cocaine is affordable, so why use the riskier version? Many scholars, including Judge James Gray, point out that "The United States brought the 'crack epidemic' on itself as a result of its prohibitionist policy on powder cocaine."[52]

The United States' goal of total abstinence from illicit psychoactive substances is unattainable. Virtually every human being ingests mood-altering chemicals, such as alcohol, caffeine, nicotine, and marijuana, as well as a myriad of prescription drugs which alleviate anxiety, depression, and insomnia.[53] As mentioned in chapter 12,[54] scientific evidence reveals that intoxication is a drive almost as basic as hunger, thirst, or sex. The psychopharmacologist Ronald Siegel refers to it as "the fourth drive"; as he put it, "Our nervous system ... is arranged to respond to chemical intoxicants in much the same way it responds to food, drink, and sex."[55] Historical and archaeological studies have also reached this conclusion; they find that psychoactive substances have been used since prehistoric times.[56] For example, the coca plant has been used for at least 7,000 years; and the betel nut was chewed 11,000 years ago in Thailand and 13,000 years ago in Timor.[57]

Finally, controlled legalization would produce a safer pattern of drug consumption. As discussed in chapter 4,[58] the black market sets up incentives for the consumption of more powerful and dangerous psychoactive substances. Market forces under legalization would likely eliminate the more dangerous drugs such as crack and methamphetamine, because these substances emerged as a result of the inflated black market prices for competitive drugs. As the Dartmouth Medical School neuroscientist Michael Gazzaniga puts it: "if cocaine were reduced to the same price as crack, the abuser [of crack], acknowledging the higher rate of addiction, might forgo the more intensive high of crack, opting for the slower high of cocaine. ... we know that 120-proof alcohol doesn't sell as readily as 86 proof, not by a long shot, even though the higher the proof, the faster the psychological effect that alcohol users are seeking."[59]

The bottom line here is this: we must face the fact that people's drive to consume psychoactive substances for pleasure is not going to go away. Prohibiting the use of these drugs inevitably drives their production and distribution underground. We should wrest these drugs away from the drug lords by allowing our federal and state governments to control their production and supply, as we have done with alcohol. Doing so would not be a panacea, but it would be saner and healthier than the horror we have created by our ninety-year war against drugs.

15 Questions and Answers

Now that you've read this book, I hope you're outraged, as I am, that our federal government pursues such a harmful and futile war against its own citizens. If so, you may want to spread the word that some type of regulated legalization is urgently needed in our drug control policy. Some people may be resistant to any examination of the issue. For them it could be a religious matter; or they might have a relative enforcing the drug laws; or they could associate illicit drugs with groups they find threatening; or they could be afraid that their children would be more likely to get involved with drugs if criminal sanctions were eliminated; or they might just find the subject too frustrating or painful to think about.

We Americans have been brainwashed on this issue all our lives. Public examination of our drug control policy is practically nonexistent. Myths about the horrors of illicit drugs abound. Our ignorance about America's longest war is astonishing. One student in a college drug seminar I was conducting said, "If I'm to believe what I'm learning about the war on drugs, I would have to throw over everything I've been taught since I was born." Still, when people discover you've read this book, you may have the opportunity to share with them what you've learned. Here are some questions you're likely to get, with my suggestions as to how you might respond. Ignorance is the main stumbling block to a sane drug policy.

Q: I suppose that now you've read this book you think all drugs should be legalized?
A: Legalization, by itself, is too vague a term to be useful. It could mean anything from being on the shelf in supermarkets to being available by prescription. The issue is better framed this way: should our federal and state governments regulate the currently illicit drugs, somewhat as we do with alcohol, or should these drugs remain under the control of the drug lords? The scientific evidence presented in this book concludes that the benefits to society would be overwhelming if our governments took control away from the illegal drug cartels.

Q: Wouldn't the drug lords still exist, even if our governments regulated the prohibited drugs?

A: If illicit drugs became government regulated and accessible to adults, the drug lords would lose their profitable market and would be out of business. We no longer have drug gangs pushing alcohol as we did during alcohol prohibition.

Q: Don't illegal drugs, such as crack, cause violence?

A: Studies have found that the violence around illicit drug markets is overwhelmingly caused by drug gangs fighting each other. Crack, by itself, is not violence producing. Nor is any other illicit drug. The only drug that precipitates violence is alcohol.

Q: Aren't drugs such as heroin, cocaine, and amphetamines addictive?

A: Any drug can be addictive. But most people who use these drugs are not dependent on them. National surveys by our own government have found that two out of three regular heroin users, four out of five cocaine users, and almost nine out of ten amphetamine users are not addicted, but use them only occasionally.

Q: Aren't these hard drugs illegal because they're especially dangerous?

A: You may be surprised, as I was, to learn that deaths from cocaine and amphetamines are rare, and that pure and available heroin does not cause biological damage even to chronic users. People do die from heroin overdoses, but the overwhelming reason is that heroin from the black market is either stronger than the user expects or contaminated. The main killer drugs, by far, are tobacco and alcohol.

Q: Doesn't prohibition reduce the consumption of these hard drugs?

A: It doesn't seem to. The profits are enormous, thanks to the demand. Consequently, drug lords always find ways to get their products to consumers. Studies invariably find that, when the police crack down on illicit drug trading in one area, the transactions simply pop up elsewhere. Also, when a drug is targeted by law enforcement, consumers and producers often substitute another, usually one that's more potent. For example, the federal government's intensive effort to halt black market trading in amphetamines in the 1960s led to the emergence of cocaine.

Q: Wouldn't the consumption of illegal drugs soar if they became legally accessible?

A: Research suggests that such a scenario is unlikely. Studies comparing European countries have found that the consumption of illicit drugs is not affected by their drug control policies. For example, Italy, Spain, and Portugal do not impose criminal sanctions for possessing any psychoactive drug. Yet drug use and abuse in those countries is much the same as countries that retain criminal sanctions. Also, in the 1970s, eleven states in the United States decriminalized the possession of small amounts of marijuana, with no detectable change in consumption relative to states which retained criminal penalties.

Q: Wouldn't juveniles be more likely to be exposed to illicit drugs if they became legal for adults?

A: Our children would be better protected by the police if prohibition ended, since law enforcement is currently overwhelmed struggling to arrest the millions of Americans who possess or sell illicit drugs. Also, young people would stop being exposed to the sales pitches of drug pushers, since any legalization system would destroy the black market.

Q: Suppose we did legalize, how should we do it?

A: Most drug researchers recommend something along the lines of the way we handle alcohol. They also emphasize the benefits of treatment programs for addicts, as well as a proactive public health approach to reduce the harm that drugs can cause. But, aside from recommendations like these, no researcher or blue-ribbon commission can give the final word on precisely what kind of legalization setup would be most successful. The various levels of government would have to work that out over time. After all, it took decades to develop a system for regulating alcohol, and the system is still being fine-tuned.

Notes

Part I: Introduction

1 Mike Gray, *Drug Crazy*, pp. 107–8; James P. Gray, *Why our Drug Laws Have Failed and What We Can Do about It*, p. 128.
2 Craig Reinarman and Harry G. Levine, "Crack in context," p. 3.
3 Ibid., p. 4.
4 Gray, *Drug Crazy*, p. 107.
5 Jeffrey A. Miron and Jeffrey Zwiebel, "The economic case against drug prohibition."
6 This estimate of the annual number of homicides caused by the drug war was made by the economist Milton Friedman; see Milton Friedman and Thomas S. Szasz, *On Liberty and Drugs*, p. 71. For evidence that most drug-related homicides are caused by turf warfare between drug gangs, see Paul J. Goldstein et al., "Crack and homicide in New York City."
7 Christopher J. Mumola, Substance Abuse and Treatment, State and Federal Prisons, 1997, p. 3, table 1, cited at www.drugwarfacts.org/prison.htm.
8 Jason Ziedenberg and Vincent Schiraldi, *The Punishing Decade*, cited in Vincent Schiraldi, Barry Holms, and Phillip Beatty, *Poor Prescription*, p. 2.
9 Centers for Disease Control and Prevention, *HIV/AIDS Surveillance Report 2003*, Vol. 15, p. 12, table 3.
10 See, for example, David Satcher, *Evidence-Based Findings on the Efficacy of Syringe Exchange Programs*, summarized at www.drugwarfacts.org/syringee.htm.
11 Paige M. Harrison and Allen J. Beck, *Prisoners in 2004*, p. 9, table 12, summarized at www.drugwarfacts.org/racepris.htm.
12 Eva Bertram et al., *Drug War Politics*, p. 38.
13 American Medical Association, "About the AMA position on pain management using opioid analgesics."
14 Reinarman and Levine, "Crack in context," p. 3.
15 Ibid., p. 4.
16 Arnold S. Trebach, *The Great Drug War*, p. 12.
17 Gray, *Why our Drug Laws Have Failed*, pp. 128–9.
18 For a survey, see ibid., Appendix B; and Arnold S. Trebach and Kevin B. Zeese, *Drug Prohibition and the Conscience of Nations*, pp. 34–8.
19 Joseph D. McNamara, "Changing police attitudes support reform of national drug control polices," paper presented at the 37th annual International Congress on Alcohol and Drug Dependence, San Diego, August 20–25, 1995, cited in Craig Reinarman and Harry G. Levine, *Crack in America*, p. 348.
20 Available at www.aphf.org/survey.html. See also a 2004 survey of 300 police chiefs, where 67 percent reported that law enforcement has been "fairly" or "very"

unsuccessful at reducing the drug problem in the United States. This survey is available at www.drugstrategies.org/about.html.
21 "It's time to legalize drugs," pp. 14–15.
22 William F. Buckley, Jr., Kurt Schmoke, Joseph D. McNamara, and Robert W. Sweet, "The war on drugs is lost."
23 *America's Longest War*, p. 200.
24 *Drug War Heresies*, p. 1.
25 *Why our Drug Laws Have Failed*, p. 1.
26 Buckley et al., "The war on drugs is lost," p. 206.
27 Ibid., p. 210.
28 Ibid., p. 203.
29 "Task force reports from the ASC to Attorney General Janet Reno," 1995, quoted in Reinarman and Levine, *Crack in America*, p. 349.
30 Quoted in Reinarman and Levine, *Crack in America*, p. 348.

1 Overview

1 See, for example, James A. Inciardi, *The War on Drugs III*, pp. 314–15; or Erich Goode, *Drugs in American Society*, p. 104.
2 Inciardi, *The War on Drugs III*, p. 314.
3 www.oas.samhsa.gov/NSDUH/2k5NSDUH/2k5results.htm#Ch2, p. 229.
4 Jerrold S. Meyer and Linda F. Quenzer, *Psychopharmacology*, p. 333; *The Merck Manual of Medical Information*, p. 491; and Inciardi, *The War on Drugs III*, p. 45.
5 Mitch Earleywine, *Understanding Marijuana*, pp. 114, 204–5.
6 Nancy M. Petry and Warren K. Bickel, "Polydrug abuse in heroin addicts."
7 Robert J. MacCoun and Peter Reuter, *Drug War Heresies*, p. 361.
8 John Kaplan, *The Hardest Drug*, p. 23; *The Merck Manual of Medical Information*, p. 487; Meyer and Quenzer, *Psychopharmacology*, pp. 199, 248; and Cynthia Kuhn, Scott Swartzwelder, and Wilkie Wilson, *Buzzed*, pp. 182–3.
9 *The Merck Manual of Medical Information*, p. 487; and Kuhn et al., *Buzzed*, p. 190.
10 *The Merck Manual of Medical Information*, p. 488.
11 Ibid., p. 491.
12 National Institute on Drug Abuse, *InfoFacts: Heroin*.
13 John Morgan and Lynn Zimmer, "The social pharmacology of smokeable cocaine," pp. 137–8; and *The Merck Manual of Medical Information*, p. 492.
14 *The Merck Manual*, ibid.; and Meyer and Quenzer, *Psychopharmacology*, pp. 280–81.
15 Inciardi, *The War on Drugs III*, p. 142. See also Meyer and Quenzer, *Psychopharmacology*, pp. 286–9; and Kuhn et al., *Buzzed*, pp. 225–30.
16 Kuhn et al., ibid., p. 144; and *The Merck Manual of Medical Information*.
17 *The Merck Manual*, ibid., p. 491; and Inciardi, *The War on Drugs III*, pp. 51–2, 62–3.
18 Jerome Beck and Marsha Rosenbaum, *Pursuit of Ecstasy*; Meyer and Quenzer, *Psychopharmacology*, p. 296; and Kuhn et al., *Buzzed*, pp. 76–7.
19 Drug Abuse Warning Network, "Club drugs," p. 4.
20 Kuhn et al., *Buzzed*, p. 79.
21 Meyer and Quenzer, *Psychopharmacology*, p. 299.
22 See Goode, *Drugs in American Society*, p. 265.
23 *The Merck Manual of Medical Information*, pp. 491–2.
24 Holly Hickman, "Meth use 'choking' western hills of North Carolina."

25 *The Merck Manual of Medical Information*, p. 491.

26 Inciardi, *The War on Drugs III*, p. 51.

27 Naval Strike and Air Warfare Center, "Performance maintenance during continuous flight operations: A guide for flight surgeons," NAVMED P-6410, January 1, 2000, p. 8, available online through the Virtual Naval Hospital of the University of Iowa, at www.vnh.org/PerformMaint.

28 "Amphetamine dependence," *The Merck Manual of Diagnosis and Therapy*, section 15: Psychiatric Disorders, chapter 195: "Drug use and dependence."

29 Ibid., and National Institute on Drug Abuse, *InfoFacts: Methamphetamine*.

30 Meyer and Quenzer, *Psychopharmacology*, p. 191.

31 Kuhn et al., *Buzzed*, p. 226.

32 Hickman, "Meth use 'choking' western hills of North Carolina"; Robert E. Pierre, "Keeping pills away from drug abusers"; "Johnston sheriff fears new drug plague"; Martha Quillin, "Rural county is meth central"; "You take the high road."

33 See also www.cdc.gov/niosh/npg/pgdstart.html.

34 Inciardi, *The War on Drugs III*, p. 49; *The Merck Manual of Medical Information*, pp. 493–4; and Meyer and Quenzer, *Psychopharmacology*, pp. 352–7.

35 Meyer and Quenzer, ibid., pp. 356–7.

36 MacCoun and Reuter, *Drug War Heresies*, p. 23.

37 Ali H. Mokdad, James S. Marks, and Donna F. Stroup, "Actual causes of death in the United States, 2000," cited at www.drugwarfacts.org/causes.htm.

38 United States Surgeon General, *Reducing the Health Consequences of Smoking*, p. 160, cited in Steven B. Duke and Albert C. Gross, *America's Longest War*, p. 77.

39 *Journal of the American Medical Association*, 293, no. 3, January 19, 2005, p. 298, cited at www.drugwarfacts.org/causes.htm.

40 United States Surgeon General, *Reducing the Health Consequences of Smoking*, p. 160, cited in Duke and Gross, *America's Longest War*, p. 77.

41 Ibid.

42 Earleywine, *Understanding Marijuana*, pp. 143–4.

43 Report by the European Monitoring Centre for Drugs and Drug Addiction, quoted in "A survey of illegal drugs," p. 10.

44 www.DAWNinfo.samhsa.gov.

45 Earleywine, *Understanding Marijuana*, p. 32; SAMHSA National Survey on Drug Abuse, 1999, reported in "A survey of illegal drugs," p. 8; Philip J. Hilts, "Is nicotine addictive?"

46 SAMHSA National Survey on Drug Abuse, 1999, reported in "A survey of illegal drugs," p. 8.

47 Ibid.; See also Duke and Gross, *America's Longest War*, pp. 61–2; Goode, *Drugs in American Society*, pp. 316–17; and Tom Carnwath and Ian Smith, *Heroin Century*, p. 81.

48 SAMHSA National Survey on Drug Abuse, 1999, reported in "A survey of illegal drugs," p. 8; and J. Anthony, L. Warner, and R. Kessler, "Comparative epidemiology of dependence on tobacco, alcohol, controlled substances and inhalants," cited in MacCoun and Reuter, *Drug War Heresies*, p. 18.

49 Anthony et al., ibid., p. 19.

50 Communication from Professor Mitch Earleywine, March 31, 2004. For similar rankings, see Deborah Franklin, "Hooked—not hooked."

51 See P. A. Ebener et al., *Improving Data and Analysis to Support National Substance Abuse Policy*; and national survey results on drug use from the Monitoring the Future Study, available at www.isr.umich.edu/src/mtf, cited in MacCoun and Reuter, *Drug War Heresies*, p. 16.

52 Duke and Gross, *America's Longest War*, pp. 38–42; Goode, *Drugs in American Society*, pp. 340–43; and Paul J. Goldstein, Henry H. Brownstein,

Patrick J. Ryan, and Patricia A. Bellucci, "Crack and homicide in New York City."

53 See Paul J. Goldstein, Henry H. Brownstein, and Patrick J. Ryan, "Drug-related homicide in New York," cited in Jeffrey A. Miron and Jeffrey Zwiebel, "The economic case against drug prohibition," p. 176.

54 David Musto, *The American Disease*, p. 254.

55 See, for example, the excellent study by Diana R. Gordon, *The Return of the Dangerous Classes*.

56 David T. Courtwright, *Dark Paradise*, pp. 95–6.

57 Inciardi, *The War on Drugs III*, p. 48.

58 Eva Bertram et al., *Drug War Politics*, p. 63.

59 Ibid., p. 98.

60 H. Wayne Morgan, *Drugs in America*, p. 37.

61 Mark Thornton, "Prohibition vs. legalization."

62 Reported in the *New York Times*, February 29, 1988.

63 Bertram et al., *Drug War Politics*, pp. 115–16.

64 www.lib.ncsu.edu/congbibs/senate/101dgst2.htm; and monitoringthefuture.org, table 2.

65 Associated Press, "Gingrich wants drug dealers executed."

66 *Fresno Bee* [CA], November 30, 1999.

67 See, for example, the *Idaho Observer*, August, 2000, available at www.proliberty.com/observer/20000807.htm.

68 Paul Anderson, "Drug bill tough on smugglers," quoted in Steven Wisotsky, *Beyond the War on Drugs*, p. 200.

69 Larry Rohter, "Brazil carries the war on drugs to the air."

70 *Life* magazine, September, 1987, p. 105.

71 See Michael Massing, *The Fix*, p. 201.

72 Bertram et al., *Drug War Politics*, pp. 115–16.

73 United States Sentencing Commission, *Cocaine and Federal Sentencing Policy*, pp. 2–3. See also Eric E. Sterling, "Take another crack at that cocaine law"; Sterling was counsel to the House Judiciary Committee, principally responsible for anti-drug legislation.

74 United States Sentencing Commission, *Cocaine and Federal Sentencing Policy*, p. 150; *Sourcebook of Criminal Justice Statistics 1996* (Washington, D.C.: Bureau of Justice Statistics, 1997), p. 476, table 5.58.

75 Ibid.; also Drug Policy Alliance, *State of the States*, p. 7.

76 See Greg Winter, "A student aid ban for past drug use is creating a furor."

77 Andrews University, the MayaTech Corporation, and RAND Corporation, *Illicit Drug Policies*.

78 Ibid.

79 Eric Schlosser, "Make peace with pot."

80 James P. Gray, *Why our Drug Laws Have Failed*, p. 32.

81 Bob Herbert, "The ruinous drug laws," p. A23.

82 Schlosser, "Make peace with pot."

83 Gray, *Why our Drug Laws Have Failed*, pp. 36–7; and Bertram et al., *Drug War Politics*, p. 52.

84 Joshua W. Shenk, "America's altered states," p. 239; and Bertram et al., *Drug War Politics*, p. 139.

85 Testimony of Lee Brown before Judiciary Committee, U.S. Senate, February 10, 1994, quoted in Bertram et al., *Drug War Politics*, p. 12.

86 Shenk, "America's altered states," p. 255.

87 Christopher Connell, "Legalizing drugs would reduce crime rate," quoted in Dan Baum, *Smoke and Mirrors*, p. 334.

88 Ibid.; and Bertram et al., *Drug War Politics*, pp. 160–61.

89 Bertram et al., ibid.
90 Drug Enforcement Agency, *Illegal Price/Purity Report*, March, 1991, pp. 3, 5, 7; April, 1994, pp. 1, 4, 6; and June, 1995, pp. 1, 4, 6, cited in Bertram et al., *Drug War Politics*, Appendix 2.
91 See www.monitoringthefuture.org, table 2.
92 Statement by Joseph D. McNamara, in William Buckley, Jr., et al., "The war on drugs is lost," repr. in Gray, *Busted*, p. 207.
93 "A survey of illegal drugs," p. 6.
94 Statement by Joseph D. McNamara, in Buckley et al., "The war on drugs is lost," repr. in Gray, *Busted*, p. 204.
95 Duke and Gross, *America's Longest War*, p. 222; and Bertram et al., *Drug War Politics*, pp. 18–19.
96 Gordon, *Return of the Dangerous Classes*, ch. 6.
97 Ibid., pp. 82–3.
98 Ibid., p. 84.
99 Bertram et al., *Drug War Politics*, pp. 14–20.
100 See the study on interdiction by the Government Accounting (now Accountability) Office (GAO), available at www.fas.org/irp/gao/nsi95032.htm.
101 Duke and Gross, *America's Longest War*, pp. 203–7.
102 Ethan Nadelmann, "Drug prohibition in the U.S."
103 Bertram et al., *Drug War Politics*, p. 22.
104 See, for example, Massing, *The Fix*, p. 67.
105 See Miron and Zwiebel, "The economic case against drug prohibition," pp. 177–8; and Jeffrey A. Miron, "Violence and U.S. prohibitions of drugs and alcohol."
106 See United States Census Data and FBI Uniform Crime Reports, *Murder in America*.
107 MaCoun and Reuter, *Drug War Heresies*, p. 125.
108 Bureau of Justice Statistics, *Special Report*, cited in Duke and Gross, *America's Longest War*, p. 110; and Inciardi, *The War on Drugs III*, p. 193.
109 Duke and Gross, *America's Longest War*, pp. 113–15; and Gray, *Why our Drug Laws Have Failed*, pp. 95–100.
110 Gray, ibid., p. 73.
111 United States General Accounting Office, *Report to the Honorable Charles B. Rangel, House of Representatives, Law Enforcement*, p. 35, cited at www.drugwarfacts.org/corrupt.corrupt.htm.
112 Duke and Gross, *America's Longest War*, p. 124.
113 Ibid., pp. 135–43; and Gray, *Why our Drug Laws Have Failed*, pp. 117–22.
114 See, for example, the long-run study by researchers at the University of Kentucky, summarized at www.druglibrary.org/think/~jnr/noeffect.htm.
115 Joseph Pereira, "The informants in a drug program," quoted in Duke and Gross, p. 174.
116 Times Wire Service, "Drug czar urges pupils to turn in parents, says it's not 'snitching,'" *Los Angeles Times*, May 18, 1989, quoted in Duke and Gross, *America's Longest War*, p. 174.
117 Pereira, "The informants in a drug program," quoted ibid., p. 174.
118 Drug Policy Alliance, *State of the States*, p. 8; also Ethan Nadelmann, "Commonsense drug policy."
119 United States Surgeon General, *Evidence-Based Findings on the Efficacy of Syringe Exchange Programs: An Analysis from the Assistant Secretary for Health and the Surgeon General of the Scientific Research Completed since April 1998*, accessed May 11, 2005, at www.harmreduction.org/research/surgeongenrev/surgreview.html, cited at drugwarfacts.org/syringee.htm.
120 Patricia G. Erickson, "A public health approach to demand reduction," p. 565, cited in Bertram et al., *Drug War Politics*, p. 29; and Mathew Purdy, "Warehouse of addiction."

121 Purdy, ibid.; Elliot Currie, *Reckoning*, p. 170; and Daniel K. Benjamin and Roger Leroy Miller, *Undoing Drugs*, p. 105.
122 See SAMHSA, Office of applied Studies, National Surveys on Drug Use and Health, at www.samhsa.gov, and the Federal Drug Control Budgets at the Bureau of Justice Statistics, at www.ojp.usdoj.gov/bjs/dcf/dcb.htm.
123 See Jonathan P. Caulkins et al., *Mandatory Minimum Drug Sentences*, pp. xv–xxv, cited in Bertram et al., *Drug War Politics*, pp. 172–3.

2 The Birth of the Drug War

1 See Joseph F. Spillane, *Cocaine*, p. 40; and Richard Davenport-Hines, *The Pursuit of Oblivion*, pp. 159–60.
2 See, for example, www.november.org/thewall/cases/tanner-k/tanner-k.html.
3 Mikki Norris et al., *Shattered Lives*.
4 James P. Gray, *Why our Drug Laws Have Failed and What We Can Do about It*, p. 20.
5 See, for example, www.erowid.org/library/books/great_book.shtml.
6 Richard J. Bonnie and Charles H. Whitebread II, *The Marijuana Conviction*, pp. 1–5; and Steven B. Duke and Albert C. Gross, *America's Longest War*, p. 44.
7 James Inciardi, *The War on Drugs III*, pp. 31–3; and Mitch Earlywine, *Understanding Marijuana*, pp. 3–4.
8 For the full text of the Act, see "The Marihuana Tax Act of 1937," introduction by David Solomon, at www.druglibrary.org/schaffer/hemp/taxact/mjtaxact.htm.
9 For a summary of the details of the Tax Act, see Bonnie and Whitebread, *The Marijuana Conviction*, pp. 124–5.
10 Gray, *Why our Drug Laws Have Failed*, p. 26.
11 The Controlled Substances Act of 1970, 21 U.S.C. §§ 801 et seq.
12 H. W. Brands, *The First American*, p. 706.
13 Jeffrey A. Miron and Jeffrey Zwiebel, "The economic case against drug prohibition," p. 184, n. 3.
14 David Musto, *The American Disease*, p. 3; and Erich Goode, *Drugs in American Society*, pp. 87–9.
15 David T. Courtwright, *Dark Paradise*, p. 43.
16 Ibid.; and Musto, *The American Disease*, p. 1.
17 Courtwright, *Dark Paradise*, p. 44; and Musto, *The American Disease*, pp. 72–7.
18 Duke and Gross, *America's Longest War*, p. 55.
19 H. Wayne Morgan, *Drugs in America*, p. 1.
20 Courtwright, *Dark Paradise*, pp. 45–6; and Musto, *The American Disease*, p. 75.
21 Musto, ibid.
22 Courtwright, *Dark Paradise*, p. 47.
23 Ibid., pp. 89–91.
24 Spillane, *Cocaine*, pp. 22–3; and Duke and Gross, *America's Longest War*, p. 67.
25 Courtwright, *Dark Paradise*, p. 94.
26 Musto, *The American Disease*, p. 7.
27 Ibid., p. 3.
28 Courtwright, *Dark Paradise*, pp. 51–2.
29 *Encyclopedia Britannica*, the article on syphilis in the Micropedia.
30 Musto, *The American Disease*, p. 75.
31 Courtwright, *Dark Paradise*, p. 77.
32 Musto, *The American Disease*, pp. 8–10.
33 Spillane, *Cocaine*, pp. 95, 119–20.
34 Bonnie and Whitebread, *The Marijuana Conviction*, pp. 38–9; Musto, *The American Disease*, pp. 219–20; and Morgan, *Drugs in America*, pp. 138–9.

35 Bonnie and Whitebread, *The Marijuana Conviction*, p. 40.
36 Lawrence M. Friedman, *American Law in the 20th Century*, p. 107.
37 Courtwright, *Dark Paradise*, pp. 103–4.
38 *United States* v. *Jin Fuey Moy*.
39 *Webb et al.* v. *United States*, 249 U.S. 96 (1919), available at www.druglibrary.org/SCHAFFER/History/webb.html. See also Friedman, *American Law in the 20th Century*, p. 106.
40 Morgan, *Drugs in America*, pp. 109–11.
41 Musto, *The American Disease*, p. 182; and Courtwright, *Dark Paradise*, p. 104.
42 Eva Bertram et al., *Drug War Politics*, p. 75; and Gray, *Why our Drug Laws Have Failed*, pp. 124–5.
43 Courtwright, *Dark Paradise*, p. 104.
44 Bertram et al., *Drug War Politics*, pp. 73–4.
45 Musto, *The American Disease*, p. 204.
46 Courtwright, *Dark Paradise*, pp. 40–48; and Morgan, *Drugs in America*, ch. 3.
47 Spillane, *Cocaine*, p. 39.
48 Courtwright, *Dark Paradise*, p. 123.
49 Ibid., pp. 2–3, 110–11; see also Spillane, *Cocaine*, pp. 40–41.
50 Courtwright, *Dark Paradise*, p. 133.
51 Spillane, *Cocaine*, pp. 111–22; and Morgan, *Drugs in America*, pp. 91–6.
52 Courtwright, *Dark Paradise*, p. 121.
53 Musto, *The American Disease*, p. 65.
54 Ibid., pp. 132–4; Morgan, *Drugs in America*, pp. 108–10; Duke and Gross, *America's Longest War*, p. 86; Bertram et al., *Drug War Politics*, pp. 74–5; and Courtwright, *Dark Paradise*, p. 104.
55 Steven Wisotsky, *Beyond the War on Drugs*, p. 182.
56 See, for example, www.spartacus.schoolnet.co.uk/USApalmerR.htm.
57 *Webb et al.* v. *United States*, 249 U.S. 96 (1919), available at www.druglibrary.org/SCHAFFER/History/webb.html.

Part II: Introduction

1 Michael Massing, *The Fix*, pp. 143–4; and Dan Baum, *Smoke and Mirrors*, pp. 88–90.
2 Massing, *The Fix*, p. 144.
3 Baum, *Smoke and Mirrors*, p. 89.
4 Massing, *The Fix*, p. 146.
5 Baum, *Smoke and Mirrors*, p. 132.
6 Massing, *The Fix*, pp. 156–7, 163.
7 Ibid., p. 157.
8 Ibid., p. 163.
9 Baum, *Smoke and Mirrors*, pp. 286–9; Craig Reinarman and Harry G. Levine, "The crack attack," p. 23 and p .46, n. 3; and Steven B. Duke and Albert C. Gross, *America's Longest War*, p. xv.
10 Baum, *Smoke and Mirrors*, p. 288.
11 Ibid., p. 289.
12 Reinarman and Levine, "The crack attack," p. 46, n. 3.
13 See, for example, Duke and Gross, *America's Longest War*, pp. 135–9. Fortunately, this law, passed in 1970, was modified at the federal level in 2000. The onus was finally placed on the federal government to show that there was evidence that a drug law was being violated. But property can still be forfeited to the federal government without a conviction. Many state laws still permit asset forfeiture without bringing criminal charges. I discuss this issue in chapter 5, in the subsection entitled "The Assault on the Bill of Rights."

14 www.ojp.usdoj.gov/bjs/def/enforce.htm.
15 Jonathan P. Caulkins et al., *Mandatory Minimum Drug Sentences*, p. 16.
16 Ethan Nadelmann, "Commonsense drug policy," repr. in Mike Gray, *Busted*, pp. 176–7.

3 Crime

1 Craig Reinarman, Dan Waldorf, Sheigla B. Murphy, and Harry G. Levine, "The contingent call of the pipe," p. 89.
2 Craig Reinarmanand Harry G. Levine, "The crack attack," p. 20.
3 William J. Bennett, John J. DiIulio, Jr., and John P. Walters, *Body Count*, p. 192.
4 www.cnn.com/US/9707/22/crack.sentencing.
5 Steven B. Duke and Albert C. Gross, *America's Longest War*, p. 68.
6 Robert J. MacCoun and Peter Reuter, *Drug War Heresies*, p. 362.
7 Paul J. Goldstein, Henry H. Brownstein, Patrick J. Ryan, and Patricia A. Bellucci, "Crack and homicide in New York City." See also MacCoun and Reuter, *Drug War Heresies*, p. 122; and Jeffrey A. Miron and Jeffrey Zwiebel, "The economic case against drug prohibition," pp. 177–8.
8 Goldstein et al., "Crack and homicide in New York City," p. 116. The remaining drug-related murders could not be placed in a single category.
9 Michael Massing, *The Fix*, p. 39.
10 John P. Morgan and Lynn Zimmer, "The social pharmacology of smokeable cocaine," pp. 138–9.
11 www.csdp.org/edcs/page 24.htm#ef67.
12 Reinarman et al., "The contingent call of the pipe," p. 92; and Elliot Currie, *Reckoning*, pp. 179–80.
13 National Center on Addiction and Substance Abuse, *Behind Bars*.
14 Source: US Census Data and FBI Uniform Crime Reports. See www.drugwar facts.org/crime.htm.
15 Milton Friedman, "The war we are losing."
16 Jeffrey A. Miron, "Violence and U.S. prohibitions of drugs and alcohol."
17 See Miron and Zwiebel, "The economic case against drug prohibition," pp. 177–8.
18 "The high cost of war: A new look at crime statistics," *Prevention File*, Winter 1997, pp. 2–6, discussed and cited in James Gray, *Why our Drug Laws Have Failed and What We Can Do about It*, pp. 69–71.
19 Frederic N. Tulsky and Ted Rohrlich, "1 in 3 killers in L.A. County are punished," cited inGray, *Why our Drug Laws Have Failed*, p. 71.
20 See, for example, Isaac Ehrlich, "The deterrent effect of capital punishment."
21 See Miron, "Violence and U.S. prohibitions of drugs and alcohol"; and MacCoun and Reuter, *Drug War Heresies*, pp. 121–2.
22 See the review article by Lawrence W. Sherman, "Police crackdowns," cited in Currie, *Reckoning*, p. 205.
23 Jerome H. Skolnick, *Policing Drugs*, pp. 47–9, cited in Currie, *Reckoning*, p. 206.
24 Damien Cave and Ronald Smothers, "4th Newark police officer is shot in a violent July."
25 See Massing, *The Fix*, ch. 5.
26 Ibid., p. 70.
27 Ibid., p. 71.
28 Ibid., p. 70.
29 Ibid.
30 Daniel K. Benjamin and Roger Leroy Miller, *Undoing Drugs*, pp. 107–9.
31 "A survey of illegal drugs," pp. 5, 7, 11; and James A. Inciardi, *The War on Drugs III*, p. 193.

32 Massing, *The Fix*, p. 17.
33 Ibid., p. 29.
34 Ibid., p. 30.
35 Ibid., p. 31.
36 Ibid., p. 38.
37 Ibid., p. 48.
38 Ibid., p. 235.
39 Ibid., p. 234.
40 Ibid., p. 235.
41 Ibid., pp. 238–42.
42 Ibid., p. 261.
43 Duke and Gross, *America's Longest War*, pp. 108–9; and Inciardi, *The War on Drugs III*, p. 193.
44 Inciardi, ibid.
45 Ibid.
46 Gray, *Why our Drug Laws Have Failed*, pp. 70–71.
47 Currie, *Reckoning*, pp. 169–72.
48 Bureau of Justice Statistics, *Special Report*, cited in Duke and Gross, *America's Longest War*, p. 110.
49 Dwayne D. Simpson and S. B. Sells, "Effectiveness of treatment for drug abuse," cited in Erich Goode, *Drugs in American Society*, p. 406.
50 Lester P. Silverman and Jancy I. Spruil, "Urban crime and the price of heroin"; and Bruce L. Benson, Iljoong Kim, David W. Rasmussen, and Thomas W. Zuehlke, "Is property crime caused by drug use or by drug enforcement policy?," cited in Miron and Zwiebel, "The economic case against drug prohibition," p. 180.
51 See, for example, Gray, *Why our Drug Laws Have Failed*, ch. 8.; and Ethan Nadelmann, "Commonsense drug policy."
52 See Massing, *The Fix*, ch. 9, esp. pp. 129–31.

4 Public Health

1 Steven B. Duke and Albert C. Gross, *America's Longest War*, p. 194.
2 Daniel K. Benjamin and Roger Leroy Miller, *Undoing Drugs*, p. 19.
3 Avram Goldstein and Harold Kalant, "Drug policy," p. 80.
4 Ethan Nadelmann, "Legalization is the answer," p. 43.
5 Duke and Gross, *America's Longest War*, p. 195.
6 Craig Reinarman and Harry G. Levine, "Real opposition, real alternatives," pp. 350–51; and Ethan Nadelmann, "Commonsense drug policy," repr. in Mike Gray, *Busted*, pp. 176–7.
7 Centers for Disease Control and Prevention, *State and Local Policies Regarding IDUs' Access to Sterile Syringes*, p. 1.
8 Centers for Disease Control and Prevention, *HIV/AIDS Surveillance Report 2005*.
9 Ibid.
10 John P. Morgan and Lynn Zimmer, "Social pharmacology of smokeable cocaine," pp. 136–7; and Duke and Gross, *America's Longest War*, p. 55.
11 Centers for Disease Control and Prevention, *State and Local Policies Regarding IDUs' Access to Sterile Syringes*, p. 1; and Scott Burris, Steffanie A. Strathdee, and Jon S. Vernick, *Syringe Access Law in the United States*, pp. 39–40. For a list of the drug paraphernalia laws in the United States by state, see captus.samhsa.gov/northeast/resources/faqs/faq12.cfm, p. 2, table 2.
12 Laura Mansnerus, "Addict's suit claims police ignore needle-swap law"; and "Harm reduction: ACLU wins victory in Connecticut needle exchange case," cited at www.csdp.org/news/news/aidsupdate.htm.
13 stopthedrugwar.org/chronicle-old/438/ctneps.shtml.

14 Burris et al., *Syringe Access Law in the United States*, pp. 39–40.
15 Ibid., p. 44.
16 For a list of the surveys of drug injectors, see ibid., p. 45, n. 103.
17 Mansnerus, "Addict's suit claims police ignore needle-swap law."
18 Scott Burris, Peter Lurie, et al., "Physician prescribing of sterile injection equipment to prevent HIV infection," cited at www.drugwarfacts.org/syringee.htm.
19 Michael C. Clatts et al., "The impact of drug paraphernalia laws on HIV risk among persons who inject illegal drugs," p. 98.
20 Press release by Donna E. Shalala, secretary, Department of Health and Human Services, April 20, 1998, cited at www.drugwarfacts.org/syringee.htm.
21 For a list of these seven reports, see www.drugwarfacts.org/syringee.htm.
22 Press release by Donna E. Shalala, secretary, Department of Health and Human Services, April 20, 1998.
23 Satcher, David, *Evidence-Based Findings on the Efficacy of Syringe Exchange Programs*; also cited at www.drugwarfacts.org/syringee.htm.
24 World Health Organization, *Effectiveness of Sterile Needle and Syringe Programming in Reducing HIV/AIDS among Injecting Drug Users*, p. 28.
25 Nadelmann, "Commonsense drug policy," repr. in Gray, *Busted*, pp. 176–7.
26 James A. Inciardi, *The War on Drugs III*, p. 236.
27 Nicholas D. Kristof, "Hong Kong program."
28 Eva Bertram et al., *Drug War Politics*, p. 171.
29 National Commission on Acquired Immune Deficiency Syndrome, *The Twin Epidemics of Substance Use and HIV*, p. 19, quoted ibid.
30 Nadelmann, "Commonsense drug policy," repr. in Gray, *Busted*, p. 177.
31 Eric Lichtblau, "Nationwide raids put top drug-paraphernalia traffickers out of business."
32 www.post-gazette.com/localnews/20030912chong0912p5.asp.
33 Associated Press, "AIDS treatment resolution withdrawn at WHO meeting because of US opposition."
34 See www.ojp.usdoj.gov/bjs/dcf/correct.htm; and Drug Policy Alliance, *State of the States*, p. 4.
35 Matthew Purdy, "Warehouse of addiction: Bars don't stop flow of drugs into the prisons," cited in Bertram et al., *Drug War Politics*, p. 29.
36 Laura Maruschak, *HIV in Prisons, 2001*, p. 5, quoted at www.drugwarfacts.org/racehiv.htm.
37 Lynette Clemetson, "Links between prison and AIDS affecting blacks inside and out."
38 Ibid.
39 Ibid.
40 Drug Policy Alliance, *State of the States*, p. 7.
41 Ryan S. King, "A decade of reform," pp. 3–5; and Erik Eckholm, "States are growing more lenient in allowing felons to vote."
42 Clemetson, "Links between prison and AIDS affecting blacks inside and out."
43 William J. Bennett, John J. DiIulio, Jr., and John P. Walters, *Body Count*, p. 101.
44 Ibid., p. 94.
45 Jennifer C. Karberg and Doris J. James, *Substance Dependence, Abuse, and Treatment of Jail Inmates, 2002*, p. 6, table 7; and Christopher J. Mumola, *Substance Abuse and Treatment, State and Federal Prisoners, 1997*, p. 3, table 1. Both sources are cited at www.drugwarfacts.org/prison.htm.
46 United States Department of Health and Human Services, *Results from the . . . National Survey on Drug Use and Health*, Appendix H, table G.1.
47 Report in the *Raleigh News and Observer*, June 28, 2004, available at www.drug-rehabs.com/cocaine-possession-felony.htm.
48 Ibid.

49 Sam Howe Verhovek, "Warehouse of addiction," quoted in Bertram et al., *Drug War Politics*, pp. 251–2.
50 Ibid.
51 Daniel K. Benjamin and Roger Leroy Miller, *Undoing Drugs*, pp. 21–3; Bertram et al., *Drug War Politics*, p. 36 and p. 179, n.16; and Duke and Gross, *America's Longest War*, pp. 194–7. For a skeptical view of this relationship, see Robert J. MacCoun and Peter Reuter, *Drug War Heresies*, p. 124.
52 Jeffrey A. Miron and Jeffrey Zwiebel, "The economic case against drug prohibition," pp. 185–6; and Benjamin and Miller, *Undoing Drugs*, p. 237.
53 Duke and Gross, *America's Longest War*, p. 196.
54 Benjamin and Miller, *Undoing Drugs*, pp. 23, 114–19.
55 Joseph F. Spillane, *Cocaine*, ch. 5; H. Wayne Morgan, *Drugs in America*, ch. 2; Erich Goode, *Drugs in American Society*, pp. 87–9; and David F. Musto, *The American Disease*, pp. 6–7.
56 Benjamin and Miller, *Undoing Drugs*, pp. 117–18; and David J. Hanson, *Alcohol Beverage Consumption in the United States: Patterns and Trends*.
57 MacCoun and Reuter, *Drug War Heresies*, p. 202.
58 Benjamin and Miller, *Undoing Drugs*, pp. 129–30. Benjamin and Miller call this result "the bad-drug theorem," that is, "When drugs are illegal, more damaging drugs drive out less damaging drugs" (p. 129).
59 United States Sentencing Commission, *Report to Congress*.
60 Rick Weiss, "Results retracted on ecstasy study."
61 Charles Grob, "The politics of ecstasy."
62 United States Sentencing Commission, *Report to Congress*, p. 8, n.13.
63 George A. Ricaurte et al., "Retraction."
64 Weiss, "Results retracted on ecstasy study"; and Grob, "The politics of ecstasy," repr. in Gray, *Busted*, p. 215.
65 Weiss, "Results retracted on ecstasy study."
66 Grob, "The politics of ecstasy," repr. in Gray, *Busted*, p. 214.
67 Ibid., pp. 213–15; and C. M. Milroy, J. C. Clark, and A. R. W. Forrest, "Pathology of deaths associated with 'ecstasy' and 'eve' misuse," cited at www.drugwarfacts.org/ecstasy.htm.
68 Grob, "The politics of ecstasy," repr. in Gray, *Busted*, pp. 214–15.
69 "A survey of illegal drugs," p. 10.
70 Jerrold S. Meyer and Linda F. Quenzer, *Psychopharmacology*, pp. 296–300; and Cynthia Kuhn, Scott Swartzwelder, and Wilkie Wilson, *Buzzed*, pp. 80–82.
71 Mitch Earleywine, *Understanding Marijuana*, pp. 15–16; Lester Grinspoon and James B. Bakalar, *Marihuana, the Forbidden Medicine*, p. 23.; and Kuhn et al., *Buzzed*, p. 153.
72 Earleywine, *Understanding Marijuana*, pp. 171, 186.
73 Ibid., pp. 32, 143–4.
74 "A survey of illegal drugs," p. 10; and www.drugwarfacts.org/medicalm.htm.
75 Prepared statement by John Benson, Institute of Medicine, news conference for Marijuana and Medicine: Assessing the Science Base, 17 March, 1999; and Drug Policy Alliance, *State of the States*, p. 3.
76 United States General Accounting Office, *Marijuana*, p. 24, cited in Goode, *Drugs in American Society*, p. 252.
77 Joel Stein, "The new politics of pot."
78 Earleywine, *Understanding Marijuana*, p. 194.
79 www.norml.org/index.cfm?Group_ID=3391.
80 http://actioncenter.drugpolicy.org/ctt.asp?u=1051367&l=45408.
81 Earleywine, *Understanding Marijuana*, pp. 16, 194; Kuhn et al., *Buzzed*, p. 155; and Meyer and Quenzer, *Psychopharmacology*, pp. 334–5, box 13.1.
82 Earleywine, *Understanding Marijuana*, p. 16.

83 Grinspoon and Bakalar, *Marihuana, the Forbidden Medicine*, p. 254.
84 Richard Doblin and Mark A. R. Kleiman, "Marijuana as antiemetic medicine," p. 89.
85 Vincent Vinciguerra, T. Moore, and E. Brennan, "Inhalation marijuana as an antiemetic for cancer chemotherapy."
86 Grinspoon and Bakalar, *Marihuana, the Forbidden Medicine*, p. 24.
87 James P. Gray, *Why our Drug Laws Have Failed and What We Can Do about It*, p. 130.
88 Dean E. Murphy, "Backers of medical marijuana hail ruling."
89 Ruth Barnett, "Marijuana: good medicine."
90 www.mapinc.org/people/carter+singleton; and Sharon Coolidge, "No jail for patient who grew his own marijuana."
91 www.cannabisnews.com/news/thread3355.shtml.
92 Ethan Nadelmann, "The hospice raid and the war on drugs"; and Arianna Huffington, "A crack house divided."
93 www.drugpolicy.org/news/12_17_03raich.cfm.
94 Charles Lane, "A defeat for users of medical marijuana"; and *The Economist*, June 11, 2005, p. 31. The case is *Gonzales* v. *Raich*, case no. 03-1454.
95 Duke and Gross, *America's Longest War*, p. 238; and Benjamin and Miller, *Undoing Drugs*, pp. 183–4.
96 MacCoun and Reuter, *Drug War Heresies*, p. 361. Not all studies find marijuana and alcohol to be substitutes. A statistical study by Pacula (1998) finds that they may be complements.
97 See an evaluation of the studies comparing the effects of marijuana and alcohol on violence and traffic accidents in Earleywine, *Understanding Marijuana*, pp. 210–21.
98 MacCoun and Reuter, *Drug War Heresies*, p. 361.
99 Bertram et al., *Drug War Politics*, p. 111; and Duke and Gross, *America's Longest War*, p. 68.
100 Morgan, *Drugs in America*, pp. 155–7; and Kuhn et al., *Buzzed*, p. 214.
101 Benjamin and Miller, *Undoing Drugs*, p. 117; and Kuhn et al., *Buzzed*, p. 214.
102 Benjamin and Miller, *Undoing Drugs*, p. 44; Duke and Gross, *America's Longest War*, p. 220; and Kuhn et al., *Buzzed*, pp. 179–80.
103 Benjamin and Miller, *Undoing Drugs*, p. 44.

5 Civil Liberties

1 Barbara Whitaker, "A father is fatally shot by the police in his home, and his family is asking why"; and Anne-Marie O'Connor, "No drug link to family in fatal raid, police say."
2 David M. Bresnahan, "Cops not talking in Sallisaw."
3 Steven B. Duke and Albert C. Gross, *America's Longest War*, p. 123; and James P. Gray, *Why our Drug Laws Have Failed and What We Can Do about It*, p. 96. See the Supreme Court ruling in *Illinois* v. *Gates*, 462 U.S. 313 (1983).
4 *Wilson* v. *Arkansas* (1995).
5 *Hudson* v. *Michigan* (2006). See Joan Biskupic, "Justices allow no-knock searches."
6 Eva Bertram et al., *Drug War Politics*, p. 47.
7 William F. Buckley et al., "The war on drugs is lost," in Mike Gray, *Busted*, Mike Gray, p. 208.
8 Gray, *Why our Drug Laws Have Failed*, p. 96.
9 Duke and Gross, *America's Longest War*, ch. 7; Daniel K. Benjamin and Roger Leroy Miller, *Undoing Drugs*, ch. 8; Gray, *Why our Drug Laws Have Failed*, ch. 3; Steven B. Duke, "The drug war and the constitution," pp. 47–51; and Ted Galen Carpenter, "Collateral damage," pp. 151–2.

10 Gray, *Why our Drug Laws Have Failed*, pp. 97, 102; and Drug Policy Alliance, *State of the States*, p. 5.
11 See *Whren* v. *United States* (1996).
12 Gray, *Why our Drug Laws Have Failed*, p. 98. See *United States* v. *Leon*, 468 U.S. 897 (1983).
13 Duke and Gross, *America's Longest War*, p. 124. See *United States* v. *Montoya De Hernandez*, 473 U.S. 531, 538 (1985).
14 Duke and Gross, *America's Longest War*, p. 124.
15 Ibid., p. 125.
16 Eric Schlosser, *Reefer Madness*, pp. 62–3.
17 Gray, *Why our Drug Laws Have Failed*, p. 108.
18 Wire Reports, "Spending on informants increases," cited ibid.
19 Lisa M. Krieger, "Pot spies in the sky irk locals," cited in Gray, *Why our Drug Laws Have Failed*, p. 113.
20 *New Jersey* v. *T.L.O.*, 469 U.S. 325 (1985), cited in Duke and Gross, *America's Longest War*, p. 127 (T.L.O. was a fourteen-year-old suspected of smoking in the bathroom).
21 Duke and Gross, *America's Longest War*, pp. 135–43; Gray, *Why our Drug Laws Have Failed*, pp. 118–22; Benjamin and Miller, *Undoing Drugs*, pp. 145–8; and Drug Policy Alliance, *State of the States*, pp. 9–10.
22 Gray, *Why our Drug Laws Have Failed*, p. 118.
23 E. Blumenson and E. Nilsen, "Policing for profit," cited at www.drugwarfacts.org/forfeitu.htm.
24 www.reason.com/bi/fb90.html, cited in Benjamin and Miller, *Undoing Drugs*, p. 146.
25 John Killin, "When federal drug laws create havoc for citizens"; Gray, *Why our Drug Laws Have Failed*, p. 120; and Schlosser, *Reefer Madness*, p. 62.
26 Scott Ehlers, *Policy Briefing: Asset Forfeiture*. Washington, D.C.: Drug Policy Foundation, 1999, p. 1.
27 Ibid., pp. 6–7.
28 Gray, *Why our Drug Laws Have Failed*, pp. 119–21.
29 Blumenson and Nilsen, "Policing for Profit."
30 Schlosser, *Reefer Madness*, p. 62.
31 Mikki Norris, Chris Conrad, and Virginia Resner, *Shattered Lives*, p. 65; and Gray, *Why our Drug Laws Have Failed*, pp. 103–5, 145.
32 Gray, ibid.
33 "Exec seeks $20 million in bogus bust."
34 Drug Policy Alliance, *State of the States*, pp. 9–10. See www.unclefed.com/For TaxProfs/irs-wd/2001/0106001.pdf.
35 Steven B. Duke, "The drug war and the constitution," pp .47–51; and Duke and Gross, *America's Longest War*, pp. 128–35.
36 Duke, "The drug war and the constitution," p. 47.
37 Ibid.
38 Ibid., p. 48.
39 Wendy Kaminer, "Games prosecutors play," p. 20; and Duke, "The drug war and the constitution," pp. 48–9.
40 Lee C. Bollinger, "First Amendment," p. 298.
41 Linda Greenhouse, "Justices say doctors may not be punished for recommending medical marijuana."
42 Ibid.
43 Ibid.; and Bill Mears, "Supreme Court rejects White House appeal over medical marijuana."
44 See www.aclu.org/DrugPolicy; and Gary Greenberg, "Just say nothing."
45 www.wnyc.org/onthemedia/transcripts/transcripts_031904_dissent.html.
46 www.aclu.org/drugpolicy.

47 Ibid.
48 www.americasdebate.com.
49 See, for example, Ann Harrison, "Medical marijuana ban overturned in D.C."
50 Ibid.
51 Ibid.
52 Bertram et al., *Drug War Politics*, p. 51; and Gray, *Why our Drug Laws Have Failed*, p. 27.
53 "More than they deserve."
54 Holly Sklar, "Reinforcing racism with the war on drugs"; and Bertram et al., *Drug War Politics*, p. 51.
55 Schlosser, *Reefer Madness*, p. 55.
56 Bertram et al., *Drug War Politics*, p. 51.
57 *New York Times* editorial, August 12, 2003.
58 Jonathan Caulkins et al., *Mandatory Minimum Drug Sentences*, pp. 16–18.
59 Troy Duster, "Race in the drug war," p. 266.
60 "Harper's index," *Harper's Magazine*, May 1994; and Don J. De Benedictis, "How long is too long," both cited in Bertram et al., *Drug War Politics*, p. 51.
61 Anne Gearan, "Justice Kennedy assails 'too long' prison terms."
62 United States General Accountability Office, *Federal Drug Offenses*, pp. 9–10, cited at www.drugwarfacts.org/mandator.htm.
63 See Stephanos Bibas, "The Feeney amendment and the continuing rise of prosecutorial power to plea bargain"; and Henry Frohsin and Harriet Ivy, "The Feeney amendment."
64 *New York Times* editorial, August 12, 2003.
65 "Chief justice blasts Congress on sentencing," *New York Times* editorial, January 1, 2004.
66 Bertram et al., *Drug War Politics*, p. 160; and www.druglibrary.org/schaffer/Library/studies/cu/CU9.html.
67 Caulkins et al., *Mandatory Minimum Drug Sentences*, pp. 16, 18, 22.
68 Dirk Chase Eldredge, *Ending the War on Drugs*, p. 32; and Jacob Sullum, "Weighty matters."
69 Gray, *Why our Drug Laws Have Failed*, p. 33.
70 See "Supreme Court overturns federal sentencing guidelines," an interview with Barry Scheck, president of the National Association of Criminal Defense Lawyers, available at www.november.org/Blakely/Democracy1-14-05.html; "No rush on sentencing," *Washington Post National Weekly Edition* editorial, August 15–21, 2005, p. 25; and David D. Kirkpatrick, "Congress rekindles battle on mandatory sentences."
71 Eric Lichtblau, "Gonzales is seeking to stem light sentences."

6 Social Cohesion

1 oas.samhsa.gov/NSDUH/2k5NSDUH/tabs/Sect1peTabs67to132.htm#Tab1.73A. Table 1.73B of the survey reported that the consumption rate of illicit drugs was 9.2 percent for blacks and 8.1 percent for whites.
2 Paige M. Harrison and Allen J. Beck, *Prisoners in 2004*, p. 9, table 12.
3 United States Sentencing Commission, news release: "Changes in federal cocaine sentencing policy recommended: Findings to be submitted to Congress," April 5, 2002; Sam Vincent Medis, "Is the drug war racist," cited in Eva Bertram et al., *Drug War Politics*, p. 38; and Stuart Taylor, Jr., "How a racist drug war swells crime."
4 Taylor, "How a racist drug war swells crime"; and Bertram et al., *Drug War Politics*, p. 38.
5 Eric E. Sterling, "Drug laws and snitching."

6 Jonathan Caulkins et al., *Mandatory Minimum Drug Sentences*, p. 20.

7 Neil A. Lewis, "Justice Department opposes lower jail terms for crack."

8 Matthew R. Durose and Patrick A. Langan, *State Court Sentencing of Convicted Felons, 1998 Statistical Tables*, table 25.

9 B. S. Meierhoefer, *The General Effect of Mandatory Minimum Prison Terms*, p. 20.

10 I. J. Chasnoff, H. J. Landress, and M. E. Barrett, "The prevalence of illicit-drug or alcohol use during pregnancy and discrepancies in mandatory reporting in Pinellas County, Florida."

11 www.ojp.usdoj.gov/bis/dcf/correct.htm, p. 6.

12 Ron Harris, "Blacks feel brunt of drug war"; and Bertram et al., *Drug War Politics*, p. 39.

13 See, for example, Adam Liptak, "Texas governor pardons 35 arrested in tainted sting"; and "Targeted in Tulia, Texas?," www.cbsnews.com/stories/2003/09/26/60minutes/main575291.shtml.

14 "Targeted in Tulia, Texas?," ibid.

15 Ibid.

16 Steve Barnes, "National briefing—Southwest."

17 Peter Andreas, "Profits, poverty and illegality," cited in Bertram et al., *Drug War Politics*, p. 17; and James P. Gray, *Why our Drug Laws Have Failed and What We Can Do about It*, pp. 73–7.

18 Tom Morganthau, "Why good cops go bad," p. 34, quoted in Bertram et al., *Drug War Politics*, pp. 48–9.

19 Steven B. Duke and Albert C. Gross, *America's Longest War*, pp. 113–14.

20 Gray, *Why our Drug Laws Have Failed*, p. 73.

21 See www.hrw.org/reports98/police/uspo100.htm, reported in Steven Wisotsky, *Beyond the War on Drugs*, p. 146.

22 Arnold Markowitz, "Police corruption witness makes a dangerous friend," cited ibid., p. 147.

23 Clifford Krauss, "Corruption in uniform," cited in Bertram et al., *Drug War Politics*, p. 49.

24 Gray, *Why our Drug Laws Have Failed*, pp. 74, 76.

25 United States General Accounting Office, *Law Enforcement*, p. 8, quoted at www.drugwarfacts.org/corrupt.htm.

26 Gray, *Why our Drug Laws Have Failed*, p. 76.

27 Daniel K. Benjamin and Roger Leroy Miller, *Undoing Drugs*, p. 69.

28 Thomas A. Hagemann, "The thin blue lie," quoted in Gray, *Why our Drug Laws Have Failed*, pp. 74–5.

29 United Nations, *Economic and Social Consequences of Drug Abuse and Illicit Trafficking*, p. 39, quoted at www.drugwarfacts.org/corrupt.htm.

30 Wisotsky, *Beyond the War on Drugs*, p. 147.

7 Your Tax Dollars at Work

1 www.whitehousedrugpolicy.gov/publications/pdf/budget2002.pdf.

2 CSDP, *Revising the Federal Drug Control Budget Report*. See also www.ojp.usdoj.gov/bjs/dcf/dcb.htm.

3 National Research Council, *Informing America's Policy on Illegal Drugs*, pp. 150–51, figure 5.2. The cocaine and heroin prices are based on the STRIDE data as reported by the Office of National Drug Control Policy, *National Drug Control Strategy*, 2000, table 42. The supply data are also obtained from the Office of National Drug Control Policy, *National Drug Control Strategy*, 1997–8.

4 National Research Council, *Informing America's Policy on Illegal Drugs*, p. 151; and Robert J. MacCoun and Peter Reuter, *Drug War Heresies*, p. 31.

5 MacCoun and Reuter, ibid.
6 www.whitehousedrugpolicy.gov/publications/policy/ndcs03/table2.html; and www.oas.samhsa.gov. "Current user" means that the person had used the drug in the month prior to the interview.
7 Eva Bertram et al., *Drug War Politics*, p. 14.
8 Robert Reischauer, *The Andean Initiative*, cited in Steven B. Duke and Albert C. Gross, *America's Longest War*, p. 201.
9 Steven Wisotsky, *Beyond the War on Drugs*, p. 51.
10 Ibid., p. 54. See also Lester Grinspoon and James B. Bakalar, *Cocaine*, pp. 9–11.
11 Reed Lindsay, "The contradictions of coca eradication in Bolivia."
12 See State Department Publication 10047, available at dosfan.lib.uic.edu/erc/law/INC/1993/02.html, cited in Duke and Gross, *America's Longest War*, p. 203.
13 James Brooke, "U.S. aid hasn't stopped drug flow from South America, experts say," cited in Bertram et al., *Drug War Politics*, p. 14.
14 United States General Accounting Office, *Drug Control*, p. 2, cited at www.drugwarfacts.org/interdic.htm.
15 See the GAO report of January 8, 2003, to Charles H. Taylor of the House of Representatives, available at www.gao.gov/new.items/d03319r.pdf.
16 The Department of Agriculture report is in the *Congressional Record*, May 27, 1988, p. S7049, cited in Ethan Nadelmann, "Drug prohibition in the U.S.," p. 290.
17 Nadelmann, "Drug prohibition in the U.S.," p. 290.
18 House Judiciary Committee, Subcommittee on Crime and Criminal Justice, February, 1992, p. 93, cited in Bertram et al., *Drug War Politics*, p. 18.
19 David Clark Scott, "New cooperation seen in anti-drug strategy," cited ibid., p. 18.
20 "A survey of illegal drugs," p. 6.
21 See www.unodc.org/pdf/publications/peru_cocasurvey_2001.pdf, p. 2; and www.unodc.org/pdf/publications/peru_coca-survey_2002.pdf, p. 4.
22 *The Economist*, April 5, 2003, p. 72.
23 www.whitehousedrugpolicy.gov/news/press03/102203.html.
24 www.wola.org/Colombia/plan_col_report_card03.pdf.
25 Dan Molinski, "Cocaine supply defies war on drugs."
26 Ibid.
27 Vikki Kratz, "War on coca poisons Colombia."
28 Jeremy Bigwood, "Toxic drift."
29 *Latin American Weekly Report*, February 22, 1990, p. 1, cited in Bertram et al., *Drug War Politics*, p. 16.
30 Melvin Burke, "Bolivia: The politics of cocaine," cited ibid.
31 George Stein, "In rural Bolivia drug agents fear for their lives," cited in Wisotsky, *Beyond the War on Drugs*, p. 56.
32 Wisotsky's interview with American embassy officials, reported ibid.
33 "Church blasts U.S. anti-drug campaigns," cited ibid.
34 Larry Rohter, "Bolivian leader's ouster seen as warning on U.S. drug policy."
35 Ibid.
36 Ibid.
37 Dennis Small, "Soros wins Bolivia round."
38 *The Economist*, November 1, 2003, p. 16.
39 Rohter, "Bolivian leader's ouster seen as warning on U.S. drug policy."
40 See FY 2003 National Drug Control Budget, available at www.ojp.usdoj.gov/bjs/dcf/dcb.htm.
41 Nadelmann, "Drug prohibition in the U.S.," p. 291; Bertram et al., *Drug War Politics*, p. 33; and Duke and Gross, *America's Longest War*, p. 206.
42 James A. Inciardi, *The War on Drugs III*, ch. 6.
43 Ibid., p. 137.
44 Ibid., pp. 104–9.

45 DEA press release, February 29, 2000, cited ibid., p. 107.

46 Wisotsky, *Beyond the War on Drugs*, pp. 91–9; and Bertram et al., *Drug War Politics*, p. 21.

47 Bertram et al., ibid. Gelbard's briefing on Southeast Asia is available at dosfan.lib.uic.edu/ERC/bureaus/eap/950620GelbardSoutheastAsia.html.

48 Jerome Skolnick, "Rethinking the drug problem," quoted in Dirk Chase Eldredge, *Ending the War on Drugs*, p. 147; and "A survey of illegal drugs," p. 6.

49 Jim Abrams, "Interdiction hasn't stemmed drug flow, Congress is told," cited in Eldredge, *Ending the War on Drugs*, p. 146.

50 United States General Accounting Office, *Federal Drug Interdiction Efforts Need Strong Central Oversight*, p. 28, cited in Wisotsky, *Beyond the War on Drugs*, p. 98.

51 Transcript of the president's news conference, *New York Times*, March 7, 1981, cited in Bertram et al., *Drug War Politics*, p. 22.

52 See the National Control Budget figures at the ONDCP website, and the CPI series at the Bureau of Labor Statistics website.

53 Commission on the Advancement of Federal Law Enforcement, *Law Enforcement in a New Century and a Changing World*, p. 85, cited in Timothy Lynch, "Tabula rasa for drug policy," p. 7.

54 Nadelmann, "Drug prohibition in the U.S.," pp. 291–2; Ansley Hamid, "The political economy of crack-related violence"; and Bertram et al., *Drug War Politics*, p. 21.

55 Bertram et al., *Drug War Politics*, Appendix 2, pp. 265–7.

56 Domestic law enforcement constituted about three-quarters of the supply reduction expenditures prior to the major change in the drug control budget instituted by the Bush administration in 2004—see introduction of this chapter. Under the current budget procedures, domestic law enforcement is reduced to about half the spending on supply reduction.

57 ODALE stands for Office for Drug Abuse Law Enforcement.

58 James P. Gray, *Why our Drug Laws Have Failed and What We Can Do about It*, pp. 50–52; and Volney V. Brown, Jr., "A view from the front lines of the drug war."

59 Brown, ibid.

60 Ibid.

61 "The Koppel report: Drugs, crime, and doing time," *ABC News Special*, 1990, cited in Daniel K. Benjamin and Roger Leroy Miller, *Undoing Drugs*, pp. 80–81.

62 Duke and Gross, *America's Longest War*, p. 178.

63 United States Sentencing Commission, *Report to Congress: Cocaine and Federal Sentencing Policy*, May, 2007, p. 19, figure 2.4, cited at www.drugwarfacts.org/mandator.htm.

64 Bertram et al., *Drug War Politics*, pp. 23–4.

65 Michael Massing, *The Fix*, p. 67.

66 See, for example, Associated Press, "Drug war now many local battles"; and Bret Sigler, "Turning up heat hasn't stopped meth producers."

67 www.ojp.usdoj.gov/ovc/publications/bulletins/children/pg2.html.

68 Martha Quillin, "Rural county is meth central; and www.ojp.usdoj.gov/ovc/publications/bulletins/children/pg5.html.

69 www.cdc.gov/mmwr/preview/mmwrhtml/mm4945al.htm.

70 Ibid.; Donna Leinwand and Wade Payne, "Meth moves east"; and Gray, *Why our Drug Laws Have Failed*, pp. 127–8.

71 www.ojp.usdoj.gov/ovc/publications/bulletins/children/pg2.html.

72 Holly Hickman, "Meth use 'choking' western hills of North Carolina."

73 www.cdc.gov/mmwr/preview/mmwrhtml/mm4945al.htm; and Gray, *Why our Drug Laws Have Failed*, p. 58.

74 Hickman, "Meth use 'choking' western hills of North Carolina"; Quillin, "Rural county is meth central"; Leinwand and Payne, "Meth moves east"; and Gray, *Why our Drug Laws Have Failed*, p. 65.

75 Estimates of the DEA as reported in Leinwand and Payne, "Meth moves east."
76 Ibid.
77 www.ojp.usdoj.gov/ovc/publications/bulletins/children/pg2.html.
78 Robert E. Pierre, "Keeping pills away from drug abusers."
79 Chris Dumond, "Attorneys say region has produced most meth busts."
80 Ibid.
81 Pierre, "Keeping pills away from drug abusers."
82 Substance Abuse and Mental Health Services Administration, United States Department of Health and Human Services, *Results from the ... National Survey on Drug Use and Health* pp. 224, 226, tables G.1 and G.3, and pp. 225, 227, tables G.2 and G.4, cited at www.drugwarfacts.org/druguse.htm.
83 National Research Council, *Informing America's Policy on Illegal Drugs*, p. 150; www.whitehousedrugpolicy.gov/publications/policy/ndcs03/table2.html; and www.oas.samhsa.gov.
84 www.oas.samhsa.gov.

Part III: Introduction

1   James Ostrowski, "Drug prohibition muddles along," pp. 365–6.

8 The Perception of the Drug Czars

1   The third author is John DiIulio, Jr., who is a former deputy director in the Office of National Drug Control Policy.
2   William J. Bennett, John J. DiIulio, Jr., and John P. Walters, *Body Count*, p. 27.
3   Ibid, p. 14.
4   Ibid., p. 41.
5   Ibid.
6   Ibid., p. 56.
7   Ibid., p. 139.
8   Ibid., p. 140.
9   Ibid., pp. 146–7.
10 Ibid., p. 149.
11 Ibid.
12 Office of National Drug Control Policy, *National Drug Control Strategy*, pp. 50–51.
13 Ibid. See also Rodney Skager and Joel Brown, "On the reconstruction of drug education in the United States," pp. 325–6.
14 For a survey of the research on the effects of high-school drug education programs, see Skager and Brown, ibid., pp. 310–41.
15 Ibid., p. 321.
16 Ibid., p. 326.
17 Ibid., p. 314.
18 Ibid., p. 327.
19 Ibid.
20 Ibid., p. 322.
21 Ibid., p. 321.

9 The Czars Defend the Drug War

1   William J. Bennett, John J. DiIulio, Jr., and John P. Walters, *Body Count*, p. 45.
2   Dan Weikel, "War on drugs targets minorities over whites."

3 Bennett et al., *Body Count*, p. 101; see also Office of National Drug Control Policy, *What Americans Need to Know about Marijuana*, p. 6.

4 Bennett et al., *Body Count*, p. 101.

5 Christopher J. Mumola, *Substance Abuse and Treatment, State and Federal Prisoners, 1997*, p. 3, table 1, cited at www.drugwarfacts.org/prison.htm. Missing from this Justice Department calculation are those in local jails, INS facilities, military facilities, jails in Indian country, and juvenile facilities. In 2002, federal and state prisoners constituted only about 63 percent of all prisoners.

6 Craig Reinarman and Harry G. Levine, "Real opposition, real alternatives," p. 354.

7 oas.samhsa.gov/nsduh/2k5nsduh/AppG.htm#TabG-1.

8 Bennett et al., *Body Count*, p. 101.

9 United States Sentencing Commission, *Report to Congress: Cocaine and Federal Sentencing Policy*, May, 2007, cited at www.drugwarfacts.org/mandator.htm.

10 Fox Butterfield, "Women find a new arena for equality."

11 John Irwin, Vincent Schiraldi, and Jason Ziedenberg, *America's One Million Nonviolent Prisoners*, pp. 6–7, cited at www.drugwarfacts.org/women.htm.

12 www.famm.org/nr_sentencing_news_trends_report_11_03.htm.

13 Bennett et al., *Body Count*, p. 152.

14 Office of National Drug Control Policy, *National Drug Control Strategy*, p. 39, cited in Eva Bertram et al., *Drug War Politics*, p. 269, figure 7.

15 Susan S. Everingham and C. Peter Rydell, *Modeling the Demand for Cocaine*, p. 49, cited ibid, p. 269, figure 8.

16 The supply budget numbers are from the Office of National Drug Control Policy, 1997 and 1998, reported in National Research Council, *Informing America's Policy on Illegal Drugs*, p. 150, figure 5.2.

17 Vincent Schiraldi, Barry Holman, and Phillip Beatty, *Poor Prescription*, pp. 14–15, graph 8.

18 Robert J. MacCoun and Peter Reuter, *Drug War Heresies*, pp. 258 and 263.

19 www.csdp.org/research/nixonpot.txt, p. 6.

20 Bennett et al., *Body Count*, p. 155; and Office of National Drug Control Policy, *What Americans Need to Know about Marijuana*, p. 9.

21 Janet E. Joy, Stanley J. Watson, Jr., and John A Benson, Jr., *Marijuana and Medicine*, cited at www.drugwarfacts.org/gatewayt.htm.

22 Lynn Zimmer and John P. Morgan, *Marijuana Myths, Marijuana Facts*, p. 36.

23 Mitch Earleywine, *Understanding Marijuana*, p. 55, table 3.2; and www.samhsa.gov/oas/nhsda/2k2nsduh/Results/apph.htm#tabh.30.

24 Zimmer and Morgan, *Marijuana Myths, Marijuana Facts*, p. 35; Earleywine, *Understanding Marijuana*, p. 58; and MacCoun and Reuter, *Drug War Heresies*, pp. 347–8.

25 www.monitoringthefuture.org/data/05data.html#2005data-drugs.

26 Earleywine, *Understanding Marijuana*, p. 50.

27 Ibid.

28 Ibid.; and Zimmer and Morgan, *Marijuana Myths, Marijuana Facts*, p. 37.

29 Office of National Drug Control Policy, *What Americans Need to Know about Marijuana*, pp. 2–3.

30 Michael Lynskey et al., "Escalation of drug use in early-onset cannabis users vs. co-twin controls," summary available at www.drugwarfacts.org/gatewayt.htm.

31 Earleywine, *Understanding Marijuana*, p. 59.

32 Ibid.

33 MacCoun and Reuter, *Drug War Heresies*, pp. 350–51; Earleywine, *Understanding Marijuana*, p. 60; and Lynskey et al., "Escalation of drug use in early-onset cannabis users vs. co-twin controls."

34 Earleywine, *Understanding Marijuana*, p. 60.

35 Lynskey et al., "Escalation of drug use in early-onset cannabis users vs. co-twin controls"; and Bart Majoor, "Drug policy in the Netherlands," p. 141.
36 Joy et al., *Marijuana and Medicine*.
37 Lynskey et al., "Escalation of drug use in early-onset cannabis users vs. co-twin controls."
38 W. Hall, R. Room, and S. Bondy, *WHO Project on Health Implications of Cannabis Use*, cited at www.drugwarfacts.org/gatewayt.htm.
39 J. C. Merrill and K. S. Fox, *Cigarettes, Alcohol, Marijuana*, cited at www.drug warfacts.org/gatewayt.htm.
40 Ibid.
41 MacCoun and Reuter, *Drug War Heresies*, p. 346.
42 Earleywine, *Understanding Marijuana*, p. 64.
43 Zimmer and Morgan, *Marijuana Myths, Marijuana Facts*, p. 32.
44 Daniel K. Benjamin and Roger Leroy Miller, *Undoing Drugs*, p. 169n.
45 Cynthia Kuhn et al., *Buzzed*, p. 267.

10 The White House Versus the Scientists on Marijuana Dangers

1 Office of National Drug Control Policy, *What Americans Need to Know about Marijuana*, pp. 2–3.
2 Ibid.
3 Ibid., pp. 4–5.
4 Lester Grinspoon and James B. Bakalar, *Marihuana, the Forbidden Medicine*, p. 243.
5 Ibid., p. 250.
6 Mitch Earleywine, *Understanding Marijuana*, pp. 164 and 199.
7 W. Hall, R. Room, and S. Bondy, *WHO Project on Health Implications of Cannabis Use*, cited at www.drugwarfacts.org/marijuan.htm.
8 "A survey of illegal drugs," p. 10.
9 *The Merck Manual of Medical Information*, p. 1557.
10 Drug Enforcement Agency, *In the Matter of Marijuana Rescheduling Petition*, p. 57, quoted at www.drugwarfacts.org/marijuan.htm.
11 Leslie L. Iversen, "Long-term effects of exposure to cannabis," p. 71, quoted at www.drugwarfacts.org/marijuan.htm.
12 See, for example, Jerrold S. Meyer and Linda F. Quenzer, *Psychopharmacology*, p. 343.
13 Earleywine, *Understanding Marijuana*, p. 144. Also Lynn Zimmer and John P. Morgan, *Marijuana Myths, Marijuana Facts*, p. 133.
14 Grinspoon and Bakalar, *Marihuana, the Forbidden Medicine*, p. 235.
15 Zimmer and Morgan, *Marijuana Myths, Marijuana Facts*, p. 133.
16 Office of National Drug Control Policy, *What Americans Need to Know about Marijuana*, p. 2.
17 Bruce Mirken and Mitch Earlywine, "The 'potent pot' myth," referring to a government document entitled *Treatment Episode Data Set 1992–2001*, released by SAMSHA in December 2003.
18 Robert J. MacCoun and Peter Reuter, *Drug War Heresies*, p. 356.
19 Zimmer and Morgan, *Marijuana Myths, Marijuana Facts*, pp. 131–3.
20 Ibid.
21 Ibid., p. 133.
22 Office of National Drug Control Policy, *What Americans Need to Know about Marijuana*, p. 3.
23 Constantine G. Lyketsos et al., "Cannabis use and cognitive decline in persons under 65 years of age," cited at www.drugwarfacts.org/marijuan.htm.

24 Earleywine, *Understanding Marijuana*, pp. 150–4.
25 Ibid., p. 154. See also Meyer and Quenzer, *Psychopharmacology*, pp. 343–5.
26 W. Wilson et al., "Brain morphological changes and early marijuana use," discussed in Earleywine, *Understanding Marijuana*, pp. 151–2.
27 www.natlnorml.org/about/responsible.shtml.
28 Office of National Drug Control Policy, *What Americans Need to Know about Marijuana*, p. 2.
29 Earleywine, *Understanding Marijuana*, pp. 154–5.
30 Ibid., p. 154.
31 M. R. Polen, "Health care use by frequent marijuana smokers who do not smoke tobacco," cited ibid., p. 155.
32 Meyer and Quenzer, *Psychopharmacology*, p. 345. See, for example, D. P. Tashkin et al., "Respiratory and immunologic consequences of marijuana smoking."
33 D. P. Tashkin et al., "Heavy habitual marijuana smoking does not cause an accelerated decline in FEVI with age," cited in Earleywine, *Understanding Marijuana*, p. 155.
34 J. W. Bloom et al., "Respiratory effects of non-tobacco cigarettes," cited in Earleywine, *Understanding Marijuana*, pp. 155–6.
35 Earleywine, *Understanding Marijuana*, pp. 156–7; and Meyer and Quenzer, *Psychopharmacology*, p. 345. See, for example, Tashkin et al., "Respiratory and immunologic consequences of marijuana smoking" and the discussion in Zimmer and Morgan, *Marijuana Myths, Marijuana Facts*, p. 115.
36 See www.cnn.com/2006/HEALTH/05/24/pot.lung.cancer.reut/index.html.
37 Grinspoon and Bakalar, *Marihuana, the Forbidden Medicine*, p. 250.
38 Zimmer and Morgan, *Marijuana Myths, Marijuana Facts*, p. 109.
39 Ibid.
40 Meyer and Quenzer, *Psychopharmacology*, p. 345. See G. A. Cabral and D. A. D. Pettit, "Drugs and immunity."
41 Office of National Drug Control Policy, *What Americans Need to Know about Marijuana*, p. 2.
42 See, for example, O. H. Drummer, *Drugs in Drivers Killed in Australian Road Traffic Accidents*, cited in Earleywine, *Understanding Marijuana*, p. 211.
43 Earleywine, *Understanding Marijuana*, p. 211.
44 K. W. Terhune, C. A. Ippolito, and D. J. Crouch, *The Incidence and Role of Drugs in Fatally Injured Drivers*.
45 See, for example, A. Smiley, "Marijuana: On-road and driving simulator studies," cited in Earleywine, *Understanding Marijuana*, pp. 212–13.
46 Raymond P. Shafer et al., *Marihuana: A Signal of Misunderstanding*, ch. 3, cited at www.drugwarfacts.org/marijuan.htm.
47 Janet E. Joy, Stanley J. Watson, Jr., and John A Benson, Jr., *Marijuana and Medicine*, cited at www.drugwarfacts.org/marijuan.htm.
48 Office of National Drug Control Policy, *What Americans Need to Know about Marijuana*, p. 3.
49 Zimmer and Morgan, *Marijuana Myths, Marijuana Facts*, p. 80; Earleywine, *Understanding Marijuana*, p. 144; Grinspoon and Bakalar, *Marihuana, the Forbidden Medicine*, pp. 239–42.
50 Earleywine, *Understanding Marijuana*, p. 145.
51 Grinspoon and Bakalar, *Marihuana, the Forbidden Medicine*, p. 239.
52 Ibid., p. 242.
53 R. McGee et al., "A longitudinal study of cannabis use and mental health from adolescence to early adulthood," cited in Earleywine, *Understanding Marijuana*, p. 145.
54 Office of National Drug Control Policy, *What Americans Need to Know about Marijuana*, p. 3.

55 For example, J. S. Hochman and N. Q. Brill, "Chronic marihuana use and psychosocial adaptation." See also Zimmer and Morgan, *Marijuana Myths, Marijuana Facts*, pp. 62–4; and Earleywine, *Understanding Marijuana*, pp. 204–5.

56 J. Shedler and J. Block, "Adolescent drug use and psychological health."

57 MacCoun and Reuter, *Drug War Heresies*, p. 348.

58 Quoted in Rodney Skager and Joel Brown, "On the reconstruction of drug education in the United States," p. 319.

59 Zimmer and Morgan, *Marijuana Myths, Marijuana Facts*, p. 64.

60 See, for example, A. D. Farrell et al., "Relationship between drug use and other problem behavior in urban adolescents"; and the list of studies cited in Zimmer and Morgan, *Marijuana Myths, Marijuana Facts*, p. 190, n. 16.

61 Earleywine, *Understanding Marijuana*, p. 205.

62 Office of National Drug Control Policy, *What Americans Need to Know about Marijuana*, p. 4.

63 For example, C. Stefanis et al., "Experimental observations of a 3-day hashish abstinence period and reintroduction of use"; and the references in Zimmer and Morgan, *Marijuana Myths, Marijuana Facts*, p. 175, n. 12. See also MacCoun and Reuter, *Drug War Heresies*, pp. 355–6; Grinspoon and Bakalar, *Marihuana, the Forbidden Medicine*, p. 244; and Zimmer and Morgan, *Marijuana Myths, Marijuana Facts*, pp. 28–30.

64 R. Jones, "What have we learned from nicotine, cocaine and marijuana about addiction?," cited in MacCoun and Reuter, *Drug War Heresies*, p. 355.

65 R. Gannon, "The truth about pot," cited in Zimmer and Morgan, *Marijuana Myths, Marijuana Facts*, p. 28.

66 R. T. Jones et al., "Clinical studies of tolerance and dependence," summarized in Zimmer and Morgan, *Marijuana Myths, Marijuana Facts*, p. 28.

67 United States Department of Health and Human Services, *Drug Abuse and Drug Abuse Research*, p. 133, cited in Zimmer and Morgan, *Marijuana Myths, Marijuana Facts*, p. 29.

68 D. Franklin, "Hooked—not hooked," summarized in Earleywine, *Understanding Marijuana*, p. 32.

69 Earleywine, *Understanding Marijuana*, p. 32; and Zimmer and Morgan, *Marijuana Myths, Marijuana Facts*, p. 28.

70 Cynthia Kuhn et al., *Buzzed*, p. 27.

71 R. A. Weller and J. A. Halikas, "Objective criteria for the diagnosis of marijuana abuse," cited in Earleywine, *Understanding Marijuana*, pp. 46–7.

72 Ibid.; MacCoun and Reuter, *Drug War Heresies*, p. 356; and Grinspoon and Bakalar, *Marihuana, the Forbidden Medicine*, p. 244.

73 Earleywine, *Understanding Marijuana*, p. 130. See also Zimmer and Morgan, *Marijuana Myths, Marijuana Facts*, p. 139; and Grinspoon and Bakalar, *Marihuana, the Forbidden Medicine*, p. 250.

74 Office of National Drug Control Policy, *What Americans Need to Know about Marijuana*, p. 5.

75 Ibid.

76 Remarks by Lee Brown, director of national drug control policy, at a national conference in Arlington, Virginia, on "Marijuana Use: Prevention, Treatment, and Research," July, 1995, cited in Zimmer and Morgan, *Marijuana Myths, Marijuana Facts*, p. 88.

77 MacCoun and Reuter, *Drug War Heresies*, pp. 22 and 122.

78 Zimmer and Morgan, *Marijuana Myths, Marijuana Facts*, pp. 88–91; and Earleywine, *Understanding Marijuana*, pp. 214–21.

79 Shafer et al., *Marihuana: A Signal of Misunderstanding*, ch. 3, quoted at www.drugwarfacts.org/marijuan.htm.

80 Zimmer and Morgan, *Marijuana Myths, Marijuana Facts*, p. 90.
81 B. Spunt et al., "The role of marijuana in homicide."

11 Czars Versus the Scientists on Cocaine and Heroin

1 William J. Bennett, John J. DiIulio, Jr., and John P. Walters, *Body Count*, p. 148.
2 Ibid., p. 92.
3 See www.whitehousedrugpolicy.gov/enforce/drugcourt.html; Donald P. Lay, "Rehab justice" (the author is the senior judge for the United States Court of Appeals for the Eighth Circuit); Paul von Zielbauer, "Court treatment system is found to help drug offenders stay clean"; and "Dealing with drug use".
4 Zielbauer, "Court treatment system is found to help drug offenders stay clean."
5 Lay, "Rehab justice."
6 Bennett et al., *Body Count*, p. 178.
7 Ibid., p. 177.
8 Ibid., p. 198.
9 Zielbauer, "Court treatment system is found to help drug offenders stay clean."
10 Lay, "Rehab justice."
11 Ibid.; and Jonathan Caulkins et al., *Mandatory Minimum Drug Sentences*, p. xvi.
12 Ibid., pp. xvi, xxiv and xxv.
13 Institute of Medicine, *Dispelling the Myths about Addiction*, p. 73.
14 V. Tabbush, *The Effectiveness and Efficiency of Publicly Funded Drug Abuse Treatment and Prevention Programs in California*, cited in Steven B. Duke and Albert C. Gross, *America's Longest War*, p. 297.
15 Sam Howe Verhovek, "Warehouse of addiction," cited in Daniel K. Benjamin and Roger Leroy Miller, *Undoing Drugs*, p. 105.
16 Eric Schlosser, *Reefer Madness*, p. 72.
17 Robert J. MacCoun and Peter Reuter, *Drug War Heresies*, p. 122; and Jeffrey A. Miron and Jeffrey Zwiebel, "The economic case against drug prohibition," pp. 177–8.
18 See, for example, "A survey of illegal drugs," p. 8, table 2; and Jerrold S. Meyer and Linda F. Quenzer, *Psychopharmacology*, p. 281.
19 www.nida.nih.gov/infofax/comcaine.html; and James A. Inciardi, *The War on Drugs III*, p. 144.
20 Craig Reinarman and Harry G. Levine, "The crack attack," p. 26.
21 "A survey of illegal drugs," p. 10.
22 www.oas.samhsa.gov/NSDUH/2k5NSDUH/tabs/Sect1peTabs1to66.htm# Tab1.1A See also Reinarman and Levine, "The crack attack," pp. 32–3.
23 "A survey of illegal drugs," p. 8, table 2.
24 www.monitoringthefuture.org/data/05data.html#2005data-drugs.
25 Yuet W. Cheung and Patricia G. Erickson, "Crack use in Canada," p. 179.
26 Ibid.
27 John P. Morgan and Lynn Zimmer, "Social pharmacology of smokeable cocaine," pp. 146–7; MacCoun and Reuter, *Drug War Heresies*, p. 16; and Cheung and Erickson, "Crack use in Canada," p. 185.
28 MacCoun and Reuter, *Drug War Heresies*, p. 16.
29 See, for example, Morgan and Zimmer, "Social pharmacology of smokeable cocaine," p. 147.
30 Cheung and Erickson, "Crack use in Canada," p. 188.
31 "A survey of illegal drugs," p. 9; and Peter D. A. Cohen, "Crack in the Netherlands," pp. 219–22.
32 Sheigla B. Murphy and Marsha Rosenbaum, "Two women who used cocaine too much."

33 Ibid., p. 107.
34 Ibid., p. 108.
35 Ibid., p. 109.
36 Craig Reinarman et al., "The contingent call of the pipe," pp. 89 and 92.
37 Ibid., p. 92.
38 Ibid.
39 Duke and Gross, *America's Longest War*, p. 58.
40 Inciardi, *The War on Drugs III*, p. 116.
41 Elliot Currie, *Reckoning*, pp. 60–66, 104–12; Tom Carnwath and Ian Smith, *Heroin Century*, pp. 77–8; and Inciardi, *The War on Drugs III*, pp. 43–4.
42 Carnwath and Smith, *Heroin Century*, pp. 84–5.
43 Duke and Gross, *America's Longest War*, p. 61; John Kaplan, *The Hardest Drug*, p. 7; and Carnwath and Smith, *Heroin Century*, p. 81. See also the data from the National Survey on Drug Abuse, reported in "A survey of illegal drugs," p. 8, table 2.
44 Carnwath and Smith, *Heroin Century*, pp. 81–2; Duke and Gross, *America's Longest War*, pp. 61–2; and Currie, *Reckoning*, p. 236.
45 N. Zinberg, "The natural history of 'chipping'"; J. S. Blackwell, "Drifting, controlling and overcoming"; and M. Abdel-Mahgoud and M. K. Al-Haddad, "Patterns of heroin use among a non-treatment sample in Glasgow, Scotland."
46 Carnwath and Smith, *Heroin Century*, pp. 82–4.
47 Ibid., p. 90.
48 Duke and Gross, *America's Longest War*, p. 58.
49 Carnwath and Smith, *Heroin Century*, p. 83.
50 Cynthia Kuhn, Scott Swartzwelder, and Wilkie Wilson, *Buzzed*, p. 190.
51 Richard Davenport-Hines, *The Pursuit of Oblivion*, p. 459.
52 Duke and Gross, *America's Longest War*, pp. 58–9.
53 Michael Massing, *The Fix*, pp. 115–18.
54 MacCoun and Reuter, *Drug War Heresies*, p. 17; Currie, *Reckoning*, p. 231; and Kuhn et al., *Buzzed*, p. 189.
55 Inciardi, *The War on Drugs III*, p. 112.
56 www.oas.samhsa.gov/nhsda/2k3tabs/toc.htm.
57 "A survey of illegal drugs," p. 8, table 2. See also www.tairna.org/drugfacts/use.htm.
58 Duke and Gross, *America's Longest War*, p. 62.
59 *The Merck Manual of Medical Information*, p. 487.
60 Jerome Jaffe, "Drug addiction and drug abuse," p. 286, quoted in Duke and Gross, *America's Longest War*, p. 59.
61 Inciardi, *The War on Drugs III*, p. 115.
62 Royal College of Psychiatrists and Royal College of Physicians, *Drugs: Dilemmas and Choices*, p. 15, cited in Carnwath and Smith, *Heroin Century*, p. 154, n. 9.
63 Carnwath and Smith, *Heroin Century*, p. 138.
64 See, for example, Inciardi, *The War on Drugs III*, p. 115; and Duke and Gross, *America's Longest War*, p. 61.
65 "Opioid Dependence," *The Merck Manual of Diagnosis and Therapy*, section 15: Psychiatric Disorders, chapter 195, Drug Use and Dependence, cited at www.drugwarfacts.org/heroin.htm.
66 Kuhn et al., *Buzzed*, p. 187; and Carnwath and Smith, *Heroin Century*, p. 162.
67 Lee Robins, Darlene Davis, and Donald Goodwin, "Drug use by U.S. army enlisted men in Vietnam," p. 235, summarized in Duke and Gross, *America's Longest War*, pp. 61–2; and Davenport-Hines, *The Pursuit of Oblivion*, p. 423.
68 See World Health Organization, *Cancer Pain Relief and Palliative Care*.
69 Kuhn et al., *Buzzed*, p. 179. See also Carnwath and Smith, *Heroin Century*, pp. 137–8.

70 MacCoun and Reuter, *Drug War Heresies*, p. 16.
71 Arnold Trebach and Kevin Zeese, *Drug Prohibition and the Conscience of Nations*, p. 34.
72 Craig Reinarman and Harry G. Levine "Punitive prohibition in America," p. 327.

Part IV: Introduction

1 Eva Bertram et al., *Drug War Politics*, p. 160.
2 *Daily Mail* [London], March 10, 1998, cited in James P. Gray, *Why our Drug Laws Have Failed and What We Can Do about It*, p. 213.

12 Harm Reduction Instead of War

1 William J. Bennett, John J. DiIulio, Jr., and John P. Walters, *Body Count*, p. 14.
2 See the National Surveys on Drug Use and Health at www.oas.samhsa.gov.
3 On the theory of the symbolic character of the drug war, see, for example, Diana R. Gordon, *The Return of the Dangerous Classes*; and Eva Bertram et al., *Drug War Politics*, pp. 56–7.
4 Craig Reinarman and Harry G. Levine, "Punitive prohibition in America," p. 329.
5 See, for example, Ethan Nadelmann, "Commonsense drug policy"; and James P. Gray, *Why our Drug Laws Have Failed and What We Can Do about It*, pp. 11–12.
6 Arnold S. Trebach and Kevin B. Zeese, *Drug Prohibition and the Conscience of Nations*, pp. 34–8.
7 Robert J. MacCoun and Peter Reuter, *Drug War Heresies*, p. 297.
8 Ibid., pp. 213–14 and 297.
9 Adam J. Smith, "America's lonely drug war."
10 See Nadelmann, "Commonsense drug policy," repr. in Gray, *Busted*, p. 175.
11 Ibid., pp. 175–6; and Gray, *Why our Drug Laws Have Failed*, pp. 217–19.
12 See, for example, Ronald K. Siegel, *Intoxication*, pp. 9–10.
13 Andrew Weil, *The Natural Mind*, p. 19.
14 www.oas.samhsa.gov/NSDUH/2k5NSDUH/tabs/Sect1peTabs1to66.htm#Tab1.1A.
15 William Bennett, "The plea to legalize drugs is a siren call to surrender," p. 339.
16 William Raspberry, "Prevention and the powers of persuasion."
17 Milton Friedman, "There's no justice in the war on drugs," repr. in Gray, *Busted*, p. 169.
18 Stephen Jay Gould, "The war on (some) drugs," repr. in Gray, *Busted*, p. 257.
19 Douglas Husak, *Legalize This!*, pp. 127–33.
20 Quoted in Gray, *Why our Drug Laws Have Failed*, p. 13.
21 See *Lawrence* v. *Texas*, March 26, 2003.
22 See, for example, Ethan Nadelmann, "Thinking seriously about alternatives to drug prohibition."

13 Legalizing Marijuana

1 www.samhsa.gov/oas/nhsda/2k2nsduh/Results/apph.htm#tabh.30.
2 Federal Bureau of Investigation, *Crime in the United States*, p. 278, table 4.1, and p. 280, table 29, reported at www.drugwarfacts.org/marijuan.htm.
3 Chuck Thomas, "Marijuana arrests and incarceration in the United States."
4 See chapter 10.
5 *The Merck Manual of Medical Information*, cited in Jeffrey A. Miron and Jeffrey Zwiebel, "The economic case against drug prohibition," p. 182.

6 Quoted in Eric E. Sterling, "Principles and proposals for managing the drug problem," p. 487.
7 www.monitoringthefuture.org, table 1.
8 Robert J. MacCoun and Peter Reuter, *Drug War Heresies*, pp. 89–90.
9 Ibid., p. 88.
10 Ibid., pp. 96–8; and Steven B. Duke and Albert C. Gross, *America's Longest War*, p. 242.
11 MacCoun and Reuter, *Drug War Heresies*, pp. 256–7.
12 Ethan Nadelmann, "Europe's drug prescription," quoted in James Gray, *Why our Drug Laws Have Failed and What We Can Do about It*, p. 220.
13 www.monitoringthefuture.org, table 13.
14 Ibid., table 7.
15 Ibid., table 4.
16 Duke and Gross, *America's Longest War*, p. 194.
17 MacCoun and Reuter, *Drug War Heresies*, p. 361.
18 See chapter 10, under the subsection "Critiquing the 2003 ONDCP Report"; and Mitch Earleywine, *Understanding Marijuana*, pp. 210–21.

14 Reforming the Laws on Hard Drugs

1 *WEBB et al.* v. *United States*, 249 U.S. 96 (1919). See chapter 2.
2 James P. Gray, *Why our Drug Laws Have Failed and What We Can Do about It*, pp. 198–9.
3 Ethan Nadelmann, "Commonsense drug policy," repr. in Gray, *Busted*, p. 180.
4 Robert J. MacCoun and Peter Reuter, *Drug War Heresies*, p. 286.
5 Colin Brewer, "Recent developments in maintenance prescribing and monitoring in the United Kingdom," p. 359; and Gray, *Why our Drug Laws Have Failed*, pp. 198–9.
6 David T. Courtwright, *Dark Paradise*, pp. 163–5.
7 Ibid., p. 165.
8 William E. Schmidt, "To battle AIDS, Scots offer oral drugs to addicts." See also Eva Bertram et al., *Drug War Politics*, p. 216; and Steven B. Duke and Albert C. Gross, *America's Longest War*, p. 304.
9 See Mike Gray, *Drug Crazy*, ch. 9; Arnold S. Trebach, *The Heroin Solution*, pp. 85–117; and Gray, *Why our Drug Laws Have Failed*, pp. 199–202.
10 Gray, *Drug Crazy*, p. 192.
11 Personal interview with Dr. Marks by Judge Gray, November 18, 1993, reported in Gray, *Why our Drug Laws Have Failed*, pp. 199–202.
12 Transcript of *CBS News*, "60 Minutes," December 27, 1992.
13 Richard Davenport-Hines, *The Pursuit of Oblivion*, p. 470.
14 Transcript of *CBS News*, "60 Minutes," December 27, 1992, quoted in Gray, *Why our Drug Laws Have Failed*, p. 201.
15 Ibid.
16 Robert J. MacCoun and Peter Reuter, *Drug War Heresies*, pp. 288–96; Gray, *Why our Drug Laws Have Failed*, pp. 202–6; Nadelmann, "Commonsense drug policy," repr. in Gray, *Busted*, pp. 180–81; Mary M. Cleveland, "Downsizing the drug war and considering 'legalization'," pp. 571–2; and "A survey of illegal drugs," pp. 14–15.
17 Gray, *Why our Drug Laws Have Failed*, p. 206.
18 Ambros Uchtenhagen, Felix Gurzwiller, and Anja Dobler-Mikola, *Programme for a Medical Prescription of Narcotics*, summarized ibid., pp. 205–6.
19 "A survey of illegal drugs," pp. 14–15.
20 Nadelmann, "Commonsense drug policy," repr. in Gray, *Busted*, p. 181.

21 Gray, *Why our Drug Laws Have Failed*, p. 206.
22 MacCoun and Reuter, *Drug War Heresies*, pp. 293–4.
23 Gray, *Why our Drug Laws Have Failed*, p. 207.
24 MacCoun and Reuter, *Drug War Heresies*, p. 294.
25 Ibid., p. 384; and S. Shane, "Test of 'heroin maintenance' may be launched in Baltimore."
26 MacCoun and Reuter, *Drug War Heresies*, p. 384; and S. Shane and G. Shields, "Heroin maintenance quickly stirs outrage."
27 MacCoun and Reuter, *Drug War Heresies*, p. 385.
28 DeNeen L. Brown, "Vancouver's safer fix."
29 "A survey of drugs," p. 8. See United States Department of Health and Human Services, *Results from the . . . National Survey on Drug Use and Health*, reported at www.drugwarfacts.com/druguse.htm.
30 See, for example, Cleveland, "Downsizing the drug war and considering 'legalization'," p. 574.
31 United States Department of Health and Human Services, *Results from the . . . National Survey on Drug Use and Health*, reported at www.drugwarfacts.com/druguse.htm.
32 MacCoun and Reuter, *Drug War Heresies*, pp. 96, 230, 235–7, and 297.
33 Jeffrey A. Miron and Jeffrey Zwiebel, "The economic case against drug prohibition," pp. 185–6.
34 www.monitoringthefuture.org/data/05data.html#2005data-drugs, table 3.
35 Ibid., table 17.
36 See chapter 7, subsection "Cocaine and Heroin Prices."
37 MacCoun and Reuter, *Drug War Heresies*, pp. 194 and 197.
38 "What is 'legalization'? What are drugs?," pp. 374–5.
39 Duke and Gross, *America's Longest War*, p. 265.
40 Steven B. Duke and Albert C. Gross, "Forms of legalization," p. 629.
41 Daniel K. Benjamin and Roger Leroy Miller, *Undoing Drugs*, p. 186.
42 Gray, *Why our Drug Laws Have Failed*, p. 222.
43 Ethan Nadelmann, "Thinking seriously about alternatives to drug prohibition: Part 1," p. 4, repr. in Fish, *How to Legalize Drugs*, p. 603.
44 Nadelmann, "Thinking seriously about alternatives to drug prohibition: Part 2," p. 2.
45 Jefferson Fish, "First steps toward legalization," pp. 545–6.
46 Peter C. Rydell and Susan S. Everingham, *Controlling Cocaine*.
47 Bart Majoor, "Drug policy in the Netherlands," pp. 149–52.
48 Ibid., p. 150.
49 Ibid., pp. 141–2.
50 "Holland's drug policy: War by other means," cited in Gray, *Why our Drug Laws Have Failed*, p. 218.
51 Ibid., p. 220.
52 Ibid., p. 221.
53 Ethan Nadelmann, "Thinking seriously about alternatives to drug prohibition: Part 1," pp. 6–7, repr. in Fish, *How to Legalize Drugs*, p. 589.
54 See chapter 12, subsection "Harm Reduction Alone Ignores the Benefits of Illicit Drugs."
55 Ronald Siegel, *Intoxication*, p. 10.
56 J. Westermeyer, "The pursuit of intoxication"; and Robert S. Gable, "Not all drugs are created equal," p. 415.
57 R. J. Sullivan and E. H. Hagen, "Psychotropic substance-seeking."
58 See chapter 4, subsection "Prohibition and Potency."
59 Michael S. Gazzaniga, "Opium of the people," quoted in Duke and Gross, *America's Longest War*, p. 25.

References

Books and Reports

Andrews University, the MayaTech Corporation, and RAND Corporation. *Illicit Drug Policies: Selected Laws from the 50 States*, 2002, rev. 2003; available at www.andrews.edu/ipa/2004/chartbook/pdf.

Baum, Dan, *Smoke and Mirrors*. Boston: Little, Brown, 1996.

Bayer, Ronald, and Gerald M. Oppenheimer, eds., *Confronting Drug Policy*. New York: Cambridge University Press, 1993.

Beck, Jerome, and Marsha Rosenbaum, *Pursuit of Ecstasy: The MDMA Experience*. Albany: State University of New York Press, 1994.

Benjamin, Daniel K., and Roger Leroy Miller, *Undoing Drugs*. New York: Basic Books, 1991.

Bennett, William J., John J. DiIulio, Jr., and John P. Walters, *Body Count: Moral Poverty—and How to Win America's War against Crime and Drugs*. New York: Simon & Schuster, 1996.

Bertram, Eva, Morris Blachman, Kenneth Sharpe, and Peter Andreas, *Drug War Politics*. Berkeley: University of California Press, 1996.

Bonnie, Richard J., and Charles H. Whitebread II, *The Marijuana Conviction*. New York: Lindesmith Center, 1999.

Brands, H. W., *The First American*. New York: Doubleday, 2000.

Bureau of Justice Statistics, *Special Report: Drugs and Jail Inmates, 1989*, Washington, D.C.: U.S. Department of Justice, August 1991.

Burris, Scott, Steffanie A. Strathdee, and Jon S. Vernick, *Syringe Access Law in the United States*. Center for Law and the Public's Health at Johns Hopkins and Georgetown Universities, November 30, 2002.

Carnwath, Tom, and Ian Smith, *Heroin Century*. London and New York: Routledge, 2002.

Caulkins, Jonathan P., C. Peter Rydell, William L. Schwabe, and James Chiesa, *Mandatory Minimum Drug Sentences*. Washington, D.C.: RAND Corporation, 1997.

Centers for Disease Control and Prevention, *State and Local Policies Regarding IDUs' Access to Sterile Syringes*. December, 2005; available at www.cdc.gov/idu/facts/AED_IDU_POL.htm.

———, *HIV/AIDS Surveillance Report 2003*. Vol. 15.

———, *HIV/AIDS Surveillance Report 2005*. Vol. 17, revised June 2007.

Commission on the Advancement of Federal Law Enforcement, *Law Enforcement in a New Century and a Changing World*. Washington, D.C.: Commission on the Advancement of Federal Law Enforcement, 2000.

Courtwright, David T., *Dark Paradise: A History of Opiate Addiction in America*. Cambridge, MA: Harvard University Press, 2001.

CSDP (Common Sense for Drug Policy), *Revising the Federal Drug Control Budget Report: Changing Methodology to Hide the Cost of the Drug War?*, 2003; available at www.csdp.org/research/ondcpenron.pdf.

Currie, Elliott, *Reckoning*. New York: Hill & Wang, 1993.

Davenport-Hines, Richard, *The Pursuit of Oblivion*. New York: W. W. Norton, 2001.

Drug Enforcement Agency, *Illegal Price/Purity Report*. Washington, D.C.: U.S. Department of Justice, March 1991.

———, *Illegal Price/Purity Report*, Washington, D.C.: U.S. Department of Justice, April, 1994.

———, *Illegal Price/Purity Report*, Washington, D.C.: U.S. Department of Justice, June, 1995.

———, *In the Matter of Marijuana Rescheduling Petition*, Washington, D.C.: U.S. Department of Justice (docket #86-22), September 6, 1988.

Drug Policy Alliance, *State of the States: Drug Policy Reforms: 1996–2002*. September, 2003; available at www.drugpolicy.org/docUploads/sos_report2003.pdf.

Drummer, O. H., *Drugs in Drivers Killed in Australian Road Traffic Accidents*. (Report no. 0594), Melbourne, Australia: Monash University, Victorian Institute of Forensic Pathology, 1994.

Duke, Steven B., and Albert C. Gross, *America's Longest War*. New York: G. P. Putnam's Sons, 1993.

Durose, Matthew R., and Patrick A. Langan, *State Court Sentencing of Convicted Felons, 1998 Statistical Tables*. Washington, D.C.: U.S. Department of Justice, Bureau of Justice Statistics, December, 2001; available at www.ojp.usdoj.gov/bjs/abstract/scsc98st.htm.

Earleywine, Mitch, *Understanding Marijuana*. New York: Oxford University Press, 2002.

Ebener, P. A., J. P. Caulkins, S. A. Geshwind, D. McCaffrey, and H. L. Saner, *Improving Data and Analysis to Support National Substance Abuse Policy: Main Report*. Santa Monica, CA: RAND Corporation, 1994.

Ehlers, Scott, *Policy Briefing: Asset Forfeiture*. Washington, D.C.: Drug Policy Foundation, 1999.

Eldredge, Dirk Chase, *Ending the War on Drugs*. Bridgehampton, NY: Bridge Works Publishing Company, 1998.

Everingham, Susan S., and C. Peter Rydell, *Modeling the Demand for Cocaine*, Santa Monica, CA: RAND Corporation, 1994.

Federal Bureau of Investigation, *Crime in the United States: FBI Uniform Crime Reports 2005* Washington, D.C.: U.S. Government Printing Office, 2005.

Fish, Jefferson M., ed., *How to Legalize Drugs*. Northvale, NJ: Jason Aronson, 1998.

Friedman, Lawrence M., *American Law in the 20th Century*. New Haven, CT, and London: Yale University Press, 2002.

Friedman, Milton, and Thomas S. Szasz, *On Liberty and Drugs: Essays on Prohibition and the Free Market*. Washington, D.C.: Drug Policy Foundation, 1992.

Goode, Erich, *Drugs in American Society*, 6th ed. New York: McGraw-Hill, 2005.

Goodman, Louis, and Alfred Gilman, eds., *The Pharmacological Basis of Therapeutics*, 4th ed. New York: Macmillan, 1970.

Gordon, Diana R., *The Return of the Dangerous Classes*. New York: W. W. Norton, 1994.

Gray, James P., *Why our Drug Laws Have Failed and What We Can Do about It*. Philadelphia: Temple University Press, 2001.

Gray, Mike, ed., *Busted: Stone Cowboys, Narco-Lords, and Washington's War on Drugs*. New York: Thunder's Mouth Press/Nation Books, 2002.

————, *Drug Crazy: How We Got into this Mess and How We Can Get Out*. New York: Random House, 1998.

Grinspoon, Lester, and James B. Bakalar, *Cocaine: A Drug and its Social Evolution*, rev. ed. New York: Basic Books, 1985.

————, *Marihuana, the Forbidden Medicine*. New Haven and London: Yale University Press, 1997.

Hall, Kermit L., ed., *The Oxford Companion to the Supreme Court of the United States*. New York and Oxford: Oxford University Press, 1992.

Hall, W., R. Room, and S. Bondy, *WHO Project on Health Implications of Cannabis Use: A Comparative Appraisal of the Health and Psychological Consequences of Alcohol, Cannabis, Nicotine, and Opiate Use*. Geneva, Switzerland: World Health Organization, March, 1998.

Hanson, David J., *Alcohol Beverage Consumption in the U.S.: Patterns and Trends*, State University of New York, Sociology Department, 2003; available at www2.potsdam.edu/hansondj/Controversies/1116895242.html.

Harrison, Paige M., and Allen J. Beck, *Prisoners in 2004*. Washington, D.C.: U.S. Department of Justice, Bureau of Justice Statistics, October 2005.

Husak, Douglas, *Legalize This! The Case for Decriminalizing Drugs*. New York: Verso, 2002.

Inciardi, James A., *The War on Drugs III: The Continuing Saga of the Mysteries of Intoxication, Addiction, Crime, and Public Policy*. Boston: Allyn & Bacon, 2002.

Institute of Medicine, *Dispelling the Myths about Addiction*. Washington, D.C.: National Academy Press, 1997.

Irwin, John, Vincent Schiraldi, and Jason Ziedenberg, *America's One Million Nonviolent Prisoners*. Washington, D.C.: Justice Policy Institute, March, 1999.

Joy, Janet E., Stanley J. Watson, Jr., and John A. Benson, Jr., *Marijuana and Medicine: Assessing the Science Base*. Washington, D.C.: National Academy Press, 1999.

Kaplan, John, *The Hardest Drug: Heroin and Public Policy*. Chicago: University of Chicago Press, 1983.

Karburg Jennifer C., and Doris J. James, *Substance Dependence, Abuse, and Treatment of Jail Inmates, 2002*, Washington, D.C.: U.S. Department of Justice, Bureau of Justice Statistics, July 2005.

Krauss, Melvin, and Edward P. Lazear, eds., *Searching for Alternatives: Drug-Control Policy in the United States*. Stanford, CA: Hoover Institution Press, 1991.

Kuhn, Cynthia, Scott Swartzwelder, and Wilkie Wilson, *Buzzed*, rev. ed. New York: W. W. Norton, 2003.

Lyman, Michael D, and Gary W. Potter, eds., *Drugs in Society: Causes, Concepts, and Control*. Cincinnati, OH: Anderson, 1991.

Lynch, Timothy, ed., *After Prohibition: An Adult Approach to Drug Policies in the 21st Century*. Washington, D.C.: CATO Institute, 2000.

MacCoun, Robert J., and Peter Reuter, *Drug War Heresies*. Cambridge: Cambridge University Press, 2001.

Maruschak, Laura, *HIV in Prisons, 2001.* Washington, D.C.: U.S. Department of Justice, Bureau of Justice Statistics, January 2004.

Massing, Michael, *The Fix.* Berkeley: University of California Press, 1998.

Meierhoefer, B. S., *The General Effect of Mandatory Minimum Prison Terms: A Longitudinal Study of Federal Sentences Imposed.* Washington, D.C.: Federal Judicial Center, 1992.

The Merck Manual of Medical Information, 16th ed., 1992; available at www.merck.com.

The Merck Manual of Diagnosis and Therapy; available at www.merck.com.

Merrill, J. C., and K. S. Fox, *Cigarettes, Alcohol, Marijuana: Gateways to Illicit Drug Use,* New York: National Center on Addiction and Substance Abuse, Columbia University, 1994.

Meyer, Jerrold S., and Linda F. Quenzer, *Psychopharmacology: Drugs, the Brain, and Behaviour.* Sunderland, MA: Sinauer Associates, 2005.

Miron, Jeffrey A., *Drug War Crimes.* Oakland, CA: Independent Institute, 2004.

Morgan, H. Wayne, *Drugs in America.* Syracuse, NY: Syracuse University Press, 1981.

Mumola, Christopher J., *Substance Abuse and Treatment, State and Federal Prisons, January 1997,* Washington, D.C.: U.S. Department of Justice.

Musto, David F., *The American Disease.* New York: Oxford University Press, 1999.

National Center on Addiction and Substance Abuse, *Behind Bars: Substance Abuse and America's Prison Population.* New York: National Center on Addiction and Substance Abuse, Columbia University, 1998.

National Commission on Acquired Immune Deficiency Syndrome, *The Twin Epidemics of Substance Use and HIV.* Washington, D.C.: National Commission on Acquired Immune Deficiency Syndrome, 1991.

National Institute on Drug Abuse, *InfoFacts: Heroin.* Rockville, MD: U.S. Department of Health and Human Services; available at www.nida.nih.gov/infofacts/heroin.html.

———, *InfoFacts: Methamphetamine.* Rockville, MD: U.S. Department of Health and Human Services; available at www.nida.nih.gov/infofacts/methamphetamine.html.

National Research Council, *Informing America's Policy on Illegal Drugs.* Washington, D.C.: National Academy Press, 2001.

Norris, Mikki, Chris Conrad, and Virginia Resner, *Shattered Lives: Portraits from America's Drug War.* El Cerrito, CA: Creative Xpressions, 2000.

O'Brien, Charles P., and Jerome H. Jaffe, *Addictive States.* Green Bay, WI: Raven Press, 1991.

Office of National Drug Control Policy, *National Drug Control Strategy,* Washington, D.C.: Office of National Drug Control Policy, 1995; 1997–8; 2000.

———, *What Americans Need to Know about Marijuana.* Washington, D.C.: Office of National Drug Control Policy, 2003.

Reinarman, Craig, and Harry G. Levine, eds., *Crack in America.* Berkeley: University of California Press, 1997.

Reischauer, Robert, *The Andean Initiative: Objective and Support.* Washington, D.C.: Congressional Budget Office, March 1994; available at www.cbo.gov/showdoc.cfm?index=4885&sequence=0.

Royal College of Psychiatrists and Royal College of Physicians, *Drugs: Dilemmas and Choices.* London: Gaskell Press, 2000.

Rydell, Peter C., and Susan S. Everingham, *Controlling Cocaine: Supply versus Demand Programs.* Santa Monica, CA: RAND Corporation, 1994.

Satcher, David, *Evidence-Based Findings on the Efficacy of Syringe Exchange Programs: An Analysis from the Assistant Secretary for Health and the Surgeon General of the Scientific Research Completed since April 1998.* Washington, D.C.: U.S. Department of Health and Human Services, 2000; accessed May 11, 2005, at www.harmreduction.org/research/surgeongenrev/surgreview.html.

Schiraldi, Vincent, Barry Holman, and Phillip Beatty, *Poor Prescription: The Costs of Imprisoning Drug Offenders in the United States.* Washington, D.C.: Justice Policy Institute, July 2000; available at www.cjcj.org.

Schlosser, Eric, *Reefer Madness.* New York: Houghton Mifflin, 2003.

Shafer, Raymond P., et al., *Marihuana: A Signal of Misunderstanding*, Washington, D.C.: U.S. National Commission on Marihuana and Drug Abuse, 1972.

Siegel, Ronald K., *Intoxication.* New York: E. P. Dutton, 1989.

Skolnik, Jerome H., *Policing Drugs: The Cultural Transformation of a Victimless Crime.* Berkeley: Jurisprudence and Social Policy Program, University of California, 1986.

Spillane, Joseph F., *Cocaine.* Baltimore and London: Johns Hopkins University Press, 2000.

Tabbush, V., *The Effectiveness and Efficiency of Publicly Funded Drug Abuse Treatment and Prevention Programs in California: A Benefit Cost Analysis.* UCLA, March, 1986.

Terhune, K. W., C. A. Ippolito, and D. J. Crouch, *The Incidence and Role of Drugs in Fatally Injured Drivers.* (DOT HS Report No.808 065), Washington, D.C.: U.S. Department of Transportation, National Highway Traffic Safety Administration, 1992.

Trebach, Arnold S., *The Great Drug War.* New York: Unlimited Publishing, 2005.

——, *The Heroin Solution.* New York: Unlimited Publishing, 2006.

Trebach, Arnold S., and Kevin B. Zeese, eds., *Drug Prohibition and the Conscience of Nations.* Washington, D.C.: Drug Policy Foundation, 1990.

Uchtenhagen, Ambros, Felix Gurzwiller, and Anja Dobler-Mikola, *Programme for a Medical Prescription of Narcotics: Final Report of the Research Representatives.* Zurich: Addiction Research Institute, July 10, 1997; available at www.druglibrary.org/schaffer/heroin/programme.htm.

United Nations, *Economic and Social Consequences of Drug Abuse and Illicit Trafficking.* (United Nations International Drug Control Program, Technical Series Report #6), New York: UNDCP, 1998.

United States Census Data and FBI Uniform Crime Reports, *Murder in America, 1900–1998*; available at wwww.drugwarfacts.org/crime.htm.

United States Department of Health and Human Services, *Drug Abuse and Drug Abuse Research*, Rockville, MD: 1991.

——, *Results from the . . . National Survey on Drug Use and Health: National Findings.* Rockville, MD: 2005.

United States General Accountability Office, *Federal Drug Offenses: Departures from Sentencing Guidelines and Mandatory Minimum Sentences, Fiscal Years 1999–2001.* Washington, D.C.: USGAO, October, 2003.

United States General Accounting Office, *Drug Control: Narcotics Threat from Colombia Continues to Grow.* Washington, D.C.: USGAO, 1999.

——, *Federal Drug Interdiction Efforts Need Strong Central Oversight*, Report by the Comptroller General, June 13, 1983. Washington, D.C.: USGAO, 1983.

————, *Law Enforcement: Information on Drug-Related Police Corruption: Report to the Honorable Charles B. Rangel, House of Representatives.* Washington, D.C.: USGAO, May 1998.

————, *Marijuana: Early Experiences with Four States' Laws that Allow Use for Medical Purposes.* Washington, D.C.: USGAO, November 2002.

United States Sentencing Commission, *Report to Congress: Cocaine and Federal Sentencing Policy*, May, 2007.

————, *Report to Congress: MDMA Drug Offenses*, May, 2001.

United States Surgeon General, *Reducing the Health Consequences of Smoking: 25 Years of Progress.* Washington, D.C.: U.S. Department of Health and Human Services, 1989.

Weil, Andrew, *The Natural Mind.* Boston: Houghton Mifflin, 1972.

Wisotsky, Steven, *Beyond the War on Drugs.* Buffalo, NY: Prometheus Books, 1990.

World Health Organization, *Cancer Pain Relief and Palliative Care: Report of a WHO Expert Committee.* Geneva: WHO, 1990.

————, *Effectiveness of Sterile Needle and Syringe Programming in Reducing HIV/AIDS among Injecting Drug Users.* Geneva: WHO, 2004; available at www.euro.who.int/document/e7777.pdf.

Ziedenberg, Jason, and Vincent Schiraldi, *The Punishing Decade: Prison and Jail Estimates at the Millennium.* Washington, D.C.: Justice Policy Institute, revised estimates, May, 2000.

Zimmer, Lynn, and John P. Morgan, *Marijuana Myths, Marijuana Facts.* New York and San Francisco: Lindesmith Center, 1997.

Articles

Abdel-Mahgoud, M., and M. K. Al-Haddad, "Patterns of heroin use among a non-treatment sample in Glasgow, Scotland," *Addiction*, 91, 1996, pp. 1859–64.

Abrams, Jim, "Interdiction hasn't stemmed drug flow, Congress is told," *Boston Globe*, February 26, 1993.

American Medical Association, "About the AMA position on pain management using opioid analgesics," 2004; available at www.ama-assn.org/ama/pub/category/11541.html.

Anderson, Paul, "Drug bill tough on smugglers," *Miami Herald*, May 26, 1984.

Andreas, Peter, "Profits, poverty, and illegality: The logic of drug corruption," *NACLA Report on the Americas*, 27, no. 3, 1993, pp. 22–8.

Anthony, J., L. Warner, and R. Kessler, "Comparative epidemiology of dependence on tobacco, alcohol, controlled substances and inhalants: Basic findings from the national comorbidity study," *Experimental and Clinical Psychopharmacology*, 2, 1994, pp. 244–68.

Associated Press, "AIDS treatment resolution withdrawn at WHO meeting because of US opposition," September, 21, 2006; available at www.csdp.org/news/news/iht_whonex_092106.htm.

————, "Drug war now many local battles," *San Francisco Chronicle*, December 16, 1999.

————, "Gingrich wants drug dealers executed," *San Francisco Examiner*, August 18, 1996.

Barnes, Steve, "National briefing – Southwest: Texas: Ex-narcotics agent gets 10 years probation," *New York Times*, January 19, 2005.

Barnett, Ruth, "Marijuana: good medicine," *Los Angeles Times*, October 23, 1999.

Bennett, William, "The plea to legalize drugs is a siren call to surrender," in *Drugs in Society*, ed. Michael D. Lyman and Gary W. Potter. Cincinnati, OH: Anderson, 1991.

Benson, Bruce L., Iljoong Kim, David W. Rasmussen, and Thomas W. Zuehlke, "Is property crime caused by drug use or by drug enforcement policy?," *Applied Economics*, 24, July 1992, pp. 679–92.

Bibas, Stephanos, "The Feeney amendment and the continuing rise of prosecutorial power to plea bargain," *Journal of Criminal Law and Criminology*, 94, Winter 2004.

Bigwood, Jeremy, "Toxic drift: Monsanto and the drug war in Colombia," *Corp Watch*, June 21, 2001; available at www.globalpolicy.org/socecon/inequal/labor/monsanto0626.htm.

Biskupic, Joan, "Justices allow no-knock searches," *USA Today*, June 26, 2006.

Blackwell, J. S., "Drifting, controlling and overcoming: Opiate users who avoid becoming chronically dependent," *Journal of Drug Issues*, 13, 1983, pp. 219–36.

Bloom, J., W. T. Kaltenborn, P. Paoletti, A. Camilli, and M. S. Leibowitz, "Respiratory effects of non-tobacco cigarettes," *British Medical Journal*, 295, 1987, pp. 516–18.

Blumenson, E., and E. Nilsen, "Policing for profit: The drug war's hidden economic agenda," *University of Chicago Law Review*, 65, Winter 1998, pp. 35–114.

Bollinger, Lee C., "First Amendment," in *The Oxford Companion to the Supreme Court of the United States*, ed. Kermit L. Hall. New York and Oxford: Oxford University Press, 1992.

Bresnahan, David M., "Cops not talking in Sallisaw: Mother, shot by police in her home, may lose arm," *WorldNetDaily*, October 29, 1998; available at www.worldnetdaily.com.

Brewer, Colin, "Recent developments in maintenance prescribing and monitoring in the United Kingdom," *Bulletin of the New York Academy of Medicine*, 72, no. 2, Winter 1995.

Brooke, James, "U.S. aid hasn't stopped drug flow from South America, experts say," *New York Times*, November 21, 1993.

Brown, DeNeen L., "Vancouver's safer fix," *Washington Post*, national weekly edition, August 25–31, 2003.

Brown, Volney V., Jr., "A view from the front lines of the drug war," *Orange County Register*, September 10, 1996.

Buckley, William F., Jr., Schmoke, Kurt, McNamara, Joseph D., and Sweet, Robert W., "The war on drugs is lost," *National Review*, July 1, 1996; repr. in *Busted*, ed. Mike Gray. New York: Thunder's Mouth Press/Nation Books, 2002, pp. 198–202.

Burke, Melvin, "Bolivia: The politics of cocaine," *Current History*, 90, no. 553, 1991.

Burris, Scott, Peter Lurie, et al., "Physician prescribing of sterile injection equipment to prevent HIV infection: Time for action," *Annals of Internal Medicine*, 133, August 1, 2000.

Butterfield, Fox, "Women find a new arena for equality: Prison," *New York Times*, December 29, 2003.

Cabral, G. A., and D. A. D. Pettit, "Drugs and immunity: Cannabinoids and their role in decreased resistance to infectious disease," *Journal of Neuroimmunology*, 83, 1998, pp. 116–23.

Carpenter, Ted Galen, "Collateral damage: The wide-ranging consequences of America's drug war," in *After Prohibition*, ed. Timothy Lynch. Washington, D.C.: CATO Institute, pp. 151–2.

———, "Ending the international drug war," in *How to Legalize Drugs*, ed. Jefferson M. Fish. Northvale, NJ: Jason Aronson, pp. 293–309.

Cave, Damien, and Ronald Smothers, "4th Newark police officer is shot in a violent July," *New York Times*, July 28, 2004.

Chasnoff, I. J., H. J. Landress, and M. E. Barrett, "The prevalence of illicit-drug or alcohol use during pregnancy and discrepancies in mandatory reporting in Pinellas County, Florida," *New England Journal of Medicine*, 322, 1990, pp. 1202–6.

Cheung, Yuet W., and Patricia G. Erickson, "Crack use in Canada," in *Crack in America*, ed. Craig Reinarman and Harry G. Levine. Berkeley: University of California Press, 1997.

"Church blasts U.S. anti-drug campaigns," *Fort Lauderdale News & Sun-Sentinel*, May 6, 1982.

Clatts, Michael C., Jo L. Sotheran, Pellegrino A. Luciano, Toni M. Gallo, and Lee M. Kochens, "The impact of drug paraphernalia laws on HIV risk among persons who inject illegal drugs: Implications for public policy," in *How to Legalize Drugs*, ed. Jefferson M. Fish. Northvale, NJ: Jason Aronson, pp. 80–101.

Clemetson, Lynette, "Links between prison and AIDS affecting blacks inside and out," *New York Times*, August 6, 2004.

Cleveland, Mary M., "Downsizing the drug war and considering 'legalization': An economic perspective," in *How to Legalize Drugs*, ed. Jefferson M. Fish. Northvale, NJ: Jason Aronson, pp. 547–77.

Cohen, Peter D. A., "Crack in the Netherlands: Effective social policy is effective drug policy," in *Crack in America*, ed. Craig Reinarman and Harry G. Levine. Berkeley: University of California Press, 1997, pp. 214–24.

Connell, Christopher, "Legalizing drugs would reduce crime rate: Elders," *Los Angeles Times*, December 10, 1994.

Coolidge, Sharon, "No jail for patient who grew his own marijuana," *Cincinnati Enquirer*, May 28, 2004.

"Dealing with drug use: Treatment (not jail time) saves lives," editorial, *San Francisco Chronicle*, November 15, 2004.

De Benedictis, Don J., "How long is too long," *ABA Journal*, 79, 1993, pp. 74–9.

Doblin, Richard, and Mark A. R. Kleiman, "Marijuana as antiemetic medicine: A survey of oncologists' experiences and attitudes," *Journal of Clinical Oncology*, July 9, 1991.

Drug Abuse Warning Network, "Club drugs," *The DAWN Report*. Washington, D.C.: Office of Applied Studies, SAMHSA (Substance Abuse and Mental health Services Administration), December 2000.

Duke, Steven B., "The drug war and the constitution," in *After Prohibition*, ed. Timothy Lynch. Washington, D.C.: CATO Institute, 2000, pp. 47–51.

Duke, Steven B., and Albert C. Gross, "Forms of legalization," in *How to Legalize Drugs*, ed. Jefferson M. Fish. Northvale, NJ: Jason Aronson.

Dumond, Chris, "Attorneys say region has produced most meth busts," *Bristol Herald Courier*, August 22, 2003.

Duster, Troy, "Race in the drug war," in *Crack in America*, ed. Craig Reinarman and Harry G. Levine. Berkeley: University of California Press, 1997.

Eckholm, Eric, "States are growing more lenient in allowing felons to vote," *New York Times*, October 12, 2006.

Ehrlich, Isaac, "The deterrent effect of capital punishment—A question of life and death," *American Economic Review*, 65, 1975, pp. 397–417.

Erickson, Patricia G., "A public health approach to demand reduction," *Journal of Drug Issues*, 20, no. 4, 1990.

Evans, Richard N., "What is 'legalization'? What are drugs?," in *How to Legalize Drugs*, ed. Jefferson M. Fish. Northvale, NJ: Jason Aronson.

"Exec seeks $20 million in bogus bust," *San Diego Union-Tribune*, December 2, 1992, available at paranoia.lycaeum.org/war.on.drugs/casualties/botched.raids.

Farrell, A. D., S. J. Danish, and C. W. Howard, "Relationship between drug use and other problem behavior in urban adolescents," *Journal of Consulting and Clinical Psychology*, 60, 1992, pp. 705–12.

Fish, Jefferson, "First steps toward legalization," in *How to Legalize Drugs*, ed. Jefferson M. Fish. Northvale, NJ: Jason Aronson.

Franklin, D., "Hooked—not hooked: Why isn't everyone an addict?," In *Health*, 4, no. 6, 1990, pp. 39–52.

Friedman, Milton, "There's no justice in the war on drugs," *New York Times*, January 11, 1998; repr. in *Busted*, ed. Mike Gray. New York: Thunder's Mouth Press/Nation Books, 2002.

———, "The war we are losing," in *Searching for Alternatives*, ed. Melvyn B. Krauss and Edward P. Lazear. Stanford, CA: Hoover Institution Press, pp. 53–67.

Frohsin, Henry, and Harriet Ivy, "The Feeney amendment," *Litigation News*, Fall 2003.

Gable, Robert S., "Not all drugs are created equal," in *How to Legalize Drugs*, ed. Jefferson M. Fish. Northvale, NJ: Jason Aronson.

Gannon, R., "The truth about pot," *Popular Science*, 192, May 1968, pp. 76–9.

Gazzaniga, Michael S., "Opium of the people," *National Review*, February 5, 1990, p. 34.

Gearan, Anne, "Justice Kennedyassails 'too long' prison terms," *Arizona Republic*, August 10, 2003.

Goldstein, Avram, and Harold Kalant, "Drug policy: Striking the right balance," in *Confronting Drug Policy*, ed. Ronald Bayer and Gerald M. Oppenheimer. New York: Cambridge University Press.

Goldstein, Paul J., Henry H. Brownstein, and Patrick J. Ryan, "Drug-related homicide in New York: 1984 and 1988," *Crime and Delinquency*, 38, October 1992, pp. 459–76.

Goldstein, Paul J., Henry H. Brownstein, Patrick J. Ryan, and Patricia A. Bellucci, "Crack and homicide in New York City: A case study in the epidemiology of violence," in *Crack in America*, ed. Craig Reinarman and Harry G. Levine. Berkeley: University of California Press, 1997, pp. 113–30.

Gould, Stephen J., "The war on (some) drugs," *Harper's Magazine*, April 1990; repr. in *Busted*, ed. Mike Gray, New York: Thunder's Mouth Press/Nation Books, 2002.

Greenberg, Gary, "Just say nothing," *Legal Affairs*, May/June 2004.

Greenhouse, Linda, "Justices say doctors may not be punished for recommending medical marijuana," *New York Times*, October 15, 2003.

Grob, Charles, "The politics of ecstasy," *Journal of Psychoactive Drugs*, April–June 2002; repr. in *Busted*, ed. Mike Gray. New York: Thunder's Mouth Press/Nation Books, 2002, pp. 213–15.

Hagemann, Thomas A., "The thin blue lie," *Los Angeles Daily Journal*, October 27, 1999.

Hamid, Ansley, "The political economy of crack-related violence," *Contemporary Drug Problems*, 17, Spring 1990, pp. 31–78.

"Harm reduction: ACLU wins victory in Connecticut needle exchange case", *Drug War Chronicle*, June 2, 2006.

Harris, Ron, "Blacks feel brunt of drug war," *Los Angeles Times*, April 22, 1990.

Harrison, Ann, "Medical marijuana ban overturned in D.C.," *Alternet*, April 1, 2002; available at www.alternet.org/story/12743.

Herbert, Bob, "The ruinous drug laws," *New York Times*, July 18, 2002.

Hickman, Holly, "Meth use 'choking' western hills of North Carolina," *News & Observer*, February 29, 2004.

Hilts, Phillip J., "Is nicotine addictive? It depends on whose criteria you use," *New York Times*, August 2, 1994.

Hochman, J. S., and N. Q. Brill, "Chronic marihuana use and psychosocial adaptation," *American Journal of Psychiatry*, 130, 1973, pp. 132–40.

"Holland's drug policy: War by other means," *The Economist*, February 10, 1990.

Huffington, Arriana, "A crack house divided," www.alternet.org/drugstory/14713.

Iversen, Leslie L., "Long-term effects of exposure to cannabis," *Current Opinion in Pharmacology*, 5, no. 1, 2005.

Jaffe, Jerome H., "Drug addiction and drug abuse," in *The Pharmacological Basis of Therapeutics*, 4th ed., ed. Louis Goodman and Alfred Gilman. New York: Macmillan, 1970.

Johnson, Gary E., "It's time to legalize drugs," in *After Prohibition*, ed. Timothy Lynch. Washington, D.C.: CATO Institute, 2000, pp. 13–20.

"Johnston sheriff fears new drug plague," editorial, *News and Observer*, February 7, 2003.

Jones, R. T., "What have we learned from nicotine, cocaine and marijuana about addiction?," in *Addictive States*, ed. Charles P. O'Brien and Jerome H. Jaffe. Green Bay, WI: Raven Press, 1991, p. 112.

Jones, R. T., et al., "Clinical studies of tolerance and dependence," *Annals of the New York Academy of Sciences*, 282, 1976, pp. 221–39.

Kaminer, Wendy, "Games prosecutors play," *American Prospect*, September 1999.

Killin, John, "When federal drug laws create havoc for citizens," *Christian Science Monitor*, September 28, 1993.

King, Ryan S., "A decade of reform: Felony disenfranchisement policy in the United States," *The Sentencing Project*, October, 2006, pp. 3–5; available at www.sentencingproject.org/pubs_05.cfm.

Kirkpatrick, David D., "Congress rekindles battle on mandatory sentences," *New York Times*, May 11, 2005.

Kratz, Vikki, "War on coca poisons Colombia," *Sierra Magazine*, July/August 2002.

Krauss, Clifford, "Corruption in uniform: The long view," *New York Times*, July 8, 1994.

Krieger, Lisa M., "Pot spies in the sky irk locals," *San Francisco Examiner*, July 6, 1997.

Kristof, Nicholas D., "Hong Kong program: Addicts without AIDS," *New York Times*, June 17, 1987.

Lane, Charles, "A defeat for users of medical marijuana," *Washington Post*, June 7, 2005.

Lay, Donald P., "Rehab justice," *New York Times*, November 18, 2004.

Leinwand, Donna, and Wade Payne, "Meth moves east," *USA Today*, September 29, 2003.

Lewis, Neil A., "Justice Department opposes lower jail terms for crack," *New York Times*, March 20, 2002.

Lichtblau, Eric, "Gonzales is seeking to stem light sentences," *New York Times*, June 22, 2005.

————, "Nationwide raids put top drug-paraphernalia traffickers out of business, U.S. says," *New York Times*, February 25, 2003.

Lindsay, Reed, "The contradictions of coca eradication in Bolivia," *Narco News Bulletin*, February 15, 2003.

Liptak, Adam, "Texas governor pardons 35 arrested in tainted sting," *New York Times*, August 23, 2003.

Lyketsos, Constantine G., Elizabeth Garrett, Kung-Yee Liang, and James C. Anthony, "Cannabis use and cognitive decline in persons under 65 years of age," *American Journal of Epidemiology*, 149, no. 9, 1999.

Lynch, Timothy, "Tabula rasa for drug policy," in *After Prohibition*, ed. Timothy Lynch. Washington, D.C.: CATO Institute, 2000.

Lynskey, Michael T., et al., "Escalation of drug use in early-onset cannabis users vs. co-twin controls," *Journal of the American Medical Association*, 289, no. 4, 2003.

Majoor, Bart, "Drug policy in the Netherlands: Waiting for a change," in *How to Legalize Drugs*, ed. Jefferson M. Fish. Northvale, NJ: Jason Aronson, 1998, pp. 129–64.

Mansnerus, Laura, "Addict's suit claims police ignore needle-swap law," *New York Times*, January 1, 2001.

Markowitz, Arnold, "Police corruption witness makes a dangerous friend," *Miami Herald*, May 2, 1982.

McGee, R., S. A. Williams, R. Poulton, and T. Moffitt, "A longitudinal study of cannabis use and mental health from adolescence to early adulthood," *Addiction*, 2000, pp. 491–503.

Mears, Bill, "Supreme Court rejects White House appeal over medical marijuana," CNN.com, October 14, 2003.

Medis, Sam Vincent, "Is the drug war racist," *USA Today*, July 1993.

Milroy, C. M., J. C. Clark, and A. R. W. Forrest, "Pathology of deaths associated with 'ecstasy' and 'eve' misuse," *Journal of Clinical Pathology*, 49, 1996, pp. 149–53.

Mirken, Bruce, and Mitch Earleywine, "The 'potent pot' myth," *AlterNet*, July 30, 2004; available at www.alternet.org/story/19416.

Miron, Jeffrey A., "Violence and U.S. prohibitions of drugs and alcohol," *American Law and Economics Review*, 1–2, 1999, pp. 78–114.

Miron, Jeffrey A., and Jeffrey Zwiebel, "The economic case against drug prohibition," *Journal of Economic Perspectives*, 9, no. 4, 1995, pp. 175–92.

Mokdad, Ali H., James S. Marks, and Donna F. Stroup, "Actual causes of death in the United States, 2000," *Journal of the American Medical Association*, 291, 2004, pp. 1238, 1241–2.

Molinski, Dan, "Cocaine supply defies war on drugs," *News & Observer*, August 6, 2004.

"More than they deserve: Judges protest mandatory sentencing in drug cases," *CBS News*, January 4, 2004; available at www.cbsnews.com/stories/2003/12/31/60 minutes/printable590900.shtml.

Morgan, John P., and Lynn Zimmer, "The social pharmacology of smokeable cocaine: Not all it's cracked up to be," in *Crack in America*, ed. Craig Reinarman and Harry G. Levine. Berkeley: University of California Press, 1997, pp. 131–70.

Morganthau, Tom, "Why good cops go bad," *Newsweek*, December 19, 1994.

Murphy, Dean E., "Backers of medical marijuana hail ruling," *New York Times*, October 15, 2003.

Murphy, Sheigla B., and Marsha Rosenbaum, "Two women who used cocaine too much," in *Crack in America*, ed. Craig Reinarman and Harry G. Levine. Berkeley: University of California Press, 1997, pp. 98–112.

Nadelmann, Ethan, "Commonsense drug policy," *Foreign Affairs*, January–February 1998, pp. 111–26; repr. in *Busted*, ed. Mike Gray. New York: Thunder's Mouth Press/Nation Books, 2002, pp. 173–86.

———, "Drug prohibition in the U.S.," in *Crack in America*, ed. Craig Reinarman and Harry Levine. Berkeley: University of California Press, 1997, pp. 290–92.

———, "Europe's drug prescription," *Rolling Stone*, January 26, 1995, p. 38.

———, "The hospice raid and the war on drugs," *San Diego Union-Tribune*, September 19, 2002.

———, "Legalization is the answer," *Issues in Science and Technology*, Summer 1990.

———, "Thinking seriously about alternatives to drug prohibition: Parts 1 and 2," *Daedalus*, 121, 1992, pp. 87–132; repr. in *How to Legalize Drugs*, ed. Jefferson M. Fish. Northvale, NJ: Jason Aronson, 1998, pp. 578–616; also available at www.drugpolicy.org/library/.

O'Connor, Ann-Marie, "No drug link to family in fatal raid, police say," *Los Angeles Times*, August 28, 1999.

Ostrowski, James, "Drug prohibition muddles along: How a failure of persuasion has left us with a failed policy," in *How to Legalize Drugs*, ed. Jefferson M. Fish. Northvale, NJ: Jason Aronson, 1998.

Pereira, Joseph, "The informants in a drug program: Some kids turn in their own parents," *Wall Street Journal*, April 20, 1992.

Petry, Nancy M., and Warren K. Bickel, "Polydrug abuse in heroin addicts: A behavioral economic analysis," *Addiction*, 93, 1998, pp. 321–35.

Pierre, Robert E., "Keeping pills away from drug abusers," *Washington Post*, national weekly edition, June 23–9, 2003.

Polen, M. R., "Health care use by frequent marijuana smokers who do not smoke tobacco," *Western Journal of Medicine*, 1993, pp. 596–601.

Purdy, Mathew, "Warehouse of addiction: Bars don't stop flow of drugs into the prisons," *New York Times*, July 2, 1995.

———, "Warehouse of addiction: At Rikers, guards watch for weapons but shrug at drugs," *New York Times*, July 2, 1995.

Quillin, Martha, "Rural county is meth central," *News & Observer*, September 2, 2003.

Raspberry, William, "Prevention and the powers of persuasion," *Washington Post*, national weekly edition, July 15–21, 1996.

Reinarman, Craig, and Harry G. Levine, "Crack in context," in *Crack in America*, ed. Craig Reinarman and Harry G. Levine. Berkeley: University of California Press, 1997, pp. 1–17.

———, "The crack attack: politics and media in the crack scare," in *Crack in America*, ed. Craig Reinarman and Harry G. Levine. Berkeley: University of California Press, 1997, pp. 18–51.

———, "Punitive prohibition in America," in *Crack in America*, ed. Craig Reinarman and Harry G. Levine. Berkeley: University of California Press, 1997.

———, "Real opposition, real alternatives: Reducing the harms of drug use and drug policy," in *Crack in America*, ed. Craig Reinarman and Harry G. Levine. Berkeley: University of California Press, 1997, pp. 345–66.

Reinarman, Craig, Dan Waldorf, Sheigla B. Murphy, and Harry G. Levine, "The contingent call of the pipe," in *Crack in America*, ed. Craig Reinarman and Harry G. Levine. Berkeley: University of California Press, 1997.

Reno, Janet, "Task force reports from the ASC to Attorney General Janet Reno," *The Criminologist*, 20, no. 6, 1995, pp. 1–17.

Ricaurte, George A., Jie Yuan, George Hatzidimitriou, Branden J. Cord, and Una D. McCann, "Retraction," *Science*, 31, September 12, 2003, p. 1479.

Robins, Lee, Darlene Davis, and Donald Goodwin, "Drug use by U.S. army enlisted men in Vietnam: A follow-up on their return home," *American Journal of Epidemiology*, 99, no. 4, 1974.

Rohter, Larry, "Bolivian leader's ouster seen as warning on U.S. drug policy," *New York Times*, October 23, 2003.

———, "Brazil carries the war on drugs to the air," *New York Times*, July 25, 2004.

Schlosser, Eric, "Make peace with pot," *New York Times*, April 26, 2004.

Schmidt, William E., "To battle AIDS, Scots offer oral drugs to addicts," *New York Times*, February 8, 1993.

Scott, David Clark, "New cooperation seen in anti-drug strategy," *Christian Science Monitor*, March 16, 1993.

Shane, S., "Test of 'heroin maintenance' may be launched in Baltimore," *Baltimore Sun*, June 10, 1998.

Shane S., and G. Shields, "Heroin maintenance quickly stirs outrage," *Baltimore Sun*, June 12, 1998.

Shedler J., and J. Block, "Adolescent drug use and psychological health: A longitudinal inquiry," *American Psychologist*, 45, 1990, pp. 612–30.

Shenk, Joshua W., "America's altered states," in *Busted*, ed. Mike Gray. New York: Thunder's Mouth Press/Nation Books, 2002.

Sherman, Lawrence W., "Police crackdowns: Initial and residual deterrence," *Criminal Justice Review Annual*, ed. Michael Tonry and Norval Morris. Chicago: University of Chicago Press, 1990, pp. 18–25.

Sigler, Bret, "Turning up heat hasn't stopped meth producers," *Las Vegas Review-Journal*, August 5, 2002.

Silverman, Lester P., and Jancy I. Spruil, "Urban crime and the price of heroin," *Journal of Urban Economics*, 4, January 1977, pp. 80–105.

Simpson, Dwayne, D., and S. B. Sells, "Effectiveness of treatment for drug abuse: An overview of the DARP research program," *Advances in Alcohol and Substance Abuse*, 2, no. 1, 1982, pp. 7–29.

Skager, Rodney, and Joel H. Brown, "On the reconstruction of drug education in the United States," in *How to Legalize Drugs*, ed. Jefferson M. Fish. Northvale, NJ: Jason Aronson, 1998, pp. 310–41.

Sklar, Holly, "Reinforcing racism with the war on drugs," *Zmagazine*, December, 1995; available at www.zmag.org/zmag/zarticle.cfm?Url=articles/dec95sklar.htm.

Skolnick, Jerome, "Rethinking the drug problem," *Daedalus*, 12, no. 3, 1992.

Small, Dennis, "Soros wins Bolivia round: Area slides toward drug empire," *Executive Intelligence Review*, November 7, 2003.

Smiley, A., "Marijuana: On-road and driving simulator studies," *Alcohol, Drugs, and Driving*, 2, 1986, pp. 121–34.

Smith, Adam J., "America's lonely drug war," *Mother Jones*, December 14, 2001; repr. in *Busted*, ed. Mike Gray. New York: Thunder's Mouth Press/Nation Books, 2002, pp. 121–4.

Spunt B., P. Goldstein, H. Brownstein, and M. Fendrich, "The role of marijuana in homicide," *International Journal of the Addictions*, 29, 1994, pp. 195–213.

Stefanis, C., et al., "Experimental observations of a 3-day hashish abstinence period and reintroduction of use," *Annals of the New York Academy of Science*, 282, 1976, pp. 113–30.

Stein, George, "In rural Bolivia drug agents fear for their lives," *Miami Herald*, October 10, 1982.

Stein, Joel, "The new politics of pot," *Time*, October 27, 2002; available at www.time.com/time/covers/1101021104/story.html.

Sterling, Eric E., "Drug laws and snitching: A primer," *Frontline*, 1999; available at www.pbs.org/wgbh/pages/frontline/shows/snitch/primer.

———, "Principles and proposals for managing the drug problem," in *How to Legalize Drugs*, ed. Jefferson M. Fish. Northvale, NJ: Jason Aronson, 1998.

———, "Take another crack at that cocaine law," *Los Angeles Times*, November 13, 2006.

Sullivan, R. J., and E. H. Hagen, "Psychotropic substance-seeking: Evolutionary pathology or adaptation?," *Addiction*, 97, 2002, pp. 389–400.

Sullum, Jacob, "Weighty matters: Use of drug carrier weight in calculating sentences—drugs," *Reason*, October 1993.

"A survey of illegal drugs," *The Economist*, July 28, 2001.

Tashkin D. P., G. C. Baldwin, T. Sarafian, S. Dubinett, and M. D. Roth, "Respiratory and immunologic consequences of marijuana smoking," *Journal of Clinical Pharmacology*, 42 (suppl. 11), 2002, pp. 71S–81S.

Tashkin, D. P., M. S. Simmons, D. I. Sherrill, and A. H. Coulson, "Heavy habitual marijuana smoking does not cause an accelerated decline in FEVI with age," *American Journal of Respiratory and Critical Care Medicine*, 155, 1997, pp. 141–8.

Taylor, Stuart, Jr., "How a racist drug war swells crime," *Legal Times*, February 22, 1993.

Thomas, Chuck, "Marijuana arrests and incarceration in the United States," *Drug Policy Analysis Bulletin*, no. 7, June, 1999.

Thornton, Mark, "Prohibition vs. legalization: Do economists reach a conclusion on drug policy?" *Econ Journal Watch*, April, 2004, p. 97; available at www.econ journalwatch.org.

Treaster, Joseph B., "Warehouse of addiction: Drug therapy: Powerful tool reaching few inside prisons," *New York Times*, July 3, 1995.

Tulsky, Frederic N., and Ted Rohrlich, "1 in 3 killers in L.A. County are punished," *Los Angeles Times*, December 1, 1996.

Verhovek, Sam Howe, "Warehouse of addiction: A change in governors stalls model drug program in Texas," *New York Times*, July 4, 1995.

Vinciguerra, Vincent, T. Moore, and E. Brennan, "Inhalation marijuana as an antiemetic for cancer chemotherapy," *New York State Journal of Medicine*, 86, 1988, pp. 525–7.

Weikel, Dan, "War on drugs targets minorities over whites," *Los Angeles Times*, May 21, 1995.

Weiss, Rick, "Results retracted on ecstasy study," *Washington Post*, September 6, 2003.

Weller, R. A., and J. A. Halikas, "Objective criteria for the diagnosis of marijuana abuse," *Journal of Nervous and Mental Disease*, 176, 1980, pp. 719–25.

Westermeyer, J., "The pursuit of intoxication: Our 100-century-old romance with psychoactive substances," *American Journal of Drug and Alcohol Abuse*, 14, 1988, pp. 175–87.

Whitaker, Barbara, "A father is fatally shot by the police in his home, and his family is asking why," *New York Times*, August 28, 1999.

Wilson, W., et al., "Brain morphological changes and early marijuana use: A magnetic resonance and positron emission topography study," *Journal of Addictive Diseases*, 19, 2000, pp. 1–22.

Winter, Greg, "A student aid ban for past drug use is creating a furor," *New York Times*, March 13, 2004.

Wire Reports, "Spending on informants increases," *Los Angeles Daily Journal*, February 13, 1995.

"You take the high road," *The Economist*, November 29, 2003.

Zielbauer, Paul von, "Court treatment system is found to help drug offenders stay clean," *New York Times*, November 9, 2003.

Zinberg, N., "The natural history of 'chipping'," *American Journal of Psychiatry*, 133, 1974, pp. 37–40.

Index